SHE
COOKBOOK

SHE
COOKBOOK

Edited by Richard Ehrlich

PAVILION

First published in
Great Britain in 1995 by
Pavilion Books Limited
26 Upper Ground, London, SE1 9PD

Recipes marked **V** are suitable for vegetarians, as are all the puddings

Designed by Alan James, Write Image Limited, London

A CIP catalogue record for this book is available from the British Library

ISBN 1-85793-758 9

Printed and bound in Spain by Artes Graphicas, Toledo S.A.
D.L.TO: 977-1995

2 4 6 8 10 9 7 5 3 1

This book may be ordered by post direct from the publisher. Please contact the
Marketing Department. But try your bookshop first.

Contents

6 **Introduction**

8 **Store Cupboard**

14 **Soups**

26 **Fish & Shellfish**

44 **Poultry and Feathered Game**

66 **Meat**

88 **Savoury Tarts & Pizzas**

100 **Vegetables & Salads**

124 **Pasta, Grains & Pulses**

146 **Snacks**

158 **Sauces**

168 **Puddings**

188 **Index**

Introduction

When contemporary cooks walk into a kitchen, the one ingredient they never have enough of is time. Most of us have children. Most of us have jobs, either full- or part-time. Many of us have both. Life is very, very busy.

But the desire remains to eat well ourselves and to feed our families and friends well too. Food is not just nourishment but one of life's great pleasures, and we should do our best to maximize it within the limitations imposed by our other responsibilities. That aim underlies the recipes in this book.

As a result, certain types of recipe are conspicuously absent here. It is my belief that few modern cooks have time for making jams and other preserves, for baking elaborate cakes, for assembling the complicated creations found in cookbooks written by professional chefs. Thus, while this book covers most major areas of cookery, the most labour-intensive activities are not among them.

The accent instead is on simpler things. In an ideal world, every dish would be capable of being prepared and cooked with five ingredients and in five minutes. While that is obviously not the case, I always try to make things as simple and speedy as they can be. This applies even in more complicated dishes and in those that require long cooking.

Some of the recipes include notes on variations, a favourite culinary theme of mine. If I had my way, there would be many fewer recipes in the world and many more cooks who treat a cookery text as it should be treated: a starting point for improvisation. Where recipes call for ingredients that you don't have, or don't like, you can always – well, almost always – make substitutions based on preference and availability. As long as you pay attention to the fundamentals

of good cooking, your dish will turn out delicious.

The cooking here is geared towards keeping calories to a minimum. Whenever I make a dish, I try to use as little of the calorie-rich ingredients as possible. That is not to say that butter, cream and sugar have no place in the SHE kitchen. For some dishes they are essential, and the pleasure of the dish is destroyed if they're left out. Sensible eating achieves a balance between self-indulgence and self-denial. 'Cream today, yoghurt tomorrow' – that's a reasonable approach for anyone, regardless of whether they're trying to lose weight.

Another feature of these recipes is unashamed borrowing from other cookery writers. When I'm cooking a type of dish that I've never cooked before, I look to my collection of cookbooks for guidance. When I'm merely reading through them for ideas and inspiration, I often find dishes that look too good not to cook.

Whenever I borrow from someone else, I make changes in their ingredients and methods. But even if my result is far removed from theirs, I acknowledge the source in the introduction to my recipe. I am happily indebted to all these authors, whose hard work makes my work easier.

Some of the recipes in this book are for everyday eating, others for special occasions. I entertain quite a lot, and it saddens me to hear that other people don't do as much of it as they would like. Some are concerned about expense and others about time – especially when contemplating a dinner party after a working day. Going to work, doing the shopping, rushing home, getting the kids to bed and then cooking a meal for four or more guests is not most people's idea of fun.

It can be done, however, if you remember the two principal keys to success. The first is planning. If you haven't been able to shop and start preparing the night before, you'll arrive home laden with carrier bags and a million things to do. Don't get panicked, get organized. Sort out the ingredients for each dish and set them in place. Think about what has to be done first, second, third and fourth; then do everything in the right order.

The second key is choosing quick, easy dishes. There's pasta, of course, and many cooks choose this easy option. But most people prefer, when eating *chez* somebody else, to be given something different from the stuff they cook at home. This book has many ideas that can be prepared in minutes and cooked in well under an hour.

Dinner parties need not cost an arm and a leg, either. True, they're more expensive than not having people over. And occasionally, when finances permit, it's great to splash out on champagne, smoked salmon and a well-aged rib of beef. But luxuries do not make a dinner party memorable. It's quality that counts, not cost.

Quality refers to two things here and one is the raw materials that go into your cooking. French beans from Zimbabwe or Guatemala are wonderfully convenient, but I'd be much more impressed by home-grown Savoy cabbage stir-fried with a little garlic and ginger. Ditto for those exorbitantly priced exotic fruits sold in supermarkets. Who needs papaya if there are good English apples on the table?

The second aspect of quality in dinner-party food refers to its 'specialness': it has to show thought and attention. Again, this has nothing to do with cost. Grilling fillet steak takes minutes, but braising oxtail (which costs a quarter the price) takes hours of loving attention. The trick is to gauge what will make your guests feel that you're pampering them. If you get that right, you can feed them very cheaply indeed.

Notes on the recipes

One aspect of recipe writing that flummoxes me completely is the question of servings. I always hesitate to say that a certain recipe serves four or six or eight or whatever. In general, however, the dishes here serve four to six people. Where there's any doubt, the numbers will be obvious to any cook with a minimum of kitchen experience. I also tend to cook more food than is needed for the meal in question, since I never take the risk that someone will rise hungry from the table. I urge you to follow the same practice, and to hone your skills in the field of Creative Leftover Management.

The presentation of some of the measurements given here may seem slightly unusual. When you're pressed for time, the last thing you want to do is prepare ingredients and then measure each one out with scientific precision. Cooking is not a science. It should be relaxing, not exhausting.

That's why I try, whenever possible, to let measurements be determined by ingredients. I prefer to talk about 1 small onion rather than three ounces of onions, 1 clove of garlic rather than a teaspoon of finely chopped garlic. In the user-friendly approach taken by this book, it will matter not a bit if your onions are smaller or larger than mine.

One final note on the recipes: their origin. SHE has had two Food Editors between the magazine's re-launch in 1990 and my appointment in August 1993. My predecessors were Joy Davies and Clare Ferguson, both well respected figures in the world of cookery writing. In assembling this book we have used photographs dating from their editorships as well as my own. But all the recipes here are mine, either published under my name in SHE, created by me using earlier photography as a visual guide, or created specially for this book.

Store
Cupboard

Store Cupboard

Everyone has their own list of never-be-without-them ingredients; this is as personal a matter as the clothes you wear or the way you bring up your children. The list that follows is nothing more than my list and should not be taken as prescriptive.

One point on which I insist, however, is the need to keep an eye on what you've got – and to avoid over-buying. Supermarket surveys have shown that shoppers waste considerable sums of money buying 'exotic' ingredients that they don't use. And I'm prone to this myself on occasion, getting so enthusiastic about some ingredient or other that I buy far more than I can use within a reasonable time. Fresh herbs, for instance, lose their savour fairly quickly. If you don't use them within a few days, they'll go brown and tasteless.

And this applies even with dried ingredients such as spices. Their shelf life is not indefinite. While small quantities are more expensive than the big bags sold by Asian shops, for instance, in the long run it's cheaper than buying large quantities which will be thrown away after eight months in the back of your cupboard. As a general rule, I'd much rather see a store cupboard with ten items that see regular use than a packed treasure chest where most of the contents have been gathering dust for months.

ANCHOVIES At least 1 tin. This is one of the most useful items of all: with hardly any effort it can be made into a sauce, a snack, a sandwich or a dip.

●

BACON Green (i.e. unsmoked) streaky rather than back. I often buy fairly large quantities and freeze them in small bags. If I'm being really well organized, I cut some of the rashers into rindless shreds for instant use in pasta, braised dishes, etc.

●

BEANS AND PULSES Dried, at least one type. At the very least I keep cannellini or kidney beans and one type of lentil, usually the small French *lentilles de Puy*. Sometimes I have more. Try not to keep them for more than a year, and preferably for six months at most.

●

CAPERS One jar.

●

CREAM As needed, but most often crème fraîche or double cream.

●

CHILLIS A jar of dried (they keep indefinitely) and one or two fresh.

●

CHOCOLATE One bar (or more) of best cooking chocolate, plus a tub of cocoa powder.

●

CURRY PASTE AND POWDER One jar of the former, one tub of the latter – never more.

●

DRIED FRUITS Apricots, prunes, raisins. Don't keep them too long.

●

FLOUR Three types: plain, self-raising, strong (for bread and pizza).

●

FROZEN VEGETABLES Corn, peas and spinach. These are excellent standbys for serving as they are or for use in soups or pasta sauces.

●

GARLIC In abundance, but never more than four heads at a time. Buy the freshest, hardest heads you can find.

●

GINGER The fresh variety in abundance. Buy ginger that's rock-hard, wrinkle-free, and unbroken. Asian stores are usually the best source because of their high turnover. If you can't get good ginger, don't buy it – and don't regard the dried powder as a substitute.

HERBS A selection of dried and small quantities of fresh.

●

LEMONS AND LIMES One or the other at all times, and preferably both.

●

MUSHROOMS Dried varieties such as Italian porcini (French ceps) and Chinese black. These are expensive, but they have a wonderful pungency and can be used in small quantities.

●

MUSTARD At least one type, preferably English, Dijon, and a tin of powder.

●

NUTS I don't use them often, but there are times when blanched almonds or peanuts are absolutely essential. They seem to keep well enough for a month or so if stored in an air-tight jar away from heat and light.

●

OILS A good selection, including: plain vegetable oil (e.g. corn, sunflower, peanut); extra virgin olive oil; sesame oil; walnut or hazelnut oil.

●

ONIONS In abundance. When possible I like to have English white onions, Spanish onions, shallots and spring onions all at the same time. They serve different purposes, they're cheap (apart from shallots), and I use them immoderately.

●

PARMESAN A hunk of it, in good condition, but no more than you can use in a week or so. I keep Parmesan tightly wrapped in the butter compartment of the fridge.

●

PASTA Dried Italian, at least one type. I almost never use fresh pasta because the dried Italian stuff is so good.

●

POLENTA One bag.

●

RICE A selection. Long-grain, pudding rice, Arborio or another short-grain variety for risotto and Spanish rice dishes, wild rice (in small quantities), Basmati, Thai fragrant.

●

SAUCES IN BOTTLES A good selection, but beware of buying stuff you'll never use. My essentials are Worcestershire, some form of chilli sauce, soy sauce, Chinese oyster sauce. I am also a serious fan of Kikkoman Teriyaki Marinade.

SAUCES IN JARS One jar of something Mediterranean-style, such as tapenade, pesto, sun-dried tomato paste.

●

SPICES A large selection, especially cumin and coriander (both in powder and seeds), cayenne, paprika and chilli powder.

●

SPIRITS AND LIQUEURS Expensive but not often used, so they last a long time (if you don't drink them) and can make a huge difference in certain dishes. I try to keep one bottle of Cognac and one of Grand Marnier, which I love in puddings.

●

STOCK CUBES of chicken and beef, and home-made in the freezer. See page 16 for comments on home-made stock.

●

SUGAR A selection. I tend increasingly to use unrefined sugars, which seem to have a somewhat richer, more complex flavour than the refined varieties. I use caster sugar and granulated interchangeably, and soft brown sugar for caramels and sticky sauces.

●

TOMATOES Tinned (whole or chopped); sun-dried tomatoes, dried or in oil, and tubes of tomato purée. Tins and jars of purée tend to go off in the fridge, unless you happen to be making a dish calling for large quantities.

●

VINEGARS A good selection, including ordinary wine vinegar, cider, balsamic, sherry. The imaginative use of vinegars, combining two or more types or with citrus juice, can add complexity of flavour with no extra work.

●

WINE A selection, essential in my cooking but maybe not in yours. I always keep a bottle of dry white vermouth for cooking (and cocktails), simply because I always know it's there. And not all table wines are appropriate for cooking. I also keep cheap ruby port and fino sherry (both refrigerated). With wines as with vinegar, canny cooks can use interesting combinations to easy but impressive effect.

●

YOGHURT Greek-style or bio by preference. My fridge is never without one or the other, as I use them constantly both in sweet and in savoury dishes. I also eat it for lunch, with fresh fruit or left-over vegetables from the previous night's dinner.

Soups

Indonesian-style Chicken Soup (left, page 22), Ribollita (page 25)

Soups

If there is anyone currently residing on the planet Earth who does not like soup, I have yet to make his or her acquaintance. Soups can be light or hearty, fine-textured or chunky, mild or powerfully pungent. Whatever form they take, they're always popular with eaters and cooks alike.

The selection here ranges over quite a lot of the soupy terrain, with a general emphasis on speed and vegetables. There's also a heavy emphasis on puréed vegetable soups, which are a particular favourite of mine – and something I make constantly when people come to dinner.

It's hard to talk about soup without talking about stock, which I know is a thorny problem for most home cooks. *Fond*, the French word for stock, means base or foundation. It's a good word: stock supplies a foundation of flavour in any dish where it's deployed. And needless to say, the better the stock the better the dish. This applies especially to clear soups, where the quality of the stock will be prominent. But even a puréed soup will benefit immeasurably from the presence of a really good stock.

Unfortunately, stocks take time and planning. And even if most of the time is spent letting the stock cook unattended, the few minutes of active work need close and careful attention. What's more, you have to be around at certain crucial points.

Unsurprisingly, most home cooks 'cheat' by using cubes or tinned stock. And cookery writers – who have more time for cooking, and may therefore keep a steady supply of home-made stock – have to be aware of this fact. A dish that tastes great with the home-made stuff may be dull when made using a cube.

In my opinion, some soups must be made with proper stock. These are mostly delicate consommés and fish soups, where a cube just won't be good enough. It's a shame to make an expensive soup like *bouillabaisse* and then ruin it by using a mass-produced *fond*.

For other dishes, stock cubes or tinned stock make a perfectly acceptable substitute for the real thing. All the soups here have been tested with cubes, so I know they will work that way. The one debatable point is *ribollita* (see page 25), the great vegetable soup of Tuscany. I tested it with cubes and although it is good that way, it will be much, much better with a home-made stock.

There's a wide range of cubes, including fish and vegetable. Fish and lamb cubes I avoid, but the others are perfectly good for most soup purposes. Chicken is better than vegetable, vegetable better than beef. Stock cubes may be salty, so add extra salt with caution. Otherwise they can be used like home-made stock.

Having said everything I can think of to assuage your guilt about using stock cubes, I must add a brief word in favour of making your own. Yes, it is more work. It takes a bit of time. It requires the aid of a friendly butcher or fishmonger. But it's satisfying work, and the result gives something special to any dish in which it's used.

If you want to get into the habit, just remember that the freezer is the stock-maker's friend. Beg scraps from the butcher or fishmonger, trimmings and bones from meat, poultry or white fish. Freeze them down and then, when you've accumulated enough, make a big batch of stock and freeze it in small containers. I use both plastic tubs (for larger quantities) and ice-cube trays (for when I just need a few spoonfuls). The work is tedious, but I never regret it afterwards. Neither will you.

Crème Caroline Ⓥ

This simple soup recipe is adapted from the Roux brothers' New Classic Cuisine. *It can be made the night before.*

Preparation time: 3 minutes
Cooking time: 10 – 12 minutes

A large knob of butter
1 large Spanish onion, coarsely chopped
1 x 340 g (11 oz) tin sweetcorn, well drained
A pinch of nutmeg
A pinch of cayenne pepper

A pinch of paprika
600 ml (1 pint) milk
6 – 8 fresh chives

Melt the butter in a pan and cook the onion gently for 5 minutes, then add the sweetcorn and seasonings. Cook for 2 minutes more, then add milk and simmer for 5 minutes. Transfer to a blender and purée for 2 minutes. If you want a perfectly smooth texture you can sieve the soup, but I don't bother. Re-heat to serve hot, or refrigerate. It can be eaten hot or cold, but the Roux brothers like it cold, and so do I. Snip the chives over the top before serving.

Spinach and Lemon Soup Ⓥ

Preparation time: 10 minutes
Cooking time: 20 minutes

300 g (11 oz) floury potatoes
1–2 garlic cloves
A large knob of butter
2 x 300 g (10 oz) packets frozen spinach
450 ml (15 fl oz) chicken stock or milk
Juice of 1 large or 2 small lemons
Salt and freshly ground black pepper

To garnish
1 lemon
Chopped chives or spring onions

Peel the potatoes and garlic, and chop coarsely. Cook in about 450 ml (15 fl oz) of well salted water until the potatoes are just soft (around 20 minutes). Drain, return to the pot then add the butter and spinach.

Cook over a low heat, turning the spinach and scraping off the cooked bits, until all the spinach has defrosted.

Season with salt and pepper, cook for a few minutes more, then put the mixture in your blender with half the stock or milk. Purée until the soup is completely smooth.

If you're serving the soup cold, refrigerate until needed (at least 3 hours). When you're ready to serve, add the remaining stock or milk and re-heat if you wish. When the soup is in the bowls, put in the lemon juice and a tiny swirl of extra virgin olive oil or single cream. An extra slice of lemon plus chopped chives or spring onions make a pretty garnish.

Herb Soup Ⓥ

This is adapted from a recipe in The Best of Jane Grigson's Soups. *The original calls for coriander, but dill, chives or even plain old parsley can also be used. It's one of those brilliantly simple ideas that make you say, 'Why didn't I think of that?'*

Preparation time: 10 minutes
Cooking time: 35 minutes

3 medium onions, coarsely chopped
45 ml (3 tablespoons) extra virgin olive oil or butter
2 garlic cloves, peeled and coarsely chopped
3 small baking potatoes, peeled and coarsely chopped
1.5 litres (2½ pints) chicken or vegetable stock
1.25 ml (¼ teaspoon) cayenne pepper

1 large bunch of fresh herbs (see suggestions above), chopped
Salt and freshly ground black pepper

Gently cook the onions in the oil for 5 minutes, then add the garlic and potatoes. Stir for a few minutes, then add the stock, cayenne pepper, and seasoning to taste. Simmer until the potatoes are completely soft (15–25 minutes) then purée. The recipe may be prepared in advance to this point.

When you're ready to serve, bring the soup to a gentle simmer. Stir in the chopped herbs, heat for a few seconds then serve with good bread.

Instant Spinach Soup with Parmesan Croûtons

This soup is ridiculously quick, especially in the microwave.

Preparation time: 3 minutes
Cooking time: 10 minutes

450 g (1 lb) frozen spinach
450 ml (15 fl oz) chicken stock (a cube will do)
30 ml (2 tablespoons) dry breadcrumbs
2 small spring onions, roughly chopped
1.5 cm (½ in) slice ginger, peeled and roughly chopped
450 ml (15 fl oz) milk

For the croûtons
6 slices good white bread, crusts removed
30 ml (2 tablespoons) freshly grated Parmesan
15 ml (1 tablespoon) extra virgin olive oil

Cook the spinach in the microwave, using a large soufflé dish or bowl (about 8 minutes in an 850-watt microwave), or in a medium-sized saucepan (10–15 minutes). Meanwhile, mix together the stock, breadcrumbs, spring onions and ginger in your blender. Blend briefly, then leave aside to sit in the blender until required.

Add the cooked spinach to the blender in batches, processing each batch until well chopped. Blend for a further 1–2 minutes after the last batch of spinach has been added to get a really fine texture. Return to the vessel in which you cooked the spinach and set aside.

When you're getting ready to serve, add the milk to the soup and re-heat either in the microwave or on the hob.

To make the croûtons, cut the bread into pieces which will fit in your soup bowls. Pre-heat the grill and toast the bread on one side, then turn and grill briefly on the other. Sprinkle over the cheese and olive oil then grill just long enough to colour the cheese slightly. Ladle the soup into bowls, place a croûton on each and serve immediately.

Instant Spinach Soup with Parmesan Croûtons

Spicy Beetroot Soup

Spicy Beetroot Soup

Like nearly all beetroot soups, this takes its inspiration from borscht.

**Preparation time:
10 minutes
Cooking time:
35–40 minutes**

A good knob of butter
2 small onions, thinly sliced
2 small potatoes, thinly sliced
5 thick slices ginger, peeled
2 garlic cloves, thinly sliced
150 ml (6 fl oz) red wine or
   sherry vinegar
600 ml (1 pint) chicken stock
   or water
500 g (1 lb 2 oz) cooked beetroot,
   thinly sliced
450 ml (15 fl oz) milk
A dash of chilli sauce
Double cream or sour cream,
   optional
Salt and freshly ground pepper
Snipped chives, to garnish

Melt the butter in a pan, then add the onion, potato, ginger and garlic. Cook gently for 1–2 minutes then add the vinegar, stock or water and seasoning. Continue to cook gently until all the vegetables are soft (around 35 minutes).

Add the beetroot, mix well and cook for a further few minutes. When everything is soft, purée in the blender and return the mixture to the pan. The soup can be prepared in advance to this point.

When you're ready to serve, bring the soup back to a very gentle simmer and thin with milk to the consistency you like. Stir in the chilli sauce a few drops at a time: the aim is to give the soup a nice kick but not to make it overpowering.

Either stir in the cream (if using) just before serving or ladle the soup into individual bowls and then add a good spoonful to each one. Garnish with the chives and serve.

Carrot Soup

This simple version of an old favourite is sparked up with curry powder and large amounts of dry sherry.

**Preparation time: 10 minutes
Cooking time: 1 hour**

1.5 kg (3 lb) carrots, thinly sliced
4 garlic cloves, peeled and thinly sliced
1 litre (1¾ pints) chicken or turkey stock
300 ml (10 fl oz) fino sherry
10–15 ml (2–3 teaspoons) mild
   curry powder
2.5 ml (½ teaspoon) nutmeg
1 litre (1¾ pints) milk
80 ml (3 fl oz) double cream, optional
4 spring onions, finely chopped
Salt and freshly ground black pepper

Put the carrots and garlic in a large saucepan with the stock, sherry, curry powder and nutmeg. Bring to the boil, then reduce the heat and simmer until carrots are perfectly soft (around 1 hour). Purée in a blender and return to the pan. Set aside, covered, until needed.

When you're getting ready to serve, reheat the purée gently and whisk in enough milk to get the consistency you like. This quantity of vegetables can take as much as 1.1 litre (2 pints) milk.

Before serving, check the seasoning, divide between the bowls and dribble on a little cream, if using. Sprinkle with spring onions and serve.

Instant Pea Soup ⓥ

A well stocked store cupboard always contains a packet of frozen peas. With that in hand, you can cook this soup in minutes.

**Preparation time: 1 minute
Cooking time: 10 minutes**

A good knob of butter
A large handful of chopped fresh bread, or
   a comparable quantity of breadcrumbs
675 g (1½ lb) frozen peas
1 garlic clove, minced
225 ml (8 fl oz) stock
Milk to taste
Salt and freshly ground black pepper

Melt the butter in a large pan and cook the bread, peas and garlic with a splash of water until the peas are done (around 4–5 minutes). Season with salt and pepper, then add the stock and heat through. Purée everything in the blender and return the mixture to the pan. The soup may be prepared in advance to this point.

When you're ready to serve, re-heat the soup and thin out with as much milk as you want – it can easily take a pint or more.

Garlic and Saffron Soup

This delicate soup is based on the Spanish gazpacho blanco. It couldn't be quicker to prepare, but it makes a great impression at dinner parties.

**Preparation time: 3 minutes
Cooking time: 20 minutes**

30 ml (2 tablespoons) extra virgin olive oil
4 small garlic cloves, thinly sliced
15 ml (1 tablespoon) flour
1 large pinch of saffron, crumbled
1 chicken stock cube, crumbled
600 ml (1 pint) semi-skimmed milk
4 small slices white bread, toasted

Heat the oil in a pan and cook the garlic gently for 1 – 2 minutes before adding the flour. Cook, stirring constantly, until the flour has lost its 'raw' smell (about 2 minutes). Stir in the saffron and stock cube then gradually add the milk. Simmer very gently, stirring and scraping the flour off the bottom of the pan, until the garlic is soft (around 20 minutes). Put a slice of toast in each bowl. Ladle the soup in and serve.

Indonesian-style Chicken Soup

This is a greatly simplified adaptation of an Indonesian soup called Soto Ayam. You can use more chicken if you like and serve it either as a substantial starter or as a main course for lunch or dinner.

Preparation time: 10 minutes
Cooking time: 20 minutes

1.5 litre (2½ pints) chicken stock, preferably home-made
15 ml (1 tablespoon) vegetable oil
2–3 garlic cloves, finely chopped
6 thick slices fresh ginger, peeled and finely chopped
5 ml (1 teaspoon) turmeric or mild curry powder

225 g (8 oz) skinless, boneless chicken, thinly sliced
Chilli sauce, to taste
7.5 ml (1½ teaspoons) soy sauce
350 g (12 oz) beansprouts
250 g (9 oz) dried egg noodles
2 large spring onions, thinly sliced
Salt

Heat the stock in a pan. Bring a large pan of salted water to the boil for the noodles.

Heat the oil in a large wok or frying pan and stir-fry the garlic, ginger and turmeric or curry powder over a low heat for about 1 minute. Add the chicken, increase the heat to medium-hot and cook until it is barely done (around 3 minutes more). Reduce the heat and add the chilli sauce, soy sauce and beansprouts. Cook just long enough to heat the beansprouts through (around 1 minute). The soup can be prepared in advance to this point.

When the stock is simmering vigorously, start to cook the noodles in the water (3–5 minutes) then drain well. Add to the wok or frying pan and mix thoroughly with the chicken and beansprout mixture.

Divide between 4–6 large bowls then pour over the stock. Garnish with spring onions, and sliced boiled eggs if you wish. Serve.

Charred Soup

This 10-minute recipe uses one of my favourite vegetable techniques – fast cooking vegetables in a hot pan, so they are slightly blackened – and then turns the result into a soup. If you don't want soup, just fry the vegetables and serve as a side dish.

Preparation time: 5 minutes
Cooking time: 5–8 minutes

10 ml (2 teaspoons) vegetable oil
3 large courgettes, thinly sliced
2 celery sticks, thinly sliced
1 medium onion or leek, thinly sliced
A pinch of curry powder, optional
200 ml (7 fl oz) chicken stock
600 ml (1 pint) milk
A knob of butter, optional
Salt and freshly ground black pepper
Sherry vinegar or lemon juice, to serve

Heat the oil in a large frying pan until it is very hot. Put in all the vegetables plus a little salt and pepper and leave for 1 minute. Toss thoroughly and leave for another minute, then toss again. Cooking by this method, with a good toss every minute, the vegetables should be cooked in 5–8 minutes – very soft in some places, firm in others, and blackened selectively. Turn off the heat.

Put the stock in the blender and add the vegetable mixture in batches, puréeing each batch thoroughly before adding the next. Return the soup to the pan. The soup can be prepared in advance to this point.

To finish the soup, bring the purée to a gentle simmer and add the milk, with a knob of butter for a more luxurious effect. Heat gently until it's hot, then serve with a few drops of vinegar or lemon juice.

Low-fat Puréed Vegetable Soup Ⓥ

This is just another puréed vegetable soup, but one that is virtuously low in calories. The vegetables can be varied as you please.

Preparation time: 15 minutes
Cooking time: 30–45 minutes

15 ml (1 tablespoon) extra virgin olive oil
100 g (3½ oz) floury potatoes, coarsely chopped
100 g (3½ oz) leeks, white part only, coarsely chopped
250 g (9 oz) mixed green vegetables (e.g. curly kale, broccoli, sprouts), prepared as necessary and coarsely chopped
1 large garlic clove, thinly sliced
3–4 thin slices ginger
600 ml (1 pint) semi-skimmed milk
Salt and freshly ground black pepper
Chopped fresh herbs, to garnish

Heat the oil in a large pan and add the vegetables, garlic and ginger. Cook gently for 5–10 minutes, to soften without browning, then season with salt and pepper. Pour in the stock and bring to the boil. Reduce the heat and simmer until the vegetables are soft (25–35 minutes). Purée the soup in the blender and then return to the pan. The soup can be prepared in advance to this point.

Just before serving, bring the soup to a gentle simmer and add milk. Heat just long enough for the soup to get really hot and serve garnished with the herbs.

Variation

The soup can also be garnished with a dollop of Greek or bio yoghurt and it can be given a little extra oomph with dry sherry, sherry vinegar, chilli sauce or lemon juice.

Low-fat Puréed Vegetable Soup

Cabbage and Potato Soup Ⓥ

This is a winter warmer of distinction. If you don't want to use the fat from the bacon, use extra virgin olive oil or butter instead.

**Preparation time:
15 minutes
Cooking time:
30–50 minutes**

4 – 6 rashers streaky bacon, rinds
    removed and cut into shreds
2 garlic cloves, finely chopped
7.5 ml (1½ teaspoons) fennel or
    coriander seeds
450 g (1 lb) waxy potatoes, chopped
    into 1.5 cm (½ in) thick pieces
1 small head cabbage, preferably Savoy,
    halved, cored and thinly sliced
100 ml (4 fl oz) dry white wine or
    vermouth
1 litre (1¾ pints) chicken, beef or
    vegetable stock
Salt and freshly ground black pepper

Put the bacon pieces in a large pan with a splash of water and cook gently until they become translucent and start giving up some of their fat. Add the garlic, spices and potatoes, season with salt and pepper. Cook for a further 1–2 minutes. Add the cabbage and toss, then pour in the wine and stock and bring to the boil. Turn down the heat and simmer until the potatoes are disintegrating and the cabbage is done the way you like it. This can take anything from 25–45 minutes. Serve.

Leek and Cannellini Bean Soup

This is a modified version of a recipe in Lindsey Bareham's A Celebration of Soup. The original calls for the outer leaves of curly endive lettuce, which gives a sharper flavour. I've compensated by adding lemon juice at the end of the cooking time. Served with good bread, this makes an excellent weekend lunch.

**Preparation time: 10 minutes.
Cooking time: 35 minutes.**

45 ml (3 tablespoons) extra virgin olive oil
3 garlic cloves, finely chopped
1 small red chilli pepper, dried or fresh, seeded and
    finely chopped
450 g (1 lb) leeks, white parts only, finely chopped
1 litre (1¾ pints) chicken stock
225 g (8 oz) tin of cannellini or other white beans
Juice of ½ lemon
Salt and freshly ground black pepper

Heat the oil in a pan and gently cook the garlic and chilli for a minute or so, taking care not to let the garlic brown. Add the leeks and stock then simmer for about 20–30 minutes or until the leeks are completely soft.

In the meantime, drain the beans and mash them lightly with a fork, if you wish. Add to the soup and simmer for a few minutes, then mix in the lemon juice and cook for 30 seconds or so. Serve with lots of crusty bread.

Ribollita

The name of this great soup from Tuscany means 'twice-boiled', a reference to the traditional practice of making it a day ahead and re-heating it before serving. The vegetables can be varied, as long as you include cabbage and beans.

Preparation time: 20 minutes
Cooking time: 1 hour

50 ml (2 fl oz) extra virgin olive oil
2 large onions, coarsely chopped
2 large carrots, coarsely chopped
4 garlic cloves, peeled and smashed
4 celery sticks, thickly sliced
125 g (4 oz) bacon or pancetta, preferably thickly sliced
2.5 ml (½ teaspoon) dried thyme or mixed herbs
2.5 ml (½ teaspoon) fennel seeds
1 small head Savoy or Primo cabbage, cored
1 small head red cabbage, cored
1 large baking potato, peeled and roughly chopped, optional
1.1 litre (2 pints) chicken stock
1 x 400 g (14 oz) tin cannellini beans, drained
Salt and freshly ground black pepper

Heat the oil in a large pan or flameproof casserole. Add the onions, carrots, garlic and celery with a little salt and a lot of black pepper. Cook gently for a couple of minutes, then add the bacon or pancetta and the herbs. Cover and continue cooking while you prepare the cabbages. They should both be left in fairly large pieces, each half cut lengthwise in 4 crescent-shaped sections and the leaves roughly separated.

Add the cabbage to the pot with the potato (if using) and pour in the stock. Bring to the boil, then turn down and simmer, partly covered, for around 45 minutes, stirring occasionally. Add the beans for the last 10 minutes or so, just long enough to soften them. If you wish, you can scoop out around half the beans and purée them in the blender with some of the stock before returning to the pan or casserole and cooking for a few more minutes.

If you want to serve the soup now, cook it for an extra 15 minutes. To serve later, leave to cool and refrigerate overnight. To re-heat, place the pan or casserole over a low heat or in a 170°C/325°F/Gas 3 oven. Serve with good bread, and with more olive oil for a really luxurious effect.

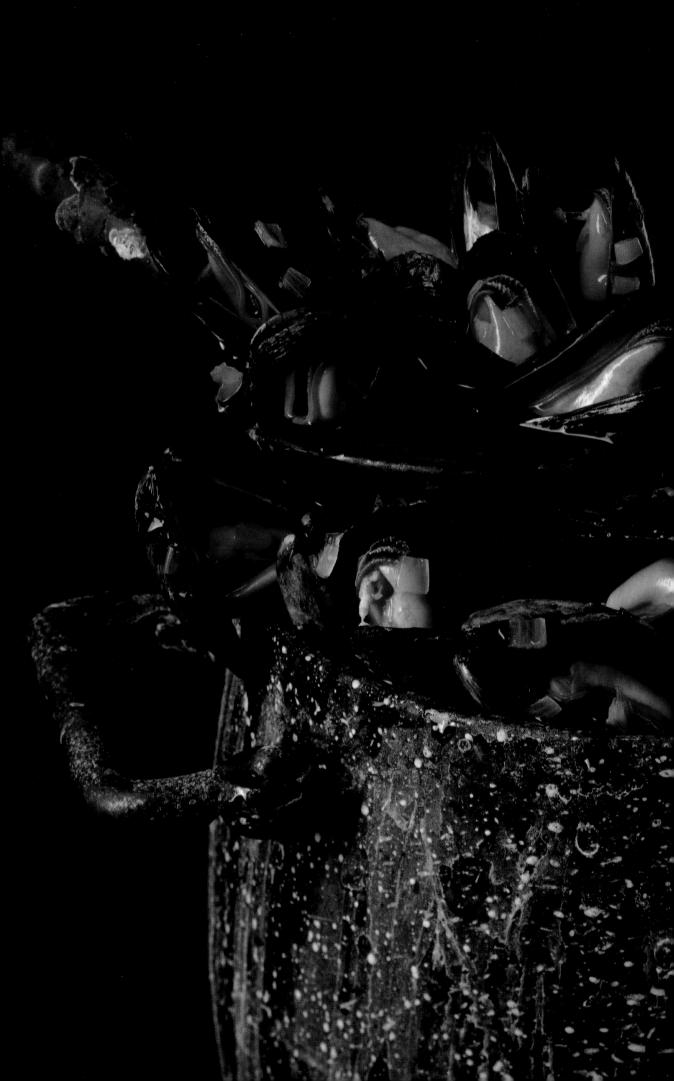

Fish
& Shellfish

Mussels with Shallot Vinegar (page 39)

Fish
& shellfish

Home cooks have a curious attitude towards fish. They want to eat more of it, largely because of its reputation as a 'healthy' food, yet they're often intimidated by the task of preparing it. A 1993 survey by Young's, the frozen fish company, found that only one in ten women below the age of 35 could prepare a whole fish for cooking. Even if the figures may be somewhat better among older cooks, that's a dispiriting finding. It suggests that fillets or cutlets are the only acceptable way of buying fish.

And there's nothing wrong with fillets, of course. Most of the recipes here use them, and they're great things as long as they're fresh or well frozen. (Frozen fish can be just as good as fresh, and sometimes – if your local supplies are limited – even better.)

But a whole fish is a wonderful thing, whether it's a large one or a small one for individual servings. It's also easier to judge freshness if you're buying whole fish. Look for bright eyes and skin, robust, red gills, firmness when the fish is picked up, and a clean, sweet, 'un-fishy' smell.

Fish can be cooked instantly, on its own or with a handful of flavourings. It can also be sauced with good results, in a spicy Thai curry, a tomato sauce, or a Spanish dish such as Hake in Salsa Verde (recipe on page 37). Which you use will depend partly on the season. In summer my favourite fish dishes are those I can prepare as quickly and lightly as possible. The microwave comes in very handy here, as in the recipe for Sole Fillets with Julienne Vegetables from Nicola Selhuber, winner of the first SHE/This Morning 'Family Cook of the Year' competition.

Better still are fish dishes that don't need cooking at all. I love raw fish in any form, whether it's Japanese *sushi*, Mexican *ceviche*, or a marinated *fish tartare* using a noble sea fish such as halibut, turbot or salmon. (Fresh water fish must not be eaten raw.) You'll find several uncooked dishes in this chapter and I can't recommend them too highly.

Fish also tastes wonderful on the barbecue or grill, though it needs careful choosing and handling. I've never found those wire fish-holders to be much use. You need a firm-fleshed fish if using steaks or fillets, or a whole fish that's small enough to be cooked (and turned) with ease. Tuna, monkfish and red mullet are all top choices at top prices. Salmon is somewhat cheaper and good in thick steaks.

At the lower end of the price scale, don't overlook oily fish such as mackerel and sardines. These are at their best on the barbecue, perfect with bread and a salad. Other summer stars include: round white fish such as hake, haddock, John Dory, sea bream, whiting; flat fish such as flounder, sole, plaice, turbot, skate; and oily fish such as herring.

One final word about fish: buy it from a good fishmonger. All specialist food retailers have been hit by the growth of supermarkets, and fishmongers close down at an alarming rate. Fish from a specialist may cost somewhat more, but you're likely to get better, more informative service. And if you don't support your local, it will shut down. Once that happens, your range of cooking options is narrowed irreversibly.

Salad of Baked Tuna, Red Mullet, Fennel and Beans

This recipe is inspired by a dish I ate at one of my favourite restaurants in London, Clarke's. I've substituted summery French beans for the dried broad beans served at Clarke's.

Preparation time: 15 – 20 minutes
Cooking time: 15 – 20 minutes

450 g (1 lb) tuna steaks
2 large or 4 small red mullet
15 ml (1 tablespoon) vegetable oil
450 g (1 lb) French beans or broad beans
30 ml (2 tablespoons) extra virgin olive oil
5 ml (1 teaspoon) balsamic vinegar
4 small bulbs fennel
2.5 ml (½ teaspoon) lemon juice
Salt and freshly ground pepper
Salad leaves, to serve

Pre-heat the oven to 240°C/475°F/Gas 9. Skin and bone the tuna then cut it into 5 cm (2 in) strips. Place the tuna and red mullet in a non-stick baking dish, brush with oil, and bake at the top of the oven until barely cooked (around 10 minutes for the tuna, 15 for the mul-

let). Remove and leave to cool in the pan.

Meanwhile, heat a large pot of well salted water to boiling point. Trim the beans and cut into 5 cm (2 in) lengths then boil for about 2 minutes so they are still very crunchy. Refresh under running water and drain.

To make the vinaigrette mix together the olive oil with the balsamic vinegar, and a little salt and plenty of black pepper.

To serve, remove the mullet from the bone, top and tail the fennel and slice it very thinly lengthwise. Toss the beans and fennel with the vinaigrette. Arrange the fish on large serving plates. Add the lemon juice and remaining olive oil to the fish juices, whisk together quickly and pour over the fish. Arrange the salad leaves on each plate and serve.

Variation

To make this dish more substantial, use dried beans (as they do at Clarke's) or lentils. You could also cook the fish on the barbecue and serve them hot.

Vegetable-topped Lemon Sole

This is adapted from a recipe by Nicola Selhuber, winner of SHE's 1994 Family Cook of the Year competition. Nicola says that a cheaper fish such as dab or plaice can be used instead of lemon sole. If you don't have a microwave, cook the vegetables in a pan before steaming them with the fish for 15 minutes or so.

Preparation time: 20 minutes
Cooking time: around 10 minutes

8 skinless fillets lemon sole or other flat fish
1 garlic clove
125 g (4 oz) chestnut mushrooms
1 large carrot
1 courgette
2 – 3 spring onions
15 ml (1 tablespoon) butter or extra virgin olive oil
2 small tomatoes
Salt and freshly ground pepper

Season the fish with salt and freshly ground black pepper. Roll the fillets loosely to form sausage shapes. Chop the garlic finely and cut the mushrooms into slices 2.5 mm (⅛ in) thick. Slice the remaining vegetables, except the tomatoes, into the same thickness.

If you are using a microwave, place the vegetables in a non-metallic bowl with the butter or oil and cook at full power for 2 – 3 min-

utes, stirring once or twice. They should end up half-cooked and softened but with a good deal of bite.

If you are not using a microwave, place the vegetables and oil or butter in a pan and cook over a moderate heat until just softened.

If you are using a microwave, put the fish in a non-metallic baking dish and spoon over the vegetables. Slice tomatoes thinly and place on the vegetables. Cover with cling film and cook at full power for around 5 minutes, until the fish flakes easily with a fork. Do not overcook.

If you don't have a microwave, place the fish on a plate with the vegetables and tomatoes on top, as for the microwave and steam over a pan of simmering water until the fish flakes easily, taking care not to overcook it.

Serve immediately with parsleyed potatoes or plain rice.

Variation

Use dried Chinese mushrooms or fresh shiitakes instead of chestnut mushrooms and cook the fish with a splash of white wine and a few drops of vinegar.

Low-fat Fried Fish

Ceviche with Avocado

The sharpness of the fish makes a perfect counterpoint for the unctuousness of a ripe avocado. If you prefer, you can just serve the fish on top of the halved avocados.

Preparation time: 10 minutes
Marinating time: 10 – 24 hours

450 g (1 lb) fish such as mackerel, cod,
   monkfish or sea trout
1 small onion
1 small green chilli
Juice of 6 limes or 3 lemons
2.5 ml (½ teaspoon) dried thyme
   or oregano
15 ml (1 tablespoon) extra virgin olive oil
Freshly ground black pepper
4 ripe avocados
Crusty bread, to serve

Skin and bone the fish and cut into 1.5 x 2.5 cm (½ x 1 in) chunks. Chop the onion and chilli finely. Put fish and onion in a non-metallic bowl and mix well with the citrus juice, herbs, oil and plenty of black pepper. The fish should be well coated with liquid but not swimming in it so pour a little away if there seems to be too much. Cover tightly and refrigerate for at least 10 hours and up to 24. Give it a stir every few hours.

Remove the fish from fridge one hour before serving as it will not taste at its best if it's icy-cold.

Just before serving, halve the avocados, remove the stones and peel. Working quickly but carefully, slice thinly and arrange in a fan around your serving plates. Spoon the *ceviche* into the centre of the plates and sprinkle with a little coarse salt. Serve immediately with lots of crusty bread.

To vary the recipe, sprinkle on fresh herbs (basil, sorrel, chervil) just before serving. You can also add peeled, diced tomatoes 30 minutes before serving.

Low-fat Fried Fish

This should be made with thickish fillets of cod or haddock.

**Preparation time:
2 minutes
Cooking time:
8 – 12 minutes**

4 fillets of white fish, each
   weighing about 150 g (5 oz)
15 ml (1 tablespoon) flour
30 ml (2 tablespoons) vegetable oil

Dry the fish well and put the flour in a fine-meshed sieve. Brush the flesh side of the fillets with oil. Heat a non-stick frying pan over a gentle heat for a couple of minutes. Hold the sieve over the fish and tap it lightly to release a fine dusting of flour. Season with salt and pepper and put the fillets in the pan, floured side down. Turn the heat up to medium and cook for at least 3 minutes.

In the meantime, brush the skin lightly with oil. When the flesh side has turned light gold, carefully turn the fillets and cook skin side down until done. This will take from 4 – 8 minutes, depending on the thickness of the fish. Serve immediately with lemon wedges or malt vinegar.

Mérou à la Tahitienne (Raw Fish Salad)

This recipe, a very snazzy relative of ceviche, is adapted from Richard Olney's A Provençal Table. *Use any leaf which will form a cup for easy eating.*

Preparation time: around 30 minutes
Resting time: at least 4 hours

900 g (2 lb) firm, skinless, boneless white
   fish such as cod, cut into 1 cm (⅓ in)
   cubes
Juice of at least 3 lemons
450 g (1 lb) ripe tomatoes
A small handful of fresh mint
A large handful of fresh flat-leaf parsley
3 garlic cloves, finely chopped
1 medium onion, finely chopped

1 large yellow pepper, seeded and finely
   diced
1 large red pepper, seeded and finely diced
A large pinch of cayenne pepper
5 ml (1 teaspoon) fennel seeds
120 ml (8 tablespoons) extra virgin olive oil
Salt and freshly ground pepper
Mixed salad leaves such as Cos, Webb,
   radicchio, chicory and Little Gem

Put the fish in a large bowl and pour in enough lemon juice to cover. Refrigerate for 45 minutes, tossing occasionally, then drain well, rinse in cold water and pat dry. Wipe out the bowl and put the fish back in.

Meanwhile, peel, seed and dice the tomatoes and leave to drain in a colander. Mix the fish with the remaining ingredients up to and including the olive oil, tossing gently with your fingers to keep it from breaking up. Taste and add more lemon juice, salt and pepper, as necessary. Refrigerate for at least 3 hours. Toss and taste again just before serving.

To serve, arrange the leaves on a big, colourful platter and spoon some of the fish into each one. Olney recommends 15 ml (1 tablespoon) in each, with the remaining fish and leaves served separately, but you can use more fish in each leaf if you prefer. Eat with your fingers.

Pescado en Escabeche

Escabeche (pronounced ess-kah-BAY-chay) is an aromatic brine used with poultry, vegetables and especially fish. The recipe here is inspired by Victoria Wise's book Mexican Cooking.

Preparation time: 15 minutes
Cooking time: 6 minutes for the *escabeche* and 5 for the fish
Steeping time: at least 1 hour

1 large onion
1 green and 1 red or yellow pepper
3 – 4 garlic cloves
1.25 ml (¼ teaspoon) ground cumin
1.25 ml (¼ teaspoon) allspice
1.25 ml (¼ teaspoon) ground cinnamon
1 fresh chilli, optional
5 ml (1 teaspoon) oregano
2 cloves
5 black peppercorns
2 bay leaves
100 ml (4 fl oz) wine vinegar or cider vinegar
15 ml (1 tablespoon) sugar
30 ml (2 tablespoons) vegetable oil or olive oil
4 small whole fish such as mackerel, trout, mullet or whiting

To make the *escabeche*, finely slice the onion, peppers and garlic then put them in a pan with the spices, herbs, vinegar and sugar, half the oil and 100 ml (4 fl oz) of water. Bring to the boil then turn down the heat and simmer for 5 minutes. You can prepare the dish in advance up to this stage.

Pat the fish dry and score each side deeply, on the diagonal. Bring the *escabeche* back to a simmer, if you've prepared it in advance. Heat the remaining oil in a frying pan large enough to hold the fish in a single layer. When it's very hot, fry the fish until lightly browned on both sides (1 – 2 minutes). Add the *escabeche* and simmer, covered, for 5 minutes. Turn off the heat and leave to steep for at least an hour. Either serve the fish now or leave to cool, uncovered, then re-cover and refrigerate overnight. Serve with tortillas or bread.

Fish Tartare with Tomatoes and Basil

This is fiddly to make, but a delight to look at – and eat. Use salmon, halibut, tuna, or smoked cod or haddock.

**Preparation time:
20 – 30 minutes**

450 g (1 lb) fish
(see suggestions above)
2 spring onions
6 – 8 sprigs of flat-leaf parsley
45 ml (3 tablespoons) extra virgin olive oil
8 large tomatoes or 12 small ones
1 small bunch fresh basil
Salt and freshly ground black pepper
Lemon wedges, to serve

Skin and bone the fish and slice it into thin shreds no more than 2.5 cm (1 in) long (this will be easiest if the fish is very cold). Mince the spring onions (including the green part) and the parsley, and stir into the fish with 30 ml (2 tablespoons) of the oil. Season well with lots of black pepper and a little salt. Cover tightly and refrigerate until needed. You can prepare this dish up to 2 hours in advance, but remove at least 20 minutes before serving so that it isn't too cold.

Meanwhile, core the tomatoes and cut in half lengthwise. Using a small, sharp knife and a teaspoon, carefully remove the seeds, jelly and internal ribs. Pat dry on kitchen towels and refrigerate until needed. Wash the basil and dry well, then pinch the leaves off the stems.

To serve, brush the tomato halves with the remaining oil (using more if needed) and season with salt and pepper. To serve, you can either spoon the tartare into the tomato halves and decorate with basil or serve the tartare in the centre of 4 plates with the basil-topped tomatoes around it. Serve with lemon wedges.

This can be varied by adding chillis or fresh ginger, and by using walnut oil instead of olive plus a little vinegar. If you like, you can serve the fish with a salad of bitter leaves (frisée and radicchio) instead of tomatoes.

Thai-style Fish Curry

This is a greatly simplified version of a classic dish. It can also be made with small whole fish or with chicken, cut into chunks.

Preparation time: 15 minutes
Cooking time: 20 minutes

2 stalks lemon grass, trimmed
1 green or red chilli, seeded
3 thick slices ginger, peeled
4 garlic cloves, peeled
1 large onion, peeled
3 kaffir lime leaves, optional
30 ml (2 tablespoons) vegetable oil
15 ml (1 tablespoon) soy sauce
15 ml (1 tablespoon) Thai fish sauce (*nam pla*), optional
4 pieces, good white fish such as cod, haddock, skate, whiting, hake, each weighing about 175 – 225 g (6 – 8oz)
250 g (9 oz) long-grain rice
A small handful of fresh coriander, chopped

To make the topping, mince the lemon grass, chilli, ginger, garlic and onion in a food processor, and (if using) shred the lime leaves. Heat half the oil in a non-stick pan and gently fry the mixture for 4 – 5 minutes, to soften and bring out the aromas. Mix with the soy sauce and fish sauce (if using). You can prepare the dish in advance up to this point.

Pre-heat oven to 200°C/400°F/Gas 6. Put the fish in a flat-bottomed dish which is large enough to hold it in one layer. Season with black pepper. Spread the topping evenly over the fish and drizzle over the remaining oil. Bake at the top of the oven until the fish is barely cooked (around 25 minutes). Meanwhile, bring a large pot of salted water to the boil and cook the rice. When it is just tender, drain in a colander without rinsing.

To serve, spread the rice over a platter and place the fish on top scraping out the last drop of sauce. Sprinkle over the coriander and serve immediately.

Flash-roasted Fish with Parsley Butter Sauce

Although this dish comes under the heading of fish, it's equally well suited to chicken and steak. If you make this dish with steak, omit the breadcrumbs. Use 6 pieces of rump, rolled sirloin or fillet steak, each cut 2.5 cm (1 in) thick. Brown the steaks early in the proceedings so the smoke has time to dissipate.

Preparation time: 3 minutes
Cooking time: 15 – 35 minutes

45 – 60 ml (3 – 4 tablespoons) dry breadcrumbs
5 ml (1 teaspoon) salt
6 whole fish, such as red mullet, trout or whiting
45 – 60 ml (3 – 4 tablespoons) vegetable or olive oil
1 quantity Parsley Butter Sauce (see p. 161)

Pre-heat oven to 230°C/450°F/Gas 8. This should be done 1 hour before you want to eat if serving chicken, 45 minutes for fish, 30 minutes for steak. Mix the breadcrumbs, salt, and a good grinding of black pepper.

If you are cooking steak, brown each portion in a frying pan first so it has some colour. Heat enough vegetable oil to cover the bottom of a non-stick pan in a fine film. When it's very hot, brown the steaks for around 1 minute on each side. Don't crowd them in the pan (brown in batches if necessary), and don't be tempted to overcook them. You can prepare them in advance up to this point.

Place the fish or chicken on a flat rack in a large roasting tin. Brush generously with the oil, then sprinkle on a light, even coating of breadcrumbs. Sprinkle the bottom of the pan with water so the drippings don't burn. Roast at the top of the oven for around 25 minutes (30 minutes for chicken breasts, 35 minutes for legs). If cooking steaks, roast for around 10 minutes for rare and 15 minutes for medium-rare. Baste the fish, chicken or steak with the drippings 3 or 4 times, especially towards the end of cooking, and brush with more oil if the meat or breadcrumbs are getting too brown. Once cooked, the heat can be turned off and the fish, chicken or steak can be left for 10 – 15 minutes, loosely covered, if necessary.

To serve, place a portion of fish, chicken or steak on each plate and spoon over some of the Parsley Butter Sauce. Serve immediately.

Pan-fried Salmon with Double Ginger

Seafood Salad with Red-oil Dressing

Preparation time: 20 minutes
Cooking time: 10 – 15 minutes

100 ml (4 fl oz) extra virgin olive oil
2 garlic cloves, finely chopped
30 ml (2 tablespoons) tomato purée
2.5 ml (½ teaspoon) mild chilli powder
2.5 ml (½ teaspoon) paprika
1 kg (2.2 lb) mussels, cleaned
450 g (1 lb) squid, cleaned and cut into rings or strips
Dry white wine, optional
2 – 3 red onions, chopped
Juice of 1 lemon
Salt and freshly ground black pepper

Gently heat the oil in a small pan. Add the garlic and let it warm for a few moments, then add the tomato purée, chilli powder and paprika. Continue to cook for a few minutes, taking care not to let the garlic get too brown, then remove from the heat and leave to infuse for up to 3 hours.

Heat a large pan over a medium heat and add the mussels along with a good splash of water or dry white wine. Cover and cook, shaking a few times, until the mussels are done (around 5 – 8 minutes). Strain the mussels through a colander, reserving the cooking liquor. Place the mussels in a bowl and pour over a little of the liquor saving the rest for a fish stock or soup.

Add the squid to the same pan with another splash of water or wine and cook, stirring, until just done (around 3 minutes). Drain and refrigerate, with the mussels, if not serving immediately.

To serve, strain the flavoured oil through a fine sieve and toss with the squid, onions and lemon juice. Arrange the mussels on a large serving platter and scatter the dressed squid on top. Season with black pepper (and salt, if needed) and serve immediately.

Pan-fried Salmon with Double Ginger

The quantity of ginger in this recipe may seem extravagant, but raw and cooked ginger are radically different and both wonderful in their own way. Use wild salmon if you can get it.

Preparation time: 5 minutes
Cooking time: 5 – 10 minutes

5 ml (1 teaspoon) sesame oil
2 salmon fillets, each weighing about 150g (5 oz)
50 g (2 oz) piece fresh ginger, peeled and finely chopped
5 ml (1 teaspoon) dry mustard
5 ml (1 teaspoon) coarse salt
5 ml (1 teaspoon) freshly ground black pepper
5 ml (1 teaspoon) peanut oil

Rub the sesame oil into the flesh of the fish. Pat 5 ml (1 teaspoon) of the ginger onto the flesh side of each fillet, spreading it with your fingers for even distribution. Do the same with the mustard, and salt and pepper, aiming again for even distribution.

Heat the peanut oil in a large non-stick frying pan over a medium heat. When the oil is hot, put in the salmon, flesh-side down. Cook for 2 minutes precisely, then turn. They will need anything from 3 – 8 minutes more cooking, depending on how you like your salmon and the thickness of the fillets. The skin of the fish will be deeply browned and very crisp – delicious for those who like it.

When the fillets are done, put them on heated plates and sprinkle over the remaining ginger. Serve immediately with steamed potatoes and a green vegetable.

Barbecued Prawn and Bacon Brochettes

I ate this dish at London's Neal Street Restaurant. The dill mayonnaise, devised by owner Antonio Carluccio, goes equally well with fish, vegetables or chicken. Left-over mayonnaise can be reused for 2 – 3 days. (NB: Old people, children and pregnant women are advised not to eat raw egg.)

Preparation time: 30 minutes
Cooking time: 5 – 10 minutes

8 thin slices green streaky bacon
16 uncooked prawns (8 if they're very large)
Freshly ground black pepper

For the mayonnaise
1 egg, size 1
1.25 ml (¼ teaspoon) fine salt
10 ml (2 teaspoons) wine vinegar
50 ml (2 fl oz) extra virgin olive oil
175 ml (6 fl oz) vegetable oil
Juice of 1 lime
15 ml (1 tablespoon) fresh dill, minced
1.25 ml (¼ teaspoon) cayenne pepper

Bring a pan of unsalted water to the boil. Remove the rind from the bacon and halve each slice, then blanch for 1 minute to tone down the saltiness. Pat dry and leave to cool.

Shell and remove the veins from the prawns, halve them if they are very large, and season with pepper. Wrap a slice of bacon around each prawn or piece of prawn, thread onto 4 skewers and refrigerate until needed.

To make the mayonnaise, put egg, salt and vinegar into a food processor and whiz for 10 seconds. Combine the oils and, with the motor running, pour into the bowl in a thin, steady stream. Turn off the motor when the mixture is thick and make sure all the oil has been incorporated. Scoop into a clean bowl and whisk in half the lime juice. Taste to check that the lime is detectable but not overpowering and add more if necessary. Stir in the dill and cayenne pepper, and refrigerate, covered, until needed.

Heat the barbecue until it is hot then cook the prawns until just tender (4 – 8 minutes), turning 2 or 3 times. Serve immediately with the mayonnaise passed separately.

These brochettes may also be cooked under a grill, or in a hot frying pan; they'll probably need slightly less time in a frying pan .

Salmon en Croûte

This easy recipe exploits the convenience of ready-made puff pastry. This recipe for 2 will use half a packet, so wrap the rest tightly in cling film and freeze it. The salmon can be cooked the night before, then cooled and refrigerated. The same procedure can be used with fillet of beef, substituting red wine for the vermouth in the sauce.

Preparation time: 15 minutes
Cooking time: 15 minutes

30 ml (2 tablespoons) olive oil or clarified butter
½ a 340 g packet puff pastry or 2 sheets puff pastry
2 skinless salmon fillets, each weighing about 150 g (5 oz)

For the sauce
A small knob of butter
2 spring onions, finely chopped
A small pinch of dried thyme
60 ml (4 tablespoons) dry vermouth

Well in advance of cooking, heat a non-stick frying pan until it's very hot then add the olive oil or butter. When it sizzling hot, cook the fillets for 1 – 2 minutes on each side until they are well browned. Remove from the pan and leave to cool (5 – 10 minutes), then cover. If you're working more than 2 hours in advance, wrap the fish in foil and refrigerate. If you don't want to have your salmon browned, skip this stage and cook it for longer in the oven.

To make the sauce, melt the butter in a small pan and cook the spring onions gently for a few minutes until softened. Add the thyme and wine, turn up the heat and boil rapidly to reduce to around 30 ml (2 tablespoons) of sauce. Season and leave to cool. This can all be done up to a day before you want to serve the dish.

Pre-heat the oven to 230°C/450°F/Gas 8. Roll out the pastry on a lightly floured surface to 15 cm (6 in) square and 5 mm (¼ in) thick. Cut the puff pastry into 2 equal pieces (if using a single block) and place on a non-stick baking sheet (if using pastry sheets, roll each piece to a rectangle 3 x 6 in and 5 mm (¼ in) thick). Bake in the centre of the oven for 15 minutes until golden-brown and well puffed up.

Put the fish on another baking sheet and bake for 8 – 10 minutes, or until it is cooked the way you like it. Unseared salmon will need 2 – 3 minutes more. If the puff pastry is done first, let it rest in a warm place for 10 minutes.

In the meantime, re-heat the sauce gently. As soon as the fish is done, gently split each pastry square so it opens like a book. Put one piece of fish inside each, spoon over a little sauce and close. Serve immediately with steamed French beans or mangetout.

Hake in Salsa Verde

This is based on a recipe in Pepita Aris's Recipes from a Spanish Village. *Cod or haddock cutlets can be used instead of hake.*

Preparation time: 15 minutes
Cooking time: 25 – 30 minutes

16 – 20 fresh mussels
30 ml (2 tablespoons) extra virgin olive oil
2 large knobs of butter
1 medium onion, finely chopped
3 small garlic cloves, finely chopped
4 hake, cod or haddock cutlets, each weighing
   about 175 g (6 oz)
15 ml (1 tablespoon) plain flour
275 g (10 oz) French beans, topped, tailed, and cut
   in 1.5 cm (½ in) pieces
350 ml (12 fl oz) fish stock
175 ml (6 fl oz) dry white wine
Salt and freshly ground pepper
A small handful of parsley, chopped

Clean the mussels and discard any that do not close. Heat the oil and butter in a covered pot which will hold the fish in one layer, and gently cook the onion (without colouring) for a few minutes. Add the garlic and continue cooking until everything is soft. Lightly dust the fish with flour. Push the onion and garlic to the sides of the pan and put in the fish. Cook until lightly browned, then turn and brown the other side.

Add the beans, stock and wine, and season with salt and pepper. Bring to a gentle simmer, and cook for 1 – 2 minutes. Add the mussel s and parsley, and continue cooking until the mussels have opened (5 – 7 minutes). Serve in deep plates or shallow soup bowls, with plenty of bread.

Red Mullet with Sherry Vinegar

Red mullet, one of my favourite fish, has a strong, almost meaty flavour which needs little embellishment. This illustrates one of the best and easiest ways of cooking it. The seasonings may be varied as you like.

Preparation time: 5 minutes
Cooking time: 25 minutes

4 red mullet, each weighing about 175 – 225 g (6 – 8 oz)
1 spring onion, finely chopped
1 thick slice of lime, quartered
15 ml (1 tablespoon) extra virgin olive oil
10 ml (2 teaspoons) sherry vinegar
Salt and freshly ground black pepper

Pre-heat the oven to 180°C/350°F/Gas 4. Clean the fish thoroughly, then pat dry and season both inside and out with salt and pepper. Put some of the spring onion and a lime wedge in the cavity of each fish, then place in a lightly oiled roasting tin and drizzle over the olive oil. Bake just above the centre of the oven for 25 – 30 minutes, then swirl the vinegar in the pan and serve immediately with the cooking juices drizzled on top.

Fish Cutlets with Spicy Tomato Sauce

Preparation time: 2 minutes
Cooking time: 20 minutes

4 hake cutlets, each weighing about 225 g (8 oz)
30 ml (2 tablespoons) extra virgin olive oil
3 plump garlic cloves, finely chopped
1 – 2 dried red chillis, seeded and crumbled
300 ml (10 fl oz) tomato sauce (see page 161)
A small handful of coriander
Halved black olives, optional
Salt and freshly ground black pepper

Season the fish on both sides and dust with a little flour. Heat the oil over a moderate heat in a large lidded frying pan. Add the garlic and chillis to the pan and cook for a few minutes without browning, stirring constantly.

Add the fish and brown lightly on both sides, then pour in the tomato sauce. Bring to a simmer, cover and cook until the fish is just tender (around 10 – 15 minutes). Carefully lift the fish onto a serving platter and spoon over the sauce. If the sauce is very runny, it can be reduced by boiling hard for a couple of minutes. Sprinkle with the coriander and olives, if using.

You can also put the fish and sauce in the microwave rather than simmering it on the hob. It will take around 5 – 8 minutes at full power.

Mussels with Shallot Vinegar

Mussels are the cheapest of molluscs but also one of the best. Here they're cooked very simply and served with a pungent dipping sauce like those served in France with a plateau de fruits de mer.

Preparation time: 20 minutes
Cooking time: 5 – 10 minutes

2 kg (4.4 lb) mussels
15 ml (1 tablespoon) vegetable oil or extra virgin olive oil
1 large onion, finely chopped
2 garlic cloves, finely chopped
100 ml (4 fl oz) dry white wine or vermouth

For the sauce
225 g (8 oz) shallots, finely chopped
225 ml (8 fl oz) red wine vinegar
45 ml (3 tablespoons) extra virgin olive oil, optional
Salt and freshly ground black pepper

Clean the mussels and pull off the 'beards' from the shells. Discard any that remain open when tapped firmly on the edge of the sink. Leave in a bowl or colander with a little water. (Soaking in water will dilute the flavour and eventually kill the mussels.)

To make the sauce, mix the shallots, vinegar and oil (if using). Season and refrigerate for at least 30 minutes so the flavours can blend.

Gently heat the oil in a wok, large saucepan or stock-pot and cook the onion and garlic for 3 – 4 minutes to soften slightly. Increase the heat and put in the mussels, tossing them in the oil and letting them sizzle for a few moments. Pour in the wine, stir again, then cook, covered, until the mussels are all open and cooked. This can take anything from 4 – 10 minutes, depending on your pot. Give them an energetic stir every minute or so.

Serve the mussels in a large bowl (discarding any that are still closed) with the sauce passed separately in small bowls. Each diner should scoop up a little sauce with each mussel. The mussel cooking liquor can be strained and frozen for use with fish dishes.

Remojón

This delicious salad is adapted from a recipe in Elizabeth Luard's Flavours of Andalucia. *Originally made with salt cod, it is now more commonly found with tinned tuna, but I prefer this version with smoked fish.*

Preparation time: 20 – 25 minutes
Cooking time: 10 minutes
Marinating time: 1 hour

75 ml (5 tablespoons) extra virgin olive oil
2 large red peppers, seeded and cut into 1.5 cm (½ in) strips
350 – 400 g (12 – 14oz) smoked cod or haddock, skinned, boned and thinly sliced
1 garlic clove, finely chopped
1 tin anchovies, drained and finely chopped
1 large bunch spring onions, cut on the bias 5 mm (¼ in) thick
125 g (4 oz) green olives, stoned and coarsely chopped
30 ml (2 tablespoons) sherry or wine vinegar
6 small oranges
4 – 6 large leaves Cos lettuce
Freshly ground black pepper

Gently heat the oil in a large frying pan and sauté the peppers until they are soft but still retain a little of bite (around 10 minutes). Meanwhile, mix the smoked fish, anchovies, garlic, spring onions and olives in a bowl and season with plenty of black pepper.

Add the cooked peppers to the bowl along with the vinegar and toss well. Leave to marinate for 1 hour.

Peel the oranges and remove as much of the pith as you can. Cut into slices 1.5 cm (½ in) thick or separate into segments. Segments make for easier eating but take more work. Five minutes before serving, toss the orange with the other salad ingredients.

To serve, put a lettuce leaf on each plate and spoon the salad along its whole length; take care not to overfill, as they are intended to be eaten with the fingers, but supply forks for any salad that ends up back on the plate.

Grilled Sardines

Grilled Sardines

People don't make enough use of sardines, a cheap, nutritious delicacy which is usually plentiful from around February through to the end of the summer. They're at their best when simply grilled or barbecued. The sardines can be served on a bed of salad leaves if you wish.

Preparation time: 1 minute
Cooking time: 3 – 6 minutes

675 g (1 ½ lb) fresh sardines
30 – 45 ml (2 – 3 tablespoons) vegetable oil
Coarse sea salt
Lemon wedges, to serve

Heat the barbecue or grill until it is medium-hot. Meanwhile, put the fish in a large dish and toss gently but thoroughly with the oil, to help the fish from sticking to the wire mesh of the grill or barbecue. Gently shake off the excess oil and place them on the grill, taking care not to crowd them. Cook for 2 – 3 minutes then brush with a little more oil and sprinkle with a little salt. Turn carefully and continue to cook for 1 – 3 minutes more, or until the fish are barely done.

Serve the fish either as they are cooked or all at once with the lemon wedges.

Brandade (Fish Spread)

This is very loosely modelled on the famous Brandade de Morue, a French dish made with salt cod. I usually serve it on toast, as a nibble with drinks or a starter, but it could also form the centrepiece of a cold lunch.

Preparation time: 10 minutes
Cooking time: 10 – 15 minutes

A bay leaf
2 large garlic cloves
300 g (10 oz) fresh cod or haddock
300 g (10 oz) smoked cod or haddock
A large handful of parsley
1 tablespoon fresh thyme or 1 teaspoon dried
75 ml (5 tablespoons) walnut oil
2 hard-boiled eggs, finely chopped

Put 5 cm (2 in) of water in a small frying pan with the garlic and bay leaf and boil for 5 minutes. Turn down the heat to a gentle simmer, add the fish and poach until barely cooked (5 – 10 minutes). Remove the fish, bay leaf and garlic from the pan and drain well. Remove the skin and bones from both the fresh and smoked fish and chop in 2.5 cm (1 in) pieces.

If you have a food processor, add the garlic and process until finely chopped; you'll need to scrape the sides a few times . Add the parsley and process until coarsely chopped then add the fish and thyme and process to a medium-fine paste (around 30 – 45 seconds). Slowly pour in the oil and process again to mix well. Finally, scrape into a bowl and stir in the eggs.

If working by hand, finely chop the garlic, parsley, fish and thyme with a large kitchen knife. Mix in the oil and eggs and serve.

Pan-fried Mullet with Wilted Fennel

The fennel is optional, but makes a nice touch for a one-dish summer meal.

Preparation time: 5 minutes
Cooking time: 8 – 20 minutes

15 ml (1 tablespoons) extra virgin olive oil
4 red mullet, each weighing around 175 – 225 g
  (6 – 8oz)
60 ml (4 tablespoons) chicken stock, dry white
  wine or dry vermouth
4 thin strips orange rind, shredded
1 large sprig of fresh rosemary, needles only
Salt and freshly ground black pepper

For the fennel
30 ml (2 tablespoons) extra virgin olive oil
4 medium bulbs fennel, thinly sliced and fronds
  reserved for the garnish, optional
Juice of 1 – 2 limes

Heat the oil in a large frying pan and fry the fish until just done (around 3 minutes each side). Turn the fish carefully to keep them from breaking up. Turn the heat right down, add the remaining ingredients, and cook, covered, for a further 2 minutes.

This may be served immediately, but I think it's even better if left to cool while you cook the fennel.

Heat the remaining oil in another large pan, add the fennel and season with salt and pepper. Cook over a moderate heat, stirring occasionally, until the fennel is soft but retains a firm bite (around 15 minutes). Leave to cool, then add the lime juice and toss.

To serve, make a generous fringe of fennel around the serving plates and put a fish in the centre. Garnish with the fennel fronds if you wish. This could be served with a potato salad, but slices of toast go equally well.

Gravadlax with Potatoes 'en Chiffonade'

Squid with Chillis

Some people are intimidated by the thought of cleaning squid, even though it's very easy (and a lot of fun). But supermarkets often sell prepared rings and any fishmonger will clean squid for you – so there's no excuse not to cook this delicious, simple sauté.

**Preparation time: 5 minutes for prepared squid,
15 minutes if you're preparing it yourself
Cooking time: 3 – 5 minutes**

15 ml (1 tablespoon) vegetable oil
450 g (1 lb) squid, cleaned and cut in rings or shreds
4 – 5 spring onions, thickly sliced
2 – 3 mild red chillis, seeded and thinly sliced
50 ml (2 fl oz) dry white wine or vermouth
15 ml (1 tablespoon) extra virgin olive oil
15 ml (1 tablespoon) red wine vinegar
Salt and freshly ground black pepper

Heat the oil in a frying pan until it's blazing hot then stir-fry the spring onions and chillis for a minute or so. Add the squid, season and cook until the squid is just done (around 3 minutes). Turn off the heat and add the wine or vermouth, allowing it to bubble until the sauce is reduced by around half, then swirl in the olive oil and vinegar.

   Mix well, and serve immediately with rice or potatoes – or even a slice of bread.

Gravadlax with Potatoes 'en Chiffonade'

Gravadlax is, for my money, one of the greatest dishes in the world.

**Preparation time: 15 minutes
Marinating time: at least 2 hours
Cooking time: 20 minutes**

12 – 16 slices fresh salmon, around 1.5 cm (½ in) thick
5 ml (1 teaspoon) coarse salt
2.5 ml (½ teaspoon) coarsely ground black pepper
120 ml (8 tablespoons) finely chopped fresh dill
550 g (1¼ lb) new potatoes
100 ml (4 fl oz) fromage frais (*not* low-fat) or Bio yoghurt
30 ml (2 tablespoons) extra virgin olive oil
30 ml (2 tablespoons) wine vinegar
2 spring onions or 1 small red onion, finely chopped
5 – 6 leaves Cos lettuce
Lemon wedges, to serve

Lay the fish on a large plate and rub the salt and pepper into it. Scatter over the dill, pressing into the flesh firmly. Cover tightly with cling film, then seal inside an airtight container. Refrigerate for at least 2 hours and up to 8.

   Meanwhile, boil, microwave or steam the potatoes until they're just done; (they mustn't be overcooked). Leave to cool, then halve or quarter (if necessary) and toss with the fromage frais or yoghurt, oil, vinegar and spring onions or red onion.

   When you're ready to serve, shred the lettuce and spread out over the serving plates. Put potato salad on each one, and lay the salmon slices round the edges. Serve with lemon wedges.

Poultry
& feathered game

Chicken with Forty Cloves of Garlic (page 56)

Poultry
& feathered game

There's a saying about the food-loving people of Kwangtung (Canton), in China, that they'll eat anything with wings except an aeroplane and anything with legs except a table. I'm the same way, especially when it comes to birds. I could give up meat if I were forced to, but I can't imagine life without free-range chicken, farmed duck, goose, quails and feathered game.

I'm not the only one, of course: chicken sales in particular have soared in recent years. That's partly because chicken has become a cheap food, but with lower cost has come lower quality. The intensively reared type live their short lives in inhumane conditions and they have hardly any taste at all. So buy only free-range birds – now readily available – if you possibly can.

The other reason for chicken's popularity is that it's lower in fat than red meat. In fact, this isn't necessarily true of intensively reared birds. A 1989 study found that carcasses from intensively reared chickens contained 22 per cent fat – nearly a tenfold increase from the nineteenth century. Some cooks deal with this by eating only the leaner breasts, and by removing the skin before cooking. But chicken legs have more flavour, and cooking without the skin is more likely to cause dryness. All of which make good reasons for buying the leaner, free-range birds rather than the intensively reared variety.

Among other birds I am unenthusiastic about poussins, which are nice to look at but killed at an age when they've hardly any time to develop flavour. If you want a really small bird, quail is a wonderful treat. So is guinea fowl, either from France or from the UK. Both these birds are now farmed

extensively, but their wild origins are apparent in their flavour.

Better still is farmed duck, one of the great treats for a dinner party. Boned-out breasts are popular and easy, and you can buy them in pre-prepared portions to make your life easier. But when I'm cooking either breasts or legs for four, I buy two birds. I cut the legs and breasts off the carcass, freeze whichever portion I'm not using and make a stock with the carcass. This works out cheaper and yields a bonus in the form of richly flavoured stock.

British cooks should always take advantage of the multitude of excellent game found here. This is one of the glories of British cuisine and a point that I appreciate fully as an American expatriate: in the USA, feathered game is nothing like as common as it is here. I like all the wild birds, though my budget doesn't usually stretch to the pricier items such as partridge and grouse. You can get just as much pleasure from pheasant and wild duck and recipes for both are included here.

One plea I would make for poultry is not to overcook it. I simply cannot understand the taste for dry, stringy breast meat and legs that are falling off the bone. Overcooking has had an apparent endorsement from people concerned with food-safety, who rightly deplore the propagation of salmonella in chickens through poor farming practice. But safe cooking is not synonymous with overcooking. You don't need to remove all flavour and juiciness in order to kill salmonella bacteria. Time your chicken carefully, pay attention to it, and take it off the heat when it's just done. You'll be feeding your family and friends safely, and you'll enjoy the food at its best.

Chicken and Cucumbers with Spicy Peanut Sauce

You can use ordinary chicken either roasted or poached, but a smoked bird lends extra tang (and cuts down on your work).

Preparation time: 20 minutes
Resting time: 30 minutes

1 x 1.5 – 2 kg (3 – 4 lb) smoked chicken
7.5 ml (1½ teaspoons) ground cumin
7.5 ml (1½ teaspoons) ground coriander
2.5 ml (½ teaspoon) turmeric
2.5 ml (½ teaspoon) paprika
25 ml (1½ tablespoons) vegetable oil
150 g (5 oz) blanched peanuts
300 ml (10 fl oz) Greek-style or bio yoghurt
1 – 2 fresh red chillis, seeded and finely chopped
2 spring onions, finely chopped
1 – 2 cucumbers, seeded and shredded
7.5 ml (1½ teaspoons) sesame oil
Salt and freshly ground black pepper

Joint the chicken, cut the meat off the bone and slice into long shreds. Refrigerate, covered, until needed.

Meanwhile, mix together the spices in a small bowl. Heat the oil in small frying pan and add the peanuts. Stir-fry until they're lightly browned as evenly as possible, then add the spices and stir-fry until they start smelling fragrant (around 1 minute). Leave to cool for a few minutes.

Put the peanuts and all the spices (you'll have to scrape to get them all out of the pan) in a blender or food processor and chop them as finely as possible. Add the yoghurt and mix again until well blended. Stir in the chillis and onions by hand. Season with salt and pepper then refrigerate the sauce for at least 30 minutes to let the flavours blend.

Shortly before you want to eat, mix the sesame oil into the sauce and arrange the cucumbers and chicken on a platter. Spoon some of the sauce onto the chicken and serve immediately. Hand the remaining sauce separately.

'Kung Pao' Chicken Thighs

Thighs are perfect – in both size and shape – for barbecuing. The fiery dipping sauce adapts the flavours of the classic Sichuan dish Kung Pao chicken; you'll find the real thing in Yan-Kit So's Classic Chinese Cookbook.

Preparation time: 10 minutes
Cooking time: 15 – 20 minutes

4 thin slices ginger, finely chopped
2 garlic cloves, finely chopped
2 spring onions or 1 small onion, finely chopped
1 small chilli, preferably dried, seeded and thinly
    sliced
60 ml (4 tablespoons) soy sauce
30 ml (2 tablespoons) dry sherry
30 ml (2 tablespoons) red wine vinegar
100 ml (4 fl oz) chicken stock or water
65 g (2½ oz) dry-roasted peanuts
5 – 10 ml (1 – 2 teaspoons) vegetable oil
5 ml (1 teaspoon) sugar
8 – 12 chicken thighs

Mix together the ginger, garlic, spring onions or onion and chilli in a bowl. Measure out the soy sauce, sherry, vinegar and stock or water in a measuring cup or small bowl. Using a food processor or rolling pin, crush the peanuts until they resemble very coarse breadcrumbs.

Heat the oil to a medium heat in a pan. Add the minced seasonings and stir-fry for 1 – 2 minutes, until everything is slightly coloured and very fragrant. Add the liquids and sugar then boil hard for a minute or so. Turn off the heat. The dish can be prepared in advance to this point, then re-heated before serving.

Pre-heat the barbecue or grill to a medium heat. When it's ready, cook the chicken pieces until well browned on all sides (around 10 – 20 minutes in all). Watch carefully – chicken can go from perfection to dryness in no time at all. Just before serving, re-heat the sauce and add the nuts, stirring well for a few moments to blend thoroughly. Serve the sauce in bowls so your guests can dip the chicken themselves.

Variations

The chicken can be marinated in the sauce (without the peanuts), then the nuts can be fried in oil and scattered over the chicken just before serving.

The chicken can also be cubed and cooked on skewers, then tossed with the sauce and served on Chinese noodles or leaves of Cos lettuce.

Pollo con Adobo

This delicious version of a Mexican classic is based on a recipe in Authentic Mexican Cooking *by Rick Bayless. While it can be made with small dried chillis, the chillis mentioned are available from the Cool Chilli Company (01973 311714). The adobo paste takes time to prepare, but these quantities make much more than is needed for one dish. See the suggestions at the end of the recipe for using the remainder.*

Preparation time: 30 minutes
Cooking time: 25 – 35 minutes

1 head (10 – 12 cloves) garlic
50 g (2 oz) mixed chillis, e.g. guajillo, ancho and pasado;
    or 25g (1 oz) ordinary dried red chillis
1.25 ml (¼ teaspoon) whole cumin seeds
2.5 cm (1 in) piece cinnamon stick
1 clove
5 black peppercorns
10 ml (2 teaspoons) salt
5 ml (1 teaspoon) thyme
5 ml (1 teaspoon) oregano
2 bay leaves, crumbled
60 ml (4 tablespoons) wine or cider vinegar
1 medium onion, thinly sliced
1 green pepper, thinly sliced
30 ml (2 tablespoons) vegetable oil
8 chicken pieces, total weight about 900 g (2 lb)
Salt and freshly ground black pepper

Heat a heavy, uncoated frying pan over a low heat. Separate the garlic cloves without peeling, and cook them in the pan until deeply browned all over (around 15 minutes). In the same pan, 'toast' the chillis one at a time for around 30 seconds on each side, then remove the seeds and stems. If you're using small dried chillis, skip the toast-ing and just seed. As each chilli is done, crumble it and put it into a spice blender. A coffee blender will be fine, as long as it's cleaned scrupulously both before and afterwards.

Add the cumin, cinnamon, clove and peppercorns to the chillis, and blend to a fine powder; turn out into a mixing bowl. When the garlic is done, squeeze the flesh out of the skins and put through a garlic press or mash with a mortar and pestle. Add to the chilli-spice mixture along with the salt, thyme, oregano, bay leaves and vinegar. Blend thoroughly then transfer to a glass jar and refrigerate until needed. Adobo will keep for a month or more – if it doesn't get used before.

To make the chicken, fry the onion and pepper in half the oil until just soft (around 10 minutes). Remove to a bowl and heat the remaining oil; if your pan is not non-stick, you will need a little more. Season the chicken with salt and pepper and fry over a medium heat until it's browned as uniformly as possible. Add 30 ml (2 tablespoons) of adobo and keep cooking until the chicken is barely done (15 – 25 minutes). Serve on a platter with the onions and peppers. Pass rice or tortillas separately.

Variations

Left-over adobo can be mixed with vegetable oil and used as a marinade for pork, lamb, beef or chicken – you'll need around 10 ml (2 teaspoons) per pound of meat.

A small spoonful can be added to stews, soups, beans or rice, mixed with yoghurt as a topping for baked potatoes, or used to deglaze the roasting pan from a joint.

Flash-roasted Moroccan Chicken

This dish is adapted from Nigel Slater's The 30 – Minute Cook*. The original is fried at a high heat, but it's friendlier (i.e., less smoky) to use the oven when guests are nearby.*

Preparation time: 10 minutes
Marinating time: 30 minutes – 1 hour
Cooking time: 40 minutes

6 chicken pieces, breast or leg
1 – 2 fresh red chillis, seeded and finely chopped
1 – 2 dried red chillis, seeded and finely chopped
3 – 4 garlic cloves, finely chopped
Juice of 1 lemon
60 ml (4 tablespoons) extra virgin olive oil
10 ml (2 teaspoons) ground cinnamon
225 ml (8 fl oz) water or chicken stock
A dash of white wine, optional
60 ml (4 tablespoons) raisins
60 ml (4 tablespoons) pine nuts
Salt and freshly ground black pepper
Fresh mint, to garnish

Place the chicken in a roasting tin. Mix the chillis, garlic, lemon juice, olive oil and cinnamon with some salt and freshly ground black pepper. Rub or brush the mixture onto the chicken and marinate for at least 30 minutes – an hour or more would be better.

Pre-heat the oven to 230°C/450°F/Gas 8. Add a splash of water to the roasting tin and bake at the top of the oven for around 30 – 35 minutes. Baste a few times, and top up with water if the juices in the pan seem to be drying out.

When the chicken's cooked, remove to a serving platter and keep warm in the turned-off oven (door slightly ajar). Put the roasting tin on the hob over a medium heat and pour in the stock or water. Add a splash of white wine, if you've got it. Deglaze the pan, scraping all the delicious bits stuck onto the bottom, then put in the raisins and pine nuts. Cook hard for about 2 minutes, season to taste with salt and pepper then pour over the chicken. Garnish with the mint and serve immediately with rice, bread, couscous, or burghal.

Flash-roasted Moroccan Chicken

Sautéed Chicken with Bacon and Courgettes

Sautéed Chicken With Bacon and Courgettes

Served with baked potatoes or even just slices of toast, this makes a wonderful midweek meal for 2.

**Preparation time:
10 minutes
Cooking time: 40 minutes**

2 slices smoked streaky bacon,
  rinds removed, shredded
1 medium onion, thinly sliced
5 – 10 ml (1 – 2 teaspoons)
  vegetable oil
3 – 4 smallish courgettes,
  cut in 5 mm (¼ in) slices
2 chicken breasts or legs
100 ml (4 fl oz) water, stock or
  white wine (or a combination)
Salt and freshly ground black
  pepper

Stir-fry the bacon over a medium heat until a little of its fat starts to run. Add the onion and continue frying, stirring regularly, until the onion is barely softened (around 3 – 4 minutes). Remove to a bowl and wipe out the pan if there's a lot of fat in it.

Put half the oil in the pan, turn up the heat to high and add the courgettes with a good grinding of pepper. Fry briskly, stirring every minute or so until they're still quite crunchy but lightly browned in spots. Add a small splash of water and scrape the pan bottom to deglaze, then transfer to a bowl.

Add the remaining oil to the pan, swirl it around and put in the chicken pieces skin side down. Brown lightly (around 2 minutes), then season with a little salt and pepper and turn. Brown the second side, then turn the heat down and stir in the bacon and onions. Cook for a further 1 minute, pour in the liquid, and cook (covered) for around 30 minutes. When it is done, add the courgettes and heat through.

Duck Breasts 'au poivre' with Red Onion Relish

This can be made with either ordinary duck or the smaller, leaner Barbary ducks available from Sainsbury's and other supermarkets. If you don't eat all the onions, they can be used with other dishes.

**Preparation time: 5 minutes
Cooking time: 1 – 1¼ hours**

2.5 – 5 ml (½ – 1 teaspoon) black
  peppercorns
2 duck breasts
225 g (8 oz) red onions, thinly sliced
15 ml (1 tablespoon) red wine vinegar
15 – 30 ml (1 – 2 tablespoons) extra virgin
  olive oil
1 bay leaf, broken into 4 pieces
50 ml (2 fl oz) chicken stock
15 ml (1 tablespoon) Crème de Cassis,
  optional

Grind or pound the peppercorns coarsely and rub into the flesh side of the duck breasts. Meanwhile, put the onions, vinegar, oil and bay leaf in a heavy-based frying pan. Cook at the gentlest possible heat, stirring occasionally, until the onions are very soft (around 45 minutes). They can also be microwaved for 12 – 15 minutes, stirring 2 or 3 times. The dish can be prepared in advance to this point and the onions re-heated just before serving.

If you've cooked the onions in the pan you're using for the duck, wipe it out and place over a medium heat. Slap in the duck breasts, skin side down. Leave them to cook until the skin is deeply browned and most of the subcutaneous fat is rendered out. This can take anything from 4 – 10 minutes, depending on the duck. Now spoon out the excess fat, turn the duck and cook on the flesh side until the meat is done the way you like it (another 5 – 10 minutes). Remove to a plate and cover with aluminium foil to keep warm.

Deglaze the pan with the stock and Cassis (if using), then boil down to a thick syrup. Slice the duck breasts around 5 mm (½ in) thick and fan out on warm serving plates. Spoon a little sauce on each one, and serve with the onion relish.

Chicken Pilaff with Vegetables

This recipe assumes that your roast chicken, like mine, is cooked à point. If it's well-done, cook it just long enough to heat through (around 2 minutes).

**Preparation time: 15 minutes
Cooking time: 25 – 30 minutes**

225 g (8 oz) long-grain rice
½ roast chicken
30 ml (2 tablespoons) vegetable oil
5 ml (1 teaspoon) whole cumin seeds
5 ml (1 teaspoon) whole coriander seeds
1 bay leaf
1 large onion, coarsely chopped
350 ml (12½ fl oz) chicken stock
1 green pepper, seeded and shredded
1 red pepper, seeded and shredded
225 g (8 oz) mushroom, thickly sliced
30 ml (2 tablespoons) crème fraîche,
  optional
Salt and freshly ground black pepper

Wash the rice under the cold tap and drain for 5 minutes. Cut the chicken from the bone and pull into pieces about 2.5 cm (1 in) thick.

Heat the oil in a heavy casserole and add the cumin, coriander, bay leaf and onion. Cook gently for 5 minutes, then add rice and stir well to coat with oil. Pour in the stock, cover and simmer gently for 5 minutes. Add the peppers, stir to mix and cook for another 5 minutes. Add the chicken and mushrooms, stir again and cook for another 5 minutes. Mix in crème fraîche (if using) and serve immediately with a green salad.

This dish will easily serve 4, and the left-over left-overs (if there are any) will be delicious cold for lunch the next day.

Chicken Pilaff with Vegetables (page 51)

Barbecued Chicken Croquettes with Sun-dried Tomatoes

The tomatoes must be the type sold in oil; they can be chopped quickly with the garlic and herbs in your food processor, which must be used afterwards for the chicken.

Preparation time: 15 – 20 minutes
Cooking time: 6 – 8 minutes

3 skinless, boneless chicken breasts or 6 thighs
6 small sun-dried tomatoes, finely chopped
2 garlic cloves, finely chopped
6 leaves fresh tarragon or 3 leaves fresh sage,
    finely chopped
Oil for brushing
½ lemon
Salt and freshly ground black pepper

Cut the chicken into chunks and process in the food processor to a fine paste. Add the tomatoes, garlic and herbs and whiz until everything is well mixed. Season with salt and plenty of pepper then form the mixture into small patties about 7.5 cm (3 in) wide and 2.5 cm (1 in) thick. Refrigerate, covered, until needed.

When the barbecue is hot, brush one side of the patties generously with oil; this is essential to prevent sticking. Barbecue for around 3 – 4 minutes, then brush the other side with oil and cook on the other side until just done. Remove to a serving platter, squeeze over some lemon juice, and serve immediately.

These croquettes may also be cooked on the grill, or in a hot frying pan.

Roast Chicken

I've experimented with many techniques for roast chicken, and my favourite is a foolproof method from Jacques Pépin, published in Ken Hom's East Meets West. Vary the seasonings to your taste. The recipe here is designed for dinner parties requiring 2 chickens; this may be too much, so use the left-overs for the pilaff on page 51 – or cook 1 chicken instead of 2.

Preparation time: 5 minutes
Cooking time: 70 minutes plus 5 – 15 minutes' resting time

2 bay leaves
2 garlic cloves or 1 small onion, halved
2 x 1.5 – 2 kg (3 – 4 lb) free-range chickens
60 ml (4 tablespoons) softened butter
Salt and freshly ground pepper

Pre-heat the oven to 230°C/450° F/Gas 8. Put the bay leaves and onion or garlic in the chicken cavities and place on a poultry roasting rack in a roasting pan, breast-side down. Smear with the butter, season well with salt and pepper, and put a little water in the pan to keep the pan juices from burning.

Roast in the centre of the oven for 20 minutes, then turn the oven down to 180°C/350° F/Gas 4 and baste with the melted butter. Roast for another 40 minutes, then turn the heat up to 230°C/450°F/Gas 8. Turn the chickens over so the breasts face up, baste again and season with more salt and pepper. Return to the oven for another 5 – 10 minutes, until the breasts are lightly browned. If you like chicken well done, cook at this final stage for 15 – 20 minutes.

To test, prick a leg just below the joint between drumstick and thigh. If the juices run clear, with the faintest hint of pink, the chicken is done. You can also test by pressing the breast firmly with your finger. If it feels quite firm, with no hint of softness, the bird should be cooked. Leave to rest in the turned-off oven, with the door open, for up to 15 minutes. You can make a gravy in the meantime if you wish.

Baked Chicken with Fresh Herbs

This is a fat-free dish but delicious in spite of that.

Preparation time: 5 minutes
Cooking time: 45 – 60 minutes

4 chicken legs or breasts
4 sage leaves
1 large onion, finely chopped
A small handful of flat-leaf parsley,
    finely chopped
1 large sprig of tarragon, finely chopped
100 ml (4 fl oz) dry white wine or
    vermouth
Salt and freshly ground black pepper

Pre-heat the oven to 180°C/350°F/Gas 4.
Trim the chicken of all visible fat and place
in a roasting tin. Tuck a sage leaf under each
piece, making sure the leaf is completely
covered. Scatter the onion and remaining
herbs around the chicken, pour over the
wine and season with salt and pepper. Bake
in the centre of the oven, basting 3 – 4 times
with wine and pan juices, until the chicken
is just cooked (around 45 – 60 minutes).

Chicken with Polenta and Bagna Cauda

Bagna Cauda, the famous anchovy sauce of Piedmont, is usually served with raw vegetables. Here the sauce is spooned onto polenta and then topped with a flash-roasted chicken breast. You can skip the polenta and serve the chicken on its own if you like.

Preparation time:
20 minutes
Cooking time: 25 – 30
minutes plus cooking time
for the polenta

1 quantity Basic Polenta
    (see page 143)
4 boneless free-range chicken breasts,
    wings removed
A small handful of flat-leaf parsley,
    coarsely chopped

For the sauce
1 dried red chilli, finely chopped, or a
    dash of chilli sauce
4 – 5 garlic cloves, finely chopped
4 sun-dried tomatoes, finely chopped
200 ml (7 fl oz) extra virgin olive oil
1 tin anchovies, drained and coarsely
    chopped

Pour the cooked polenta into a dish that will form a slab around 1.25 cm (½ in) thick.
Prepare the chicken, if necessary.

Heat the chilli, garlic and tomatoes in 30 ml (2 tablespoons) of the oil until they begin to smell fragrant. Add the anchovies and cook, stirring frequently, until they begin
to break. Now add the remaining oil, a little at a time, until the sauce is fairly smooth
(around 5 – 10 minutes). The recipe can be prepared in advance to this point and kept,
covered, on the hob.

Pre-heat the oven to 230°C/450°F/Gas 8. Season the chicken with a little salt and
plenty of freshly ground black pepper. Cut out 4 slabs of polenta big enough to hold a
single breast apiece. Lightly oil a large roasting pan and put in the chicken and polenta
(don't amalgamate yet – use 2 pans if you don't have one large enough to hold everything). Brush chicken and polenta with a little extra virgin olive oil and roast at the top
of the oven for around 25 – 30 minutes. The polenta will take up some of the chicken
juices, which is fine. If the chicken is done before the polenta is ready, remove and cover
lightly with foil.

Gently re-heat the sauce and warm 4 serving plates. Put a slab of polenta on each plate,
spoon over a bit of the sauce and top with a chicken breast. (You could also spoon the
sauce over the chicken.) Sprinkle with chopped parsley and serve immediately with
steamed green vegetables.

Chicken with Polenta and Bagna Cauda

Chicken with Thai Flavours

This dish adapts Thai flavours to Western-style cooking. If your chicken is on the fatty side, trim away every bit you can see.

Preparation time: 5 minutes
Cooking time: 35 – 45 minutes

15 ml (1 tablespoon) peanut oil or vegetable oil
2 stalks lemon grass, finely chopped
4 garlic cloves, finely chopped
1 – 2 dried red chillis, seeded and crumbled
2 small onions or 6 spring onions, finely chopped
3 – 4 kaffir lime leaves, finely shredded
450 ml (15 fl oz) coconut milk
30 ml (2 tablespoons) Thai fish sauce, optional
4 chicken breasts or legs

Heat the oil to a medium heat in a small pan and stir-fry the lemon grass, garlic, chillis, onions and lime leaves for 1 minute. Add the coconut milk and fish sauce then bring to the boil before turning down heat and simmering for 10 minutes. This dish can be prepared in advance to this point, and refrigerated overnight if necessary.

Pre-heat the oven to 230°C/450°F/Gas 8. Make a few deep slashes through the skin of each piece of chicken and place in a roasting tin with the sauce. Bake in the top of the oven, basting 2 – 3 times, until the chicken is just cooked (around 25 minutes for breasts, 30 – 35 minutes for legs). The sauce can be reduced if it's too liquid by boiling on the hob for a few minutes. Serve with rice and a plain green vegetable.

Chicken with Forty Cloves of Garlic

The name of this recipe is frightening, but long cooking removes at least some of the breath-polluting attributes of garlic. And after-effects are acceptable, because this is one of the greatest dishes in the world.

Preparation time: 5 minutes
Cooking time: 1¼ – 1½ hours

1.5 – 2 kg (3 – 4 lb) chicken, preferably free-range
80 – 100 ml (3 – 4 fl oz) extra virgin olive oil
4 – 5 heads of garlic
Fresh herbs of your choice, e.g. sage, thyme, rosemary, tarragon
Flour-water paste for sealing casserole, optional
Salt and freshly ground black pepper

Pre-heat the oven to 180°C/350°F/Gas 4. Separate the garlic into cloves and remove the outer papery husks but do not peel them. Put the oil in the casserole over a low heat and roll the chicken around in it, turning to coat well. Add the garlic and herbs and coat them too, then season well with salt and pepper.

Now cover the casserole and seal it in one of two ways to lock in the garlic-scented steam. For the traditional method (and a lovely impression at the table), roll out a large ball of flour-water paste into a long strip. Pat it down around the rim of the casserole and press the lid on to make a tight seal. The easier method, which always works for me, is to use a double thickness of aluminium foil. Cut the foil to a size larger than the casserole lid, then place it over the casserole, making sure the edges hang over the sides and clamp the lid on tightly.

In either case, cook the chicken in the oven for around 1¼ – 1½ hours, until the chicken is done (see the Roast Chicken recipe on page 53).

This dish should be served with toasted French bread. Squeeze a clove of cooked garlic onto each slice then squash it down and dribble with a little of the perfumed oil.

Chicken Brochettes with Watercress Salad

The chicken will taste even better if it's marinated overnight.

Preparation time: 5 minutes
Cooking time: 10 minutes

675 g (1½ lb) boneless chicken pieces, leg or breast
Juice of 1 lemon
7.5 ml (1½ teaspoons) dried thyme or 30 ml
    (2 tablespoons) fresh
45 ml (3 tablespoons) extra virgin olive oil
2 bunches watercress, trimmed of their thick stems
5 ml (1 teaspoon) balsamic vinegar
Salt and freshly ground black pepper

Skin the chicken and trim off any visible fat, then cut into cubes around 2 cm (¾ in) square. Combine the lemon juice, thyme and 1 tablespoon of the oil. Put the chicken in a glass or ceramic bowl and toss well with the marinade. Leave to marinate for at least 15 minutes, or overnight in the fridge.

Pre-heat the grill for 5 minutes and thread the chicken onto 4–6 skewers. Grill the brochettes, turning 2–3 times, until just done (around 10 minutes).

Meanwhile, put the watercress in a bowl and toss with the remaining oil, the vinegar and a little salt and pepper. Divide between 4–6 serving plates to make a 'nest' for the chicken.

To serve, either put the brochettes on each plate or remove from the skewers beforehand.

Chicken Tajine with Dried Fruit

Moroccan tajines – braises of meat or poultry – are one of the few dishes that successfully combine chicken and fruit. This is loosely based on a recipe in Paula Wolfert's Good Food From Morocco *which uses prunes. Apricots or apples may be substituted.*

Preparation time: 30 minutes
Cooking time: 40 minutes

350 g (12 oz) dried fruit – prunes, apricots or apples
7.5 cm (3 in) cinnamon stick or 15 ml (1 tablespoon)
    ground cinnamon
30 ml (2 tablespoons) vegetable oil
A small handful of whole, blanched almonds or
    almond flakes
1 x 1.75 – 2 kg (3½ – 4 lb) chicken or 8 chicken
    pieces, preferably free-range
10 ml (2 teaspoons) ground cumin
2 large onions, coarsely chopped
2 garlic cloves, finely chopped
5 ml (1 teaspoon) turmeric
5 ml (1 teaspoon) ground ginger or coriander
Salt and freshly ground black pepper

Place the fruit in a pan with the cinnamon stick (if using) and enough water to cover. Bring to the boil, then turn down the heat and simmer until the fruit is just soft (15 – 20 minutes). Meanwhile, joint the chicken (if whole) and cut into 8 pieces.

Heat the oil in a heavy-based casserole and quickly brown the almonds; remove to a bowl using a slotted spoon. In the same oil, lightly brown the chicken all over, seasoning with salt and pepper as you turn them, then remove. (You'll probably have to do this in batches.) Top up with more oil if necessary, then add the cumin, onions, garlic, turmeric and coriander or ginger; if you're using cinnamon powder, it too should go in at this point. Cook over a gentle heat for a few minutes to brown the onions lightly, adding a splash of water if the spices are catching on the bottom.

Return the chicken to the pot with the fruit, their soaking liquid, and the cinnamon stick (if using). Add enough water to cover the chicken by three-quarters (about 225 ml/8 fl oz) and bring to the boil. Turn down the heat and cook at a gentle simmer until the chicken is done (around 30 minutes). Scatter over the almonds and serve immediately with plain boiled rice.

Baked Chicken and Fennel

Baked Chicken and Fennel

Chicken and fennel make a great partnership. Here, the chicken is cooked on a bed of the vegetable which flavours the chicken as it cooks. If you don't use the crème fraîche, this dish will be brilliantly low in calories.

**Preparation time:
5 minutes
Cooking time:
35 – 40 minutes**

4 chicken breasts or legs
1 garlic clove, finely chopped
4 smallish fennel bulbs, thickly
    sliced
5 ml (1 teaspoon) dried mixed
    herbs
100 ml (4 fl oz) chicken stock or
    dry white wine
30 ml (2 tablespoons) crème
    fraîche
Salt and freshly ground black
    pepper
Finely chopped fresh herbs,
    e.g. coriander, dill or tarragon,
    to garnish

Pre-heat oven to 200°C/400°F/Gas 6 and trim the chicken of all visible fat, if there is any; you can skin it if you really want to eliminate extra calories. Put the garlic, fennel and dried herbs in a roasting pan which will hold the chicken in a single layer, then lay the chicken pieces on top.

Season with salt and pepper, pour over the liquid and bake in the centre of the oven until the chicken is just done (around 35 minutes for breasts, 40 for legs). Baste several times and add the crème fraîche (if you're using it) around 5 minutes before the end of the cooking time. The fennel should be soft and full of flavour. Sprinkle on the fresh herbs and serve immediately.

Fragrant Rice with Chicken

You can use pork or lamb instead of the chicken for this dish. You can also omit the chicken altogether and serve the rice on its own.

**Preparation time:
10 – 15 minutes
Cooking time: 20 minutes**

350 g (12 oz) long-grain rice
1 stalk lemon grass, finely chopped
4 kaffir lime leaves, thinly sliced, optional
2 garlic cloves, quartered
1 boneless chicken breast, preferably
    free-range, finely shredded
10 ml (1 teaspoon) vegetable oil
2.5 ml (½ teaspoon) Thai fish sauce
    (*nam pla*)
5 ml (1 teaspoon) soy sauce
5 ml (1 teaspoon) sesame oil
2.5 ml (½ teaspoon) vinegar, preferably
    Chinese black
½ small green chilli, seeded and finely
    chopped
6 – 8 leaves basil

Put the rice in a small pan and add 1½ times the volume of water (about 700 ml/1¼ pints). Mix in the lemon grass, lime leaves and garlic and bring to the boil. Reduce the heat, cover and simmer until the rice is barely cooked (15 – 20 minutes). Meanwhile, fry the chicken lightly in the vegetable oil.

When the rice is ready, mix in the Thai fish sauce, soy sauce, sesame oil, vinegar and chilli. Fluff up with a fork, cover and leave to infuse for 5 minutes away from the heat.

Top the rice with chicken and basil and serve with extra soy sauce if you wish.

Lemon Chicken

This great combination appears, in different guises, in many national cuisines. The version here is designed for quick cooking, which preserves the freshness of the citrus.

**Preparation time: 5 minutes
Cooking time: around 30 – 35
minutes**

4 chicken pieces
15 ml (1 tablespoon) vegetable or
    olive oil
5 ml (1 teaspoon) flour
1 clove garlic, finely chopped
100 ml (4 fl oz) dry white wine
1 bunch spring onions, green bits
    included, finely shredded
225 g (8 oz) mushrooms, brown or
    shiitake, thickly sliced
1 large lemon
Salt and freshly ground black pepper

If using chicken legs, separate the thighs from the drumsticks. Heat the oil in a large frying pan and brown the chicken pieces lightly on both sides (around 5 minutes). Stir the flour and garlic into the oil, season with salt and pepper and pour in the wine. Cover the pan and cook at a gentle simmer. Add the onions after 10 minutes and the mushrooms after 20. Turn the chicken once or twice during the cooking time.

Meanwhile, pare the rind from the lemon and cut into very fine shreds. Squeeze out the juice and reserve. When the chicken is cooked (around 25 – 30 minutes in all), pour in the lemon juice and shredded rind, and continue cooking for a further minute.

Serve with plain rice or mashed potatoes to soak up the delicious juices.

Pan-Roasted Quail with Grapes and Garlic

This is something like a pan-cooked variant on Chicken with 40 Cloves of Garlic. During the game season, wood pigeons could be used instead. You'll need 2 quail per portion.

Preparation time: 2 minutes
Cooking time: 45 minutes

12 garlic cloves, unpeeled
45 ml (3 tablespoons) vegetable oil
8 quail
30 ml (2 tablespoons) Crème de Cassis or ruby port
30 ml (2 tablespoons) wine vinegar
3 – 4 slices prosciutto, quartered, optional
15 – 20 seedless grapes
Salt and freshly ground black pepper

Put the garlic in a small, heavy-based pan with 15 ml (1 tablespoon) of the oil and 45 ml (3 tablespoons) of water. Bring to a simmer, cover and cook as gently as possible until the garlic is very soft (about 30 minutes). Check the water from time to time and add more if necessary.

In a heavy, lidded frying pan (or smallish casserole), heat the remaining oil to a moderate heat and brown the birds well all over (around 5 minutes). Turn the heat down to fairly low and leave it for a minute, then pour in the liqueur or port and vinegar. Season with some salt and pepper.

Add the garlic, cover tightly and simmer until the birds are done (around 10 minutes). Do not overcook or they will be tough and dry. Add the *prosciutto* (if using) and grapes for 2 – 3 minutes only, just to heat them through.

Parcel-roasted Pheasant

Pheasant is a lean bird and needs a lot of basting if roasted in an open pan. Try this method of cooking the bird, wrapped in foil with aromatic seasonings for a deliciously robust flavour.

Preparation time: 10 minutes
Cooking time: 1 hour

1 pheasant, preferably a hen
1 garlic clove, finely chopped
1 thick slice lemon
1 piece orange peel
1 bay leaf
1 slice fresh ginger, peeled and finely chopped
A good knob of butter
15 ml (1 tablespoon) extra virgin olive oil
Freshly ground black pepper
Coarse salt

Pre-heat the oven to 200°C/400°F/Gas 6. Put a large double sheet of aluminium foil on a roasting rack then place the pheasant onto it, breast down. (If you don't have a rack that will hold the parcel securely in place, put the bird on its side.) Put the seasonings and butter in the cavity of the bird and season with black pepper. Dribble over the oil and wrap up the foil to make a sealed parcel, leaving some space around it so that the steam can circulate.

Put the bird in the oven and cook for 45 minutes. If the bird is lying on its side, remove after 25 minutes and turn so the other side is facing up. At the end of the cooking time, turn the heat up to 230°C/450°F/Gas 8. Remove the roasting tin from the oven and unwrap the parcel. Turn the bird breast-side up, season with coarse salt and roast for another 5 – 15 minutes or until the pheasant is fully cooked and the breast skin lightly browned. Serve with the cooking juices and either Mashed Potatoes (see page 114) or a Potato Gratin (see page 110).

Wild Duck with Bacon and Shallots

Wild duck is my favourite of the more affordable game birds. This recipe is sweetly luxurious and very impressive at a dinner party. Serve with mashed potatoes or grilled polenta (see page 143).

Preparation time: 10 minutes
Cooking time: 40 minutes

2 wild ducks
15 ml (1 tablespoon) vegetable oil
10 rashers streaky bacon, rinds removed, halved
20 shallots, peeled and trimmed but left whole
100 ml (4 fl oz) ruby port
100 ml (4 fl oz) raspberry vinegar
100 ml (4 fl oz) chicken stock
2 bay leaves
Juice of ½ lemon
Salt and freshly ground black pepper

Pre-heat the oven to 180°C/350°F/Gas 4. Wipe the ducks with a damp paper towel and pull off any stray bits of feather. Heat the oil in a casserole large enough to hold the birds in a single layer and gently cook the bacon until lightly browned (about 3 minutes). Now move the bacon to the sides of the casserole, put the ducks in, and brown each breast lightly for 1 minute. Finally turn the birds on their backs and brown again for 2 more minutes.

Add the remaining ingredients, season with salt and pepper and turn the heat up. When the liquid comes to a boil, cover the pot and cook the ducks until they're cooked medium-rare – with a hint of pink in the breast. Remove from the pot and cover loosely with aluminium foil while you skim the fat from the cooking liquid and boil the stock down on the hob to make the sauce. When the stock has reduced by around half, add the lemon juice.

To serve, either joint the birds or cut them in half with poultry shears (less elegant but much easier). Give each diner some bacon and shallots and pass the sauce separately.

Duck Legs with Prunes and Peppercorns

Most supermarkets sell jars of mixed peppercorns which are perfect for this dish.

Preparation time: 15 minutes
Cooking time: 7 – 8 hours

16 – 20 prunes
4 duck legs
1 large onion, thickly sliced
2 large garlic cloves, thickly sliced
2 bay leaves
15 ml (1 tablespoon) peppercorns
450 – 600 ml (15 – 20 fl oz) chicken or duck stock

100 ml (4 fl oz) fino or manzanilla sherry
30 ml (2 tablespoons) cornflour, optional

Pre-heat the oven to 140°C/275°F/Gas 1. Put the prunes in a large, heavy casserole and lay the duck legs on top (in a single layer, if possible). Add the remaining ingredients except the cornflour, cover and cook overnight, or for at least 7 hours.

To finish, you could concentrate the cooking liquid by boiling it down hard for 10 – 15 minutes or you could thicken it by mixing the cornflour with 2 tablespoons cooking liquid, then stirring it into the casserole and cooking hard for a few minutes.

The Claridge's Turkey

The Claridge's Turkey

Because turkey legs cook much more slowly than the breast, it's difficult to cook them both perfectly. You can avoid that problem with the method sometimes used at Claridge's. More work is required beforehand, but it means less work at the table – and guarantees perfect results. For the Claridge's Chestnut Stuffing, see right.

Preparation 30 minutes
Cooking time: 2 hours

6 kg (12 – 14 lb) turkey, preferably a Bronze hen
Oil and butter for greasing
Salt and freshly ground pepper

Prepare the turkey by cutting out the wishbone; this makes carving much easier. Now remove the legs, making sure you take off the 'oyster' at the top of each leg. Lay the legs, skin-side down, on a board, then make a neat incision along the whole length of the bone. Working with your fingers and the knife, gently bone out each leg. (This can take up to 10 minutes the first time you do it, but it's actually very easy.) Pull out the tendons and sinews with tweezers and lay the legs out flat. Season with salt and pepper.

Spoon the stuffing (see right) into the hollows left by the bones, taking care not to make it too thick. Roll the legs into neat sausages (ballottines) with the edges of skin meeting. Generously butter 2 pieces of aluminium foil about 45 cm (18 in) square and lay a ballottine in the centre of each, then roll the foil around them. Twist the foil ends tightly to make a neat roll.

You can treat the breasts in two ways. One is to remove them in a single piece and roll them up together with string at 2.5 cm (1 in) intervals (as in the photograph). This looks attractive, especially with a bit of parsley or herb stuffing, and is easy to carve.

But I prefer the Claridge's way, which is to roast the breasts on the bone with a slice of apple in the cavity. The wings provide stability in the roasting pan, and cooking meat on the bone is always said to give more flavour.

Cooking the turkey takes just under 2 hours in a 200°C/400°F/Gas 6 oven. The ballottines should first be steamed for 30 minutes and then roasted for 40. Season the breasts with salt and brush with oil and melted butter, then roast for around 1½ hours. Baste every 15 minutes and cover with foil if the skin is browning too quickly.

Both legs and breasts should be left in the turned-off oven, with the door open, for 15 minutes or longer while you make a gravy. Cut each breast off the bone as a whole piece and then cut slices from there.

Left-over tips

Use the remains of the turkey (or gammon, page 86) for creamy, cheesy casseroles with potatoes, beans or pasta.

Claridge's Chestnut Stuffing

Peeling chestnuts is the most odious of all kitchen chores. At Claridge's they make it easier by cutting a criss-cross incision in each, then deep-frying them for 4 – 5 minutes until the outer skin starts to peel away. This recipe makes the right quantity for the Claridge's Turkey recipe.

Preparation time: 30 minutes
Cooking time: 20 minutes

150g (5 oz) onions, coarsely chopped
100g (3½ oz) butter
1 dessert apple, peeled and finely chopped
500 g (1 lb 2 oz) sausage meat
40 g (1½ oz) fresh sage
15 g (½ oz) fresh thyme
300 g (7 oz) breadcrumbs
500g (1 lb 2 oz) chestnuts, peeled and coarsely chopped

Melt butter in a pan and gently cook the onions until they are translucent (15 – 20 minutes). Add the apple to the pan and cook long enough to soften. Leave to cool then mix thoroughly with all the remaining ingredients except the breadcrumbs and chestnuts. Mix these in last, going gently so you don't break up the nuts. Season and refrigerate until needed. For cooking method and time, see the turkey recipe.

Shaun Hill's Chestnut And Apple Stuffing

Shaun Hill, one of Britain's most distinguished chefs and cookery writers, is the owner of the Merchants House in Ludlow, Shropshire.

Preparation time: 20 minutes
Cooking time: 45 – 60 minutes

350 g (12 oz) rindless, boneless belly of pork, thinly sliced
3 medium onions, chopped
6 slices white bread soaked in 225 ml (8 fl oz) milk
1 whole nutmeg
2 – 3 cinnamon sticks
350 g (12 oz) Granny Smith apples, peeled and cut in chunks
350 g (12 oz) roast chestnuts, peeled and quartered
Salt and freshly ground black pepper

Process the pork and onions in a food processor until they're almost the consistency of sausage meat and turn out into a bowl. Remove the bread from the milk, squeeze it dry and break it into smallish pieces using your hands. Add to the pork mixture. Grate in plenty of nutmeg and cinnamon, and season with salt and lots of black pepper – the stuffing should be very spicy. You can taste it by frying or microwaving a small spoonful. Finally add the apples and chestnuts.

See Michael Roux's Christmas Stuffing (page 65) for cooking methods and times.

Roast Goose

Many people would regard my estimated cooking time for goose as being too short, but it's better to err that way than to overcook an expensive treat like goose. Just remember to watch the bird carefully from 2 hours onwards: it can quickly go from perfection to ruination.

Preparation time: 10 minutes
Cooking time: 2½ hours

1 goose, weighing about 4.5 – 6 kg (10 – 12 lb)
1 medium onion, peeled and quartered
2 bay leaves
A small handful of fresh herbs, e.g. rosemary, thyme, sage
30 ml (2 tablespoons) clear honey
15 ml (1 tablespoon) wine vinegar
Salt and freshly ground black pepper

Pre-heat the oven to 180°C/350°F, Gas Mark 4). Remove the giblets and any loose fat from the cavity of the goose and prick the skin all over (taking care not to pierce the flesh) with a small, sharp knife. Put it on a rack in your largest roasting tin and cover the ends of the drumsticks with aluminium foil to keep them from cooking too fast.

Stick the onion, bay leaves and herbs in the cavity and season it with salt and pepper. Roast at the centre of the oven for around 2½ hours, watching carefully from 2 hours onwards. The breast should feel very slightly springy to the touch and the juices in the cavity run almost clear, with just a hint of pink. The bird won't need basting because of all the subcutaneous fat, but the rendered fat should be removed with a spoon or bulb baster. Save it for cooking potatoes, vegetables and fish.

When the bird seems to be nearly done, whisk the honey and vinegar together and brush them over the skin. A further 15 – 20 minutes of cooking should help crisp up and glaze the skin. When the bird is done, cover with aluminium foil and let it rest for 20 minutes before carving.

Michel Roux's Christmas Stuffing

I've adapted this stuffing from a recipe given to me by Michel Roux of the Waterside Inn, Bray, Berkshire. Like most expert cooks, M. Roux does not recommend stuffing the main cavity because of the increase in cooking time.

Preparation time: 30 minutes
Cooking time: 45 – 60 minutes

2 very large knobs of butter
1 medium onion, finely chopped
175 g (6 oz) mushrooms, minced
85 g (3½ oz) cubed white bread soaked in 100 ml (4 fl oz) milk
675 g (1½ lb) pork fillet, minced
350 g (12 oz) pork fat, minced
A small handful of parsley, finely chopped
175 ml (6 fl oz) single cream
30 ml (2 tablespoons) cognac
2 eggs, beaten
Salt and freshly ground black pepper

Divide the butter between 2 pans and gently heat. Add the onions to one and the mushrooms to the other and cook until the onion is translucent and the mushrooms soft (around 10 minutes). Leave to cool completely.

Lightly squeeze the bread dry, then combine all the ingredients except the cream, cognac and eggs. Season with salt and pepper, and mix well. Gradually add the cream and cognac and finally the eggs. The mixture is now ready. Poach or microwave a spoonful to test for seasoning. The stuffing can be prepared in advance to this point and refrigerated or frozen until required.

If you wish, you can put some stuffing in the bird's neck cavity but it's better to roll it into 2 sausage shapes in aluminium foil then to roast it alongside the bird for 45 – 60 minutes. Alternatively, you can put it in 1 or 2 gratin dishes and bake, covered, for about the same time. The cover may be removed towards the end of cooking to brown the top.

Ken Hom's Rice and Herb Stuffing

This stuffing, one of my favourite dishes, comes from Ken Hom's East Meets West. I make it every year at Thanksgiving and it always gets polished off. The ingredients marked with an asterisk are available at Chinese markets.

Preparation time: 45 – 60 minutes
Cooking time: 45 minutes

675 g (1½ lb) glutinous rice* or pudding rice
450g (1 lb) Chinese pork sausage*, cut into 1.5 cm (½ in) chunks
30 ml (2 tablespoons) peanut oil
225 g (8 oz) shallots or onions, minced
4 spring onions, minced
100 ml (4 fl oz) Chinese rice wine* or dry sherry
700 ml (1¼ pints) of turkey or chicken stock
675 g (1½ lb) tinned water chestnuts*, finely diced
1 small red or green pepper, diced
5 ml (1 teaspoon) dried tarragon
5 ml (1 teaspoon) dried thyme
A small handful of Chinese chives* or ordinary chives,
    finely chopped
Salt and freshly ground black pepper

Put the rice in a large bowl and cover with water and soak overnight. Drain well. Chop the sausage into ½ – inch dice. Heat the oil in a wok or large frying pan and stir-fry the shallots and spring onions for 30 seconds, then add the wine and cook until nearly evaporated. Add the sausages and stir-fry for 1 minute. Add the rice and stock then season to taste. Cook, stirring occasionally, until the stock is nearly absorbed (around 8 minutes). Add the water chestnuts, pepper, and herbs; cook for another 3 minutes, stirring frequently. Remove from heat and allow to cool.

Cook the stuffing in a buttered baking dish, allowing around 45 minutes at 180°C/350°F/Gas 4).

This recipe makes 1.5 kg (3 lb) stuffing.

Meat

Chilindrón (page 81)

Meat

When people come to dinner I usually serve meat as a main course and almost invariably someone says: 'Oh good! We hardly ever eat meat at home.' For a variety of reasons – health, food-safety, conscience – meat consumption is down. But most people of my acquaintance still love the stuff. And so do I, which explains the large number of recipes in this section.

Many of the recipes here call for long, slow cooking, a method that appeals to me greatly. I love being able to put a dish in the oven and then bunk off while it gets on with the job. Since the heat is so gentle, there's no need for split-second timing. You have to plan and prepare in advance, but you're then free from most last-minute work.

Slow cooking can fit into your schedule in a variety of ways and my favourite is to leave a dish in the oven overnight: I love the idea that while the cooker's working, I'm asleep. You can also slow-cook during the day, starting the dish at breakfast and eating it, straight from the oven, in the evening. This is good for dinner parties or weekday meals.

Indeed, slow cooking is often the best bet when you have people coming to dinner. Frying or grilling requires close last-minute attention and that's often impractical if you're serving large numbers.

Another benefit of slow cooking is that it uses tough, cheap cuts of meat. I love these cuts: they're flavourful and more forgiving of mis-timing on the part of the cook. My favourites include pork belly, shoulder (as a joint or in 'spare rib chops') and hand; lamb shoulder, shank and neck fillet; and shin, clod or short ribs of beef.

Many other recipes call for frying, either in preparation or as the primary cooking method. Over the years I've switched away from the grill in favour of frying pans, using them for plain-cooked dishes that many people would make under a grill. The reason is simple. A frying pan's surface comes in direct contact with the heat source, getting much hotter than a grill. As a result, it cooks food faster – sometimes in just half the time. It's also more efficient at producing the browning reactions which play such an important part in the flavour of many foods. And rapid cooking improves flavour and prevents loss of tasty juices.

Moreover, frying is much more versatile than grilling. You can cook your basic ingredient with secondary flavourings such as herbs, spices and marinades, then make an instant sauce by deglazing the pan with wine, stock or water. You can also use a single pan to cook an entire meal.

Frying is often associated with high-calorie, high-fat cooking, but you can cut the calories by using these tips. First of all, brush food with oil rather than pouring oil into the pan. If this isn't practical, film the hot pan with oil and swirl it around for full coverage. If you've put too much oil in your pan, wipe out the excess with a kitchen towel. If you're frying fatty meat, sprinkle it lightly with salt and cook without added oil. As long as you don't move it for at least 60 seconds, it should not stick. To use a non-stick pan without added fat, pre-heat it over a medium heat. Put in the chop or steak, then turn the heat up a bit when the meat starts to sizzle.

Marinades are a contentious topic in meat cookery. Many people think the flavour doesn't penetrate in the way it's supposed to, others think it makes all the difference. I take a fence-sitting view: marinades can't hurt, and they can always be used as a dipping sauce. But if you don't have time to give all the marinating time specified in a recipe, don't lose sleep over it.

My Mother's Chuck Steak (Barbecue Version)

Marinating makes a huge difference with chuck steak cut from the shoulder end of the rib. Often sold as braising steak, it will eat as well as sirloin when marinated overnight – though you could, of course, use a more expensive cut.

Preparation time: 3 minutes
Marinating time: at least 8 hours
Cooking time: 8 – 10 minutes

2 – 4 chuck steaks, each weighing 800 g (1¾ lb)
50 ml (2 fl oz) red wine vinegar
50 ml (2 fl oz) Kikkoman soy sauce
50 ml (2 fl oz) vegetable oil
2 garlic cloves

Prick the steaks all over with a fork so the marinade can penetrate and place in a flat non-metallic container which will hold them in a single layer. Whisk together the vinegar, soy sauce and vegetable oil. Crush or chop the garlic and mix in, then pour over the steak, lifting the edges so some marinade gets underneath. Marinate the steak, turning occasionally, for at least 8 hours and preferably 24.

Get the barbecue going, with the aim of reaching a high heat. At the same time, remove meat from the fridge and scrape off the garlic (which may burn over the heat of the barbecue). Barbecue for around 4 – 5 minutes on each side, turning once and brushing with marinade a few times. This is best cooked medium-rare rather than rare – even if (like me) you usually like your beef very pink inside. At home we always ate it with plain rice and I continue to think that this is the best accompaniment.

Variations

This is just as good cold as it is hot. Wait until it's cool, slice thinly, and serve with a salad or in sandwiches.

You can also substitute Worcestershire sauce for the soy and red wine for the vinegar. For extra-special burgers, make up some of the marinade and baste them with it from the moment they go on the barbecue.

Beef Fajitas

Beef Fajitas can be served with tortillas, which are a type of Mexican pancake, often served in numerous ways – straight from the pan, fried until crisp, or wrapped round a filling and then fried or baked. Filled versions can be called burritos, quesadillas, enchiladas, or chimichangas, depending on the cooking method.

The easiest option is to re-heat the tortillas and let each diner fill them with a variety of good things, such as Beef Fajitas. This kind of mix-and-match meal is somewhat time-consuming to prepare, but tremendous fun to eat. Here is a list of other things to serve. Of course, the easy way out is to serve the fajitas on their own – and no one will complain if you do.

Salsa Cruda de dos Chiles (see page 164)
Frijoles Refritos (see page 136)
Guacamole or diced avocado tossed with lemon juice
Shredded peppers
Shredded lettuce
Shredded spring onions
A sharp cheese: feta, Manchego, mature Caerphilly, grated,
    crumbled or shredded
Sour cream or crème fraîche
Store-bought tortillas

Preparation time: none.
Cooking time: around 6 minutes

The ideal cut for Beef Fajitas is skirt steak, but rump is easier to find. The key to success lies in quick cooking over a very high heat.

450 g (1 lb) rump steak
15 – 30 ml (1 – 2 tablespoons) vegetable oil

Around 15 minutes before you want to eat, heat a heavy, uncoated frying pan or griddle until blazingly hot. Brush the meat with oil, sprinkle on a little salt and cook until it's well browned on the outside but very pink inside (around 3 minutes per side). Let it rest, covered, for 5 – 10 minutes and it will continue cooking through to the centre.

While the steak is resting, heat the tortillas through in a dry frying pan (a few seconds per side), a medium oven (around 5 minutes), or the microwave (8 at a time for around 30 seconds). Keep warm. Just before serving, cut the steak into slices around 2.5 mm (⅛ in) thick and put on a plate with the juices poured over.

Bulgogi-style Sliced Beef

Bulgogi-style Sliced Beef

Bulgogi is a Korean dish, often cooked on hotplates at the table. This version is done on the hob and delicious whether warm or piping hot. Use rump, sirloin or a cheaper cut like chuck.

Preparation time: 15 minutes
Marinating time: 2 hours
Cooking time: 10 – 15 minutes

350 g (12 oz) steak, cut in 1.5 cm
(½ in) slices
1 – 2 large spring onions, coarsely
chopped
2 small garlic cloves, coarsely chopped
5 mm (¼ in) square piece of ginger,
coarsely chopped
2.5 ml (½ teaspoon) sugar
25 ml (1 fl oz) soy sauce
25 ml (1 fl oz) water
15 ml (1 tablespoon) sesame seeds
5 – 10 ml (1 – 2 teaspoons) vegetable oil

For the dipping sauce
A small handful of coriander leaves,
coarsely chopped
½ red chilli, seeded and minced
1 large spring onion, coarsely chopped
5 – 10 ml (1 – 2 teaspoons) sesame oil
15 ml (1 tablespoon) red wine
or rice vinegar

Trim the beef of all fat and gristle and cut into manageable pieces. Put them in a mixing bowl with the spring onions, garlic, ginger, sugar, soy sauce and water. Mix the sauce ingredients together and leave for 10 minutes.

Heat the sesame seeds gently in a small pan and swirl them around until they're lightly browned and nuttily fragrant; watch carefully, as they can quickly burn. Set aside 10 ml (2 teaspoons) and decant the rest into a mortar. Mash to a smooth paste, then add to the bowl and stir well. Leave to marinate for at least 2 hours.

Put the beef slices in a sieve to drain off the excess marinade. Heat a large, heavy frying pan until it is very hot then swirl in enough oil to cover the bottom in a thin film. Add the beef leaving 2.5 cm (1 in) of space between the pieces. Cook the beef in batches turning once. If the pan is truly hot, they will take around 30 seconds per side. Since the pieces will continue to cook even out of the pan, you should err on the side of underdone. Remove to a platter and cook the next batch until all the beef is cooked. When it's all done, sprinkle with the remaining sesame seeds, and serve with rice and the sauce passed separately.

Braised Beef With Rice and Gremolata

Gremolata, the classic garnish for osso bucco, is just as good with beef – and an excellent topping for plain rice.

**Preparation time:
25 minutes
Cooking time: 3½ hours**

1.5 kg (3 lb) piece of good beef
without fat, boned and rolled
15 – 30 ml (1 – 2 tablespoons)
vegetable or olive oil
1 bottle dry white wine
3 celery sticks, minced
1 large onion, minced
2 garlic cloves, minced
2.5 ml (½ teaspoon) each of dried
rosemary, thyme and tarragon
1 x 400 g (14 oz) tin plum
tomatoes
225 ml (8 fl oz) beef stock
250 g (9 oz) long-grain rice

For the gremolada
1 garlic clove, minced
Grated rind of ½ lemon
A small handful of fresh parsley,
minced

Pre-heat the oven to 150°C/300°F/ Gas 2 and pat the meat dry. Heat the oil in a casserole that will hold the beef easily, and brown it lightly on all sides. Add the wine, vegetables, herbs, tomatoes and stock. Bring to the boil, then cover and cook for around 3 – 3½ hours, turning and basting occasionally. The dish can be prepared in advance to this point and re-heated before serving.

Around 20 minutes before you want to eat, re-heat the meat, if necessary, and mix the gremolata ingredients. Cook the rice in plenty of well salted water until just done (around 15 minutes) then drain while you remove the meat to a platter and slice it. Spread the rice around it, spoon on generous quantities of the cooking juices and sprinkle with the gremolata.

Boeuf à la Mode

French cooks use rump for this dish but topside or top rump may be substituted. It has to be started 2 days in advance, but that leaves you with little to do when your guests arrive. If you want to serve it cold, add a pig's trotter to the casserole so the stock will gel.

Preparation time: 20 minutes
Marinating time: 24 hours
Cooking time: 2 ½ hours

1.5 kg (3¼ lb) piece of boned, rolled beef
1 bottle good red wine
4 carrots, roughly chopped
1 large onion, roughly chopped
2 garlic cloves, roughly chopped
1 bay leaf
A large handful of fresh herbs, tied in a bundle with string, or a bouquet garni
Olive oil for browning
225 ml (8 fl oz) beef stock
1 pig's trotter, roughly chopped by the butcher, optional
Salt and freshly ground black pepper

Put the beef in a large bowl with the wine, vegetables and herbs. Season well with black pepper and marinate overnight. The next evening, pre-heat the oven to 180°C/350°F/Gas 4. Remove the meat from the marinade, dry well and brown in olive oil on all sides in a large casserole. Add the marinade, stock, seasoning and the pig's trotter (if using). Cover and cook for 2½ hours, turning 2 or 3 times.

To serve hot: When the meat is cooked, remove from the oven and leave to cool, then cover tightly and refrigerate overnight or leave in a cool place. The next evening, skim off the fat from the cooking liquid and re-heat in a 140°C/275°F/Gas 1 oven for 40 – 60 minutes. Slice thinly and serve with the cooking liquid.

To serve cold: Remove cooked meat from the casserole and cover with foil. When it's cool, wrap well in the foil and refrigerate. Meanwhile, remove the pig's trotter (if using) and skim the fat from the liquid then pass through a fine sieve into a jug or bowl. Remove the meat from the fridge 30 minutes before serving and slice thinly. Serve with the jellied stock and a pungent sauce like Salsa Verde (see page 161).

Italianate Burgers

These can be served either on their own, on rolls, or on a slab of baked or grilled polenta.

Preparation time: 1 minute
Cooking time: 15 – 20 minutes

450 g (1 lb) good quality minced beef
1 quantity Basic Polenta (see page 143), optional
4 – 6 thick slices Italian Mozzarella
60 – 80 ml (4 – 6 tablespoons) Tomato Sauce (see page 161)

Form the mince into 4 – 6 patties and cook them in the way you prefer, timing them so that they're done at the same time as the polenta (if using). But remember it's better to let the polenta wait for the burgers than to let the burgers wait for the polenta.

When the burgers are done, put each one on a slab of polenta and top with a dollop of sauce. Put on a slice of mozzarella and brown quickly under the grill to melt the cheese. Serve immediately with a green salad.

Roast Beef Salad with Aubergine-stuffed Peppers

This is loosely based on a dish served at London's Bibendum. Chef Simon Hopkinson uses small Spanish pimientos, but larger Italian peppers can be substituted. The meat must be free of all fat and connective tissue.

Preparation time: 15 minutes
Cooking time : 35 – 40 minutes

2 large jars red peppers in oil
Vegetable oil, for brushing
2 medium aubergines, weighing about
    1 kg (2.2 lb)
Juice of ½ lemon
15 ml (1 tablespoon) extra virgin olive oil
1 – 2 garlic cloves, finely chopped
1 small onion, finely chopped
A small handful of flat-leaf parsley,
    coarsely chopped
8 – 12 thin slices rare roast beef

Pick out the best peppers from both jars (4 if they're large, 8 if they're small) and remove any stray seeds. Put on a plate or board to drain off the excess oil.

Pre-heat the grill to a medium heat and lightly oil the aubergines. Grill at least 7.5 cm (3 in) from the heat source, turning a few times, until the skins are black and blistered (around 20 – 25 minutes) and the flesh offers no resistance when poked with a knife. Peel and chop coarsely then leave to drain in a colander for a few minutes. Mix with lemon juice and set aside.

Meanwhile, gently heat the olive oil in a pan then add the garlic and onion and cook for a few minutes. Add the aubergine and cook for around 10 minutes more, until the mixture is thick. Remove from the heat and season. Mix in the parsley and set aside to cool.

When you're ready to serve, stuff each pepper with the aubergine mixture; any that doesn't fit can be served on the side. Put the beef on cool plates with 1 or 2 peppers, depending on size. Serve immediately with some crusty bread and a salad.

Roast Beef Salad with Aubergine-stuffed Peppers

Roast Beef

The method for roast beef depends on the size of the joint. Any joint up to 2 ribs (around 2.5 kg/5 lb) can be done at a high temperature; larger joints need a medium heat throughout. Plenty of resting time is essential whichever way you cook it and this should be built into your plans. Note the recipe for left-overs preceding this one.

Preparation time: 5 minutes
Cooking time: 1 hour for small joints and up to
2½ hours for large
Resting time: 15 – 30 minutes

2.5 kg (5 lb) rib joint of beef
15 ml (1 tablespoon) dry mustard
15 ml (1 tablespoon) coarse salt
30 ml (2 tablespoons) coarsely ground black pepper
30 ml (2 tablespoons) herbes de Provence or dried rosemary

For a small joint, remove the beef from the fridge at least 1 hour before cooking. Pre-heat the oven to 230°C/450°F/Gas 8. Combine the dry ingredients and rub all over the top and sides of the joint. Roast at the centre of the oven for 50 – 65 minutes, until an oven thermometer gives a reading of 49°C/120°F. This will give a joint that is very rare at the centre; aim for a reading of 51°C/125°F if you like your beef medium-rare. If in doubt, err on the side of undercooking. When you're planning to use the left-overs, an undercooked piece is preferable.

For a larger joint, remove the beef from the fridge at least 3 hours before cooking. Pre-heat the oven to 170°C/325°F/Gas 3 and season the meat as described above. Roast for 12 minutes per pound (rare), 15 minutes per pound (medium rare), and use the temperatures above as a guideline.

When the beef is cooked, turn off the oven and open the door wide. Leave for 15 minutes (small joint) or 30 (large). If you like, prepare a gravy with the pan juices. I feel that the flavour of good roast beef needs no help. If the beef is somewhat undercooked, cut slices from both sides at the first serving. The undercooked middle section can be cooked further if necessary.

Castilian Steaks

This is modelled on a recipe in Penelope Casas' The Foods and Wines of Spain. *Use any good steak.*

Preparation and cooking time:
20 – 25 minutes

30 ml (2 tablespoon) extra virgin olive oil
1 large Spanish onion, thinly sliced
2 garlic cloves, finely chopped
15 ml (1 tablespoon) flour
225 ml (8 fl oz) chicken or beef stock
225 ml (8 fl oz) dry red or white wine
4 good steaks, each weighing 175 – 225 g (6 – 8oz)
Salt and freshly ground black pepper

Heat half the oil in a large frying pan and sauté the onion and garlic over a high heat until the onions are lightly browned (2 – 3 minutes). Turn down the heat and stir in the flour. Cook for another minute, then pour in the stock, wine and season. Cook, stirring regularly, until the liquid has reduced by around a quarter and thickened considerably (around 5 – 7 minutes). Pour into a smaller pan or jug and wipe out the pan. The dish may be prepared in advance to this point.

When you're ready to cook, re-heat the sauce. Meanwhile, heat a frying pan over a blazing heat and add the remaining oil. When it's really hot, season the steaks and cook until they're done the way you like them. Arrange on warm plates and spoon over the sauce.

Sefrina

This dish, adapted from Paula Wolfert's Good Food from Morocco, *can also be made with lamb.*

**Preparation time: 15 minutes
(plus overnight soaking if necessary)
Cooking time: 8 – 10 hours**

125 g (4 oz) chick peas, dried or tinned
1.5 kg (3 lb) boneless brisket, cut into 4 – 6 thick slices
450 g (1 lb) large new potatoes
4 eggs
2 – 3 garlic cloves, crushed
1.25 ml (¼ teaspoon) saffron threads, crumbled, or turmeric
1.25 ml (¼ teaspoon) ginger
1 litre (1¾ pints) stock or water
Salt and freshly ground black pepper

If using dried chick peas, soak overnight in plenty of water, then boil hard in fresh water for 30 minutes or so and drain well. Wash the potatoes and eggs thoroughly.

When you're ready to cook, pre-heat the oven to 140°C/275°F/ Gas 1. Put all ingredients in a heavy-based casserole in this order: chick peas, meat, potatoes, eggs (unshelled). Season with salt and pepper, sprinkle over the garlic and spices and pour in the stock or water. Cook, covered, overnight, or for at least 8 hours.

Cholent

This soothing recipe, adapted from In Search of Plenty *by Oded Schwartz, is a classic of Eastern European Jewish cooking. Serve with a salad and plenty of Dijon mustard.*

Preparation time: 15 minutes (plus overnight soaking)
Cooking time: 8 – 10 hours

225 g (8 oz) dried haricot or navy beans
30 – 45 ml (1 – 2 tablespoons) vegetable oil
2 large onions, coarsely chopped
900 g (2 lb) braising steak, in a single piece
450 g (1 lb) potatoes, peeled and quartered
175 g (6 oz) pearl barley
1 litre (1¾ pints) stock or water
Salt and freshly ground black pepper

Eight hours before you plan to start cooking, soak the beans in cold water to cover. When you're ready to cook, drain them well and pre-heat the oven to 140°C/275°F/Gas 1. Heat the oil in a heavy-based casserole and brown the onions lightly, then add the beef. Surround it with the remaining ingredients, pour over the water or stock and bring to the boil on the hob. Put in the oven and cook, covered, overnight, or for at least 8 hours.

Rack of Lamb with Mustard and Herbs

Two racks of lamb make a wonderful dish for 4 people. Get the butcher to 'chine' the rack and scrape the bone-ends for you.

Preparation time: 10 – 15 minutes
Cooking time: 25 minutes
Standing time: 10 minutes

2 racks of lamb (6 – 8 cutlets apiece)
5 ml (1 teaspoon) dried thyme
5 ml (1 teaspoon) dried rosemary
5 ml (1 teaspoon) powdered mustard
5 ml (1 teaspoon) black pepper
5 ml (1 teaspoon) coarse salt
30 ml (2 tablespoons) dry breadcrumbs, optional
30 ml (2 tablespoons) extra virgin olive oil

Pre-heat the oven to 230°C/450°F/Gas 8. If the lamb is covered with papery skin (fell), cut it away with a small sharp knife and remove all but a thin layer of fat. Trim the ends of the cutlets to 2.5 cm (1 in) from the end of the bone if the butcher hasn't done so and cover exposed bones with aluminium foil. Mix together the dry seasonings and breadcrumbs (if using).

Put the lamb on a rack in a roasting pan and roast just above the centre of the oven for 10 minutes. Brush with oil, dust with the dry seasoning mixture then drizzle over the remaining oil and cook for about 15 minutes more or until the meat feels firm but slightly springy. Cover loosely with foil and leave to stand for 10 minutes. Slice into cutlets and serve with mashed potatoes and roast vegetables.

Lamb Noisettes with Olives

I make this with flavourful olives marinated in herbs, garlic and chillis. If yours are blander, add some of these flavourings separately.

Preparation time: 2 – 3 minutes
Cooking time: 10 – 15 minutes

4 lamb noisettes, total weight 450 g (1 lb)
125 g (4 oz) green olives, pitted
15 ml (1 tablespoon) plain vegetable oil
50 ml (2 fl oz) chicken stock
50 ml (2 fl oz) white wine
A small handful of parsley or fresh coriander, chopped
Salt and freshly ground black pepper

Trim the lamb of all visible fat and chop the olives coarsely. Heat the oil in a large frying pan until almost smoking hot then add the lamb and fry until the pieces are well browned (around 2 minutes per side). Spoon out the excess fat and turn the heat down to medium.

Add the olives, stock and wine and cook, stirring regularly, until the liquid is reduced by around three-quarters. The lamb should be done by now, but poke a piece with your finger to test it. It should be firm to the touch, with just a slight hint of 'give'. Turn the heat off, sprinkle on the parsley or coriander and serve immediately with rice.

Lamb Noisettes with Olives

Lamb Shanks with Garlic, Rosemary and Tomato

This simple recipe partners lamb with classic flavourings, although the method could be adapted to any type of seasoning. Passata is sieved tomato, widely available in jars or tins.

Preparation time: 5 minutes
Cooking time: 2 – 3 hours

4 lamb shanks, knuckle removed or sawn
   part way through the bone
4 garlic cloves, peeled but left whole
1 medium onion, thickly sliced
1 bay leaf

1 sprig of fresh rosemary or 2.5 ml
   (1 teaspoon) dried
100 ml (4 fl oz) passata
300 ml (10 fl oz) chicken or beef stock
300 ml (10 fl oz) dry white wine
Salt and freshly ground black pepper

Pre-heat the oven to 170°C/325°F/Gas 3. Put the shanks in a heavy-based casserole which will hold them easily but snugly in a single layer. Now add all the remaining ingredients using more or less stock and wine as necessary to cover the lamb by around two-thirds. Season, bring to the boil on the hob, then cover and put in the oven.

There's a lot of latitude in the cooking time here – the lamb will be equally good whether just cooked or falling off the bone. It will need a minimum of 1½ hours, will be at its melting best after 2 hours, and will still be great after 3. When you remove the lamb from the oven, skim the cooking liquid of fat and reduce it, if you wish, by fast boiling on the hob for a few minutes. Test for seasoning and serve with rice, potatoes, or buttered noodles.

Pot-roasted Leg of Lamb

This is much easier than roasting the joint and tastes even better in my opinion. The method would also suit a shoulder of lamb, which is cheaper than leg, or a portion cut from either joint. Note the recipe for left-overs on page 80.

Preparation time: 10 minutes
Cooking time: around 2 hours

1 leg of lamb, weighing 2.5 kg (5 lb)
15 ml (1 tablespoon) vegetable oil
5 garlic cloves
2 – 3 sprigs of fresh rosemary, or 15 ml
   (1 tablespoon) dried

2 – 3 sprigs of fresh thyme, or 15 ml
   (1 tablespoon) dried
100 ml (4 fl oz) dry white wine
450 ml (15 fl oz) chicken stock
Salt and freshly ground black pepper

If the lamb is very fatty, trim it well. Pour the oil into a heavy casserole which will hold the lamb comfortably then add the lamb, turning it to coat lightly with oil. Season with salt and pepper, surround with the garlic and herbs, then pour in the liquids, which should cover a third of the lamb. (Use more if needed.) Bring to the boil on the hob, then cook for around 2 hours, either by simmering on the hob or by roasting in an oven heated to 170°C/325°F/Gas 3. Turn once during cooking.

When the meat is done, thoroughly skim off the fat and check the flavour of the liquid. If you wish, it can be boiled down to concentrate the flavour. Potatoes or rice make good companions, with French beans as a green vegetable.

Flash-roasted Lamb Fillet with Soy Sauce Marinade

This simple technique is perfect for dinner parties because it takes about the same time to prepare for 12 as for 4. Use neck fillets (first choice) or boned loin (much more expensive).

Preparation time: 20 minutes
Marinating time: at least 20 minutes'
Cooking time: 25 – 30 minutes

2 neck fillets, weighing 350 g (12 oz)
15 ml (1 tablespoon) vegetable oil,
   optional
Juice of 1 lime or ½ lemon
30 ml (2 tablespoons) soy sauce
15 ml (1 tablespoon) extra virgin olive oil
1 garlic clove, roughly chopped
Salt and freshly ground black pepper

Trim the lamb of fat and sinews and dry with paper towels. Place a large pan over a high heat and add the vegetable oil if it isn't non-stick. When the pan is really hot, sear the lamb quickly but evenly on all sides (around 5 minutes in all). Remove to a bowl which will hold it snugly.

To make the marinade, mix together all the liquid ingredients then add the garlic. Season with pepper than pour over the lamb. Turn the pieces to make sure they're all coated and marinate for at least 20 minutes. Once cool, this can be covered and refrigerated (with occasional turning) for up to 24 hours.

When you're ready to cook, remove the lamb from the fridge and pre-heat the oven to 230°C/450°F/Gas 8. Place the lamb on a rack which will fits in your roasting tin and leave to drain for a few minutes. Bake in the top of the oven for around 20 minutes (medium-rare) or 25 minutes (well done). Cover loosely with foil and leave to rest for 5 minutes before slicing thinly and serving.

If you get the timing right, the oven can be used for baked potatoes and braised celery, both perfect partners for this dish.

Lamb and Haricot Beans (page 80)

Lamb and Haricot Beans

This classic combination is a perfect way of using left-over braised lamb. The beans are fully cooked before the lamb goes in, as too much heat would over-cook it, and the mixture is topped with cheese and browned under the grill. Use left-over braising liquid from Pot-roasted Leg of Lamb (page 78), skimmed of all fat and topped up with stock.

Preparation time: 15 minutes
Soaking time: 8 hours
Cooking time: 2 – 3 hours

225 g (8 oz) dried haricot beans, soaked (see page 126 for methods)
400 g (14 oz) cold lamb
15 ml (1 tablespoon) extra virgin olive oil, or bacon or duck fat
1 celery stick, coarsely chopped
1 medium carrot, coarsely chopped
1 medium onion or small leek, coarsely chopped
1 – 2 garlic cloves, finely chopped
5 ml (1 teaspoon) dried mixed herbs, such as herbes de Provence
600 ml (1 pint) chicken stock and braising liquid
A large handful of flat-leaf parsley
30 – 45 ml (2 – 3 tablespoon) freshly grated Parmesan
Salt and freshly ground black pepper

Drain and rinse the soaked beans, then put in a pan with cold water to cover by 5 cm (2 in) or so. Bring to the boil, skim, and simmer for around 1½ hours, until the beans are about three-quarters cooked. Meanwhile, trim the lamb of fat and cut into 1.5 cm (½ in) pieces.

Drain the beans and rinse out the pan. Heat the oil or fat in the same pan and gently cook the vegetables and garlic for 10 minutes, stirring a few times. Add the dried herbs, beans and enough stock mixture to cover them; top up if necessary. Grind on plenty of black pepper and simmer gently (partly covered) for around 1 hour, until the beans are completely soft but not falling apart. If there's a lot of liquid left, turn the heat up and boil down until it's moist but not watery.

Season with salt and stir in the lamb. Cook for another 2 minutes or so, just to heat the lamb through. Chop the parsley and stir in. Transfer everything to a gratin or baking dish. Pre-heat the grill and sprinkle on the Parmesan. Grill until the top is crusty and golden-brown, which can take anything from 2 – 5 minutes. This filling concoction needs nothing more than a green salad.

Sweet and Spicy Spare Ribs

This sauce can be made days in advance then refrigerated. It can be used on any other cut of pork as well as spare ribs. If it's not barbecue season, cook the ribs in the oven.

Preparation time: 10 minutes
Cooking time: 40 – 55 minutes

30 ml (2 tablespoons) vegetable oil
3 thick slices ginger, finely chopped
1 medium onion, finely chopped
2 plump garlic cloves, finely chopped
1 small chilli, dried or fresh, seeded but left whole
1 x 400 g (14 oz) tin passata or whole tomatoes
30 ml (2 tablespoons) Worcestershire sauce
30 ml (2 tablespoons) maple syrup or clear honey
75 ml (5 tablespoons) dry sherry or white wine
900 g (2 lb) spare ribs

Heat the oil in a medium pan and gently cook the ginger, onion and garlic for 4 – 5 minutes to soften slightly without colouring. Add all the remaining ingredients except the ribs, roughly chopping the tomatoes if they are whole. Bring to a boil, then reduce the heat and simmer gently for at least 30 minutes. The aim is to reduce the sauce to a thick, syrupy consistency. The dish can be prepared in advance to this point, but should be re-heated thoroughly before using.

Get the barbecue going (or pre-heat the grill) and heat the sauce (on the side of the barbecue if there's room). If you can control your barbecue's heat with any precision, aim for a low-to-medium heat. Cook the ribs for 10 – 25 minutes; the timing will depend on the heat from the coals.

When you think they're about 5 minutes from being done, brush with sauce and cook for a few minutes, then turn and brush again. Serve with the remaining sauce, bringing it to the boil and removing the chilli. Provide plenty of napkins.

Variations

This recipe can be varied in numerous ways. If you're pressed for time, make the sauce from a jar of good tomato sauce with wine and chillis added. Use pork kebabs or spare rib chops instead of proper ribs. If you like very spicy food (and there are no children around), increase the amount of chilli by 2 or even 3 times.

Chilindrón

This is my adaptation of chilindrón, a Spanish dish made with dried red peppers. The meat can be pork, chicken or lamb, but a shoulder of lamb is easier and the cooking time more flexible.

Preparation time: 30 – 35 minutes
Cooking time: 2 – 3 hours

4 red peppers
4 large garlic cloves
1 large onion (weighing 300 g/11 oz)
1 x 400 g (14 oz) tin Italian plum tomatoes
15 – 30 ml (1 – 2 tablespoons) extra virgin olive oil
1 shoulder of lamb weighing 2 kg (4 lb), bone in but with shank removed
60 ml (4 tablespoon) fino sherry
2 bay leaves
Salt and freshly ground black pepper
A large handful of parsley, chopped

Pre-heat the oven to 230°C/450°F/Gas 8. Put the peppers in a roasting tin and roast near the top of the oven, turning a few times, until the skins are blackened and blistered (around 25 minutes). Leave to cool in a plastic or brown paper bag while you coarsely chop the garlic, onion and tomatoes. When the peppers are cool, peel, quarter and remove the seeds. Turn down the oven to 180°C/350°F/Gas 4.

Heat the oil in a shallow casserole that's large enough to hold the lamb. Season the lamb with salt and freshly ground black pepper and brown well on both sides. Add the garlic, onion, tomatoes, sherry, bay leaves and lamb shank. Bring to the boil, cover and roast for 1½ hours (medium-rare) to 2 ½ hours (nearly falling off the bone). Whichever result you're aiming for, add the peppers for the final 20 minutes.

To serve, skim as much fat as possible from the cooking liquid. Remove the meat to a platter and surround with peppers and cooking liquid. Sprinkle with parsley and serve immediately.

Quick Curry

This cheat's version of an Indian dish is simple enough for an ordinary meal but impressive enough to serve to guests. Use pork (very un-Indian) or lamb.

Preparation time: 5 minutes
Cooking time: 25 – 30 minutes

15 – 30 ml (1 – 2 tablespoons) vegetable oil
1 large Spanish onion, coarsely chopped
4 garlic cloves, minced
1.5 cm (½ in) piece ginger, minced
30 ml (2 tablespoons) mild/medium curry powder
4 thick shoulder lamb chops or pork spare rib chops
2 red peppers, seeded and cut into thin strips
2 green or yellow peppers, seeded and cut into thin strips
200 ml (7 fl oz) Greek-style yoghurt
Salt and freshly ground black pepper

Heat the oil in a big frying pan (preferably non-stick), until it is medium-hot then add the onion, garlic and ginger and stir-fry until the onion starts to soften (around 5 minutes). If the mixture is sticking to the pan, dribble in a splash of water. Add the curry powder, cook for a minute, then remove and wash out the pan quickly.

Return pan to a medium-high heat and sauté the chops until lightly browned (about 3 minutes each side). Add the onion mixture and the peppers and yoghurt. Season with a generous grinding of black pepper, then cover and cook for 8 – 10 minutes more, stirring once. Serve with rice.

Drunken Pork

In this recipe, inspired by ideas from both Chinese and Italian cooking, the smoky flavour of the barbecue is heightened by prodigious quantities of herb-infused wine. Cook the meat under the grill if it's not barbecue season.

Preparation time: 5 minutes
Cooking time: 10 – 15 minutes

15 ml (1 tablespoon) extra virgin olive oil
2 garlic cloves, finely chopped
1 medium onion, finely chopped
5 peppercorns, cracked
A large sprig of rosemary

300 ml (10 fl oz) dry white wine
2 large sprigs of tarragon
A large handful of flat-leaf parsley
4 – 8 pork spare rib chops or 800 g
    (1¾ lb) cubed pork shoulder
Salt

Heat the oil in a medium pan over a very low flame and cook the garlic, onion, peppercorns and rosemary until they're soft and fragrant (around 10 minutes). Pour in the wine and increase the heat to medium. Season with salt and simmer until the wine has reduced by about half (15 minutes or so), then remove the rosemary and discard. The drunken sauce can be prepared in advance to this point.

Get the barbecue going, with the aim of reaching a high heat. At the same time, remove the meat from the fridge. If you're using cubed pork, thread it onto skewers. Barbecue the meat for around 10 – 15 minutes, until it's cooked but still pink inside. Meanwhile, chop the remaining herbs coarsely and put some in the pan with the drunken mixture and re-heat.

Gently warm a large, deep serving plate. When the pork is ready, put it on the platter. Pour over the drunken sauce and toss for a moment, then scatter the remaining herbs on top. Serve with bread, potatoes, couscous, rice – anything that will soak up the inebriated juices.

Variations

Tomato purée and a pinch of saffron can be added to the pan and lamb, beef or chicken pieces can be used instead of pork.

Fragrant Pork Kebabs

This recipe provides a fairly painless way of feeding a crowd.

Preparation time: 5 minutes
Marinating time: 2 hours
Cooking time: 1 – 15 minutes

675 g (1½ lb) pork, e.g. shoulder, cut into
    2.5 cm (1 in) cubes
1.25 ml (¼ teaspoon) cayenne pepper
5 ml (1 teaspoon) ground coriander
10 ml (2 teaspoons) ground cumin
1.25 ml (¼ teaspoon) ground cloves

1.25 ml (¼ teaspoon) ground cinnamon
Juice of 1 large lemon
30 ml (2 tablespoons) extra virgin olive oil
80 ml (3 fl oz) dry white wine
Red onions and lemons, cut into chunks,
    to garnish, optional

Put the meat in a large bowl and mix in the remaining ingredients (except the garnish). Marinate for at least 2 hours, preferably all day or night. Toss every so often, if you can.

At least 30 minutes before you plan to eat, remove the lamb from the marinade and thread onto skewers, alternating with chunks of red onion and lemon, if you wish. Drain on a rack for a few minutes while you pre-heat the grill (or a grill pan) to a high but not ferocious heat.

Cook the kebabs for 10 – 15 minutes, turning 3 or 4 times, until they're browned but still a bit pink inside. Serve on a bed of couscous, bulgar wheat or rice, accompanied by a salad.

Pot-roasted Pork with Creamy Chilli Sauce

This is an easy method for shoulder of pork, a cheap, delicious cut. The clever thing about the sauce is that it's made with some of the beans you'll serve as a side dish.

Preparation time:
10 minutes
Cooking time: 2 ½ hours

1.25k g (2½ lb) boned and rolled
    shoulder of pork
225 ml (8 fl oz) white wine or
    stock
3 garlic cloves
2 juniper berries
1 bay leaf
5 peppercorns

For the sauce
225 ml (8 fl oz) cooked
    cannellini beans
30 ml (2 tablespoons) cooked
    onion and garlic
1.25 – 2.5 ml (¼ – ½ teaspoon)
    chilli powder
30 ml (2 tablespoons) tomato
    purée
2.5 ml (½ teaspoon) wine vinegar
Salt and freshly ground black
    pepper

Pre-heat the oven to 180°C/35°0F/ Gas 4. Put the meat in a heavy casserole. Bring to the boil on top of the stove, then cover and transfer to the oven. Cook, basting occasionally, until the meat and rind are soft to the touch (about 2½ hours). Once cooked, the casserole can be kept in the turned-off oven for up to 45 minutes while the sauce is prepared.

To make the sauce, put all the sauce ingredients in a blender with about 175 ml (6 fl oz) of the braising liquid. Season with salt and pepper. Purée to a smooth consistency, adding a little more liquid if you want a thinner sauce. Scrape into a saucepan for re-heating.

Pot-roasted Pork with Creamy Chilli Sauce

Braised Pork with Peppers and Spices

Spanish Stuffed Peppers

This can be made with minced pork .

**Preparation time:
15 minutes
Cooking time:
1 hour 40 minutes**

1 – 2 tablespoons extra virgin olive
     oil
3 garlic cloves, finely chopped
1 medium onion, finely chopped
1 large green pepper, finely chopped
350 g (12 oz) skinless pork,
     shoulder or hand, trimmed of fat
2.5 ml (½ teaspoon) paprika
1.25 ml (¼ teaspoon) cayenne
     pepper
1 x 400 g (14 oz) tin Italian plum
     tomatoes
100 ml (4 fl oz) dry white wine
4 – 6 red and/or yellow peppers
Salt and freshly ground black
     pepper

Heat the oil in a large frying pan. Add the garlic, onion and green pepper and fry gently, without colouring, for 10 minutes

Meanwhile, cut the pork into 2.5 mm (⅛ in) slices, then cut each slice into thin shreds. When the onion mix is well softened, increase the heat and add the pork and spices. Cook, stirring regularly, until the pork has lost its pink colour.

Add the tomatoes, chopping them roughly in the pan, then pour in the wine. Simmer gently for 30 minutes or so, until the liquid has reduced by around half and the mixture is thick and very aromatic. The dish can be prepared in advance up to this point.

Pre-heat the oven to 180°C/ 350°F/Gas 4. Cut the tops off the peppers and remove the seeds and pith (reserve the tops). Arrange in a deep dish which can hold the peppers securely then fill each 'cup' with stuffing. Put the tops on, dribble with a little more oil, and bake in the centre of the oven for around 1 hour.

Spiced Pork With Chutney

This dish combines favourite Indian flavourings in the setting of an old-fashioned pork joint. Use Sharwood's, Patak, or any other good chutney and a joint cut from the shoulder, leg or loin.

**Preparation time: 5 minutes
Seasoning time: 1 hour
Cooking time: 2 hours**

1.5 – 2.5 kg (3 – 5 lb) joint of pork, boned, with rind removed
15 ml (1 tablespoon) ground cumin
15 ml (1 tablespoon) ground coriander
15 ml (1 tablespoon) chilli powder or cayenne pepper
15 ml (1 tablespoon) black pepper
15 ml (1 tablespoon) coarse salt
30 ml (2 tablespoons) plain vegetable oil, optional
60 – 75 ml (4 – 5 tablespoons) mango chutney

Remove the meat from the fridge an hour before cooking. Mix the spices and seasonings well, and stir in the oil if using. (If the pork has a good layer of fat, the oil should not be necessary.) Smear the spice mix all over the meat and leave to sit for an hour.

Pre-heat the oven to 230°C/450°F/Gas 8. Roast the meat for 15 minutes, then reduce the heat to 180°C/350°F/Gas 4. Roast for another 1½ hours or so, basting every 15 – 20 minutes. The meat is done when the juices run clear, with a faint trace of pink and the internal temperature is 71°C/160°F. Leave to cool for 30 minutes, then cover loosely with foil.

When completely cool, smear over the chutney using as much as you need to get an even and generous coating. Cover again and set aside. If you're keeping it for more than 2 hours, refrigerate, covered, but remove from the fridge 30 minutes before serving.

Braised Pork with Peppers and Spices

The best cuts for this recipe are spare rib chops, lean slices of belly of pork, or thick pieces cut from hand or shoulder.

**Preparation time: 5 minutes
Cooking time: 5 – 8 hours**

2 garlic cloves
4 – 6 red, orange or yellow peppers, seeded and quartered lengthwise
1.5 kg (3 lb) spare ribs, or 4 large pieces of pork
5 ml (1 teaspoon) ground cumin
5 ml (1 teaspoon) ground coriander
450 ml (15 fl oz) chicken, vegetable or beef stock
Salt and freshly ground black pepper

Pre-heat the oven to 140°C/275°F/Gas 1. Peel and chop the garlic. Use the peppers to line the bottom of a large, heavy casserole. Lay the pork on top, in a single layer if possible, and scatter over the garlic. If you're using spare ribs, they'll have to be tightly bunched. Sprinkle over the spices and season well. Pour on the stock, using a little more if the peppers aren't completely covered. Cover the casserole and cook at the centre of the oven overnight, or for at least 5 hours.

Potatoes, rice or noodles are all that's needed to make a one-dish meal.

Perfect Glazed Gammon

The method here is adapted from Simply Good Food: New Basics for Today's Cook, *by Katie Stewart and Caroline Young. I think it's worth buying a whole gammon and using the left-overs for sandwiches, etc.*

Preparation time: soaking overnight, then 5 – 10 minutes
Cooking time: 4 – 4½ hours

1 whole gammon, weighing 6 kg (12 – 13 lb)
A bay leaf or fresh herbs
45 – 60 ml (3 – 4 tablespoons) Dijon mustard
45 – 60 ml (3 – 4 tablespoons) soft brown sugar, preferably unrefined

Soak the gammon overnight in cold water, then drain and pat dry.

Pre – heat the oven to 180°C/350°F/Gas 4. Tear off a piece of aluminium foil large enough to make a loose-fitting parcel for the joint. (A double thickness is advisable.) Place the foil in a large roasting tin, then place the joint onto it. Add a bay leaf or fresh herbs on top of the gammon. Draw up the edges of the foil and seal, leaving plenty of air at the top so that the heat can circulate.

Roast the joint in the centre of the oven, allowing 20 minutes per 450 g (1 lb). When it's nearly done, increase the heat to 200°C/400°F/Gas 6 and remove the joint from the oven. Tear open the foil, taking care not to scald yourself with the steam, and use a thin, sharp knife to remove the rind (which should be soft). Score the fat in a diamond pattern and coat with the mustard, then sprinkle over the sugar and press down into the surface. Return to the oven and cook for a further 20 minutes or until the surface is well browned . Allow to rest for 20 minutes before carving.

If you want a half gammon instead of a whole, Stewart and Young suggest that you cook at 190°C/375°F/Gas 5, and allow slightly longer per 450g (1lb).

Savoury tarts
& pizzas

Savoury tarts
& pizzas

Most people love something baked and golden, combining crisp pastry or dough with savoury toppings and fillings. I'm certainly one of them. The sight of a freshly baked tart or pizza fills me with an immediate hunger.

Most baked dishes take time, which militates against their use as an every-day dish for oneself and one's family. But what takes most time is the pastry or dough base and this can usually be made well in advance. If you're as keen on baked goods as I am, you'd do well to follow my example and make the pastry in large batches, using some for the dish at hand and freezing the rest for another day.

You can also, of course, buy most pastries ready-made. This is certainly true of shortcrust, which features in many of the recipes here. I love the convenience of these off-the-shelf pastries and would use them at a pinch, but their flavour is never – I mean never – as good as something you make yourself. Making shortcrust pastry is simple and foolproof using the recipe here, and I urge you to get it down as one of your basic procedures. I succeeded in doing that and I am known as something of a pastry-imbecile.

One tart method I'm particularly keen on is pre-cooking the filling, so that all that's needed once the tart's assembled is a quick heat-through in the oven. There are several recipes of that type in this chapter and I encourage you to experiment with your own ideas.

The other big emphasis in this section is on pizza, one of my favourite foods. Friends often ask, 'Is it really worth it?', when I bore them about the delights of home-made pizza. And I can see their point. You can buy pizzas frozen or chilled from any supermarket, fresh from take-aways and restaurants. You can even buy ready-made pizza bases and packets of dough mix. So why bother doing it from scratch?

There are three reasons: simplicity, taste, and good old-fashioned fun. Making pizza dough is so easy that you'll get it right on your first attempt. The dough tastes better than anything sold in supermarkets, even though some are excellent. And pizza making is very enjoyable. It's also a good way to get children helping out in the kitchen.

Pizza dough, far from ruling your life, fits into it. After 15 – 20 minutes of active work at the beginning, the dough does most of the work by itself. And it keeps in the fridge for days, needing nothing more than an occasional punching-down. Once you get the hang of it, you may want to keep a bowlful on hand 7 days a week.

Pizzas can be rolled out into circles, squares, ovals or rectangles, and you can top the base with just about anything. What's more, you can even cook them on the hob – there's a recipe for just that method in this chapter. I promise that once you've started making your own, you'll never look back.

Basic Pizza Dough ⓥ

This recipe makes enough dough for 2 – 3 large pizzas. You can make less, but if you make the full recipe you can keep whatever isn't needed in the fridge. For a slower rise, which may suit your schedule, use the lower quantity of yeast. Olive oil gives a richer base which may be slightly easier to work with.

Preparation time: 20 minutes
Resting time: 3 hours minimum
Cooking time: 15 – 25 minutes

300 ml (10 fl oz) warm water
5 – 7.5 ml (1 – 1½ teaspoons) active dried yeast
5 ml (1 teaspoon) salt
30 ml (2 tablespoons) extra virgin olive oil, optional
Around 550 g (1 ¼ lb) strong white flour

Put the water in a large mixing bowl, add the yeast and leave until it begins to froth (5 – 10 minutes). Add the salt and oil, if using.

Start adding the flour to the yeast and water mixture, starting with just a spoonful at a time than mixing it in with a wooden spoon. As you proceed, the dough will get steadily stiffer and more floury. When you've used up most of the flour, put a generous sprinkling on your work surface and coat your hands with it. Pour and scrape out the contents of the bowl and start kneading.

If you've made bread, you know how to do this. If you haven't, all it means is massaging the dough so that the water and flour gradually blend. You may need to make an occasional addition of extra flour when the dough seems sticky. Some recipes give elaborate instructions, but any action works well as long as you don't stretch the dough too much. After 10 minutes or so the dough will be smooth, springy and elastic and barely sticky, indicating that it is ready to rise.

Drizzle a little oil in the mixing bowl to prevent the dough from sticking then form the dough into a neat ball and place in the bowl. Turn so that the top surface is coated with oil. Cover tightly with cling film and a plate, and leave in the fridge (up to 10 hours) or in a warm place (2 – 3 hours) to rise.

When the dough has doubled or trebled in size, punch it down flat, reform it into a ball and leave to rise again. After another punching-down the dough is ready to use, but it can be left in the fridge for 2 – 3 days.

To bake the dough

Pre-heat the oven to 240°C/475°F/Gas 9, or as high as your oven gets, with the baking stone in place (if you're using one). Divide the dough as appropriate using a sharp knife and roll out the pieces to about 2.5 mm (⅛ in) thick. Put each piece on a baking sheet and crimp the edges so that they're slightly thicker than the interior. Brush lightly with oil, spread with the topping of your choice, and bake for 15 – 25 minutes or until the topping is cooked and the crust nicely crisped. To be sure of a crisp crust, you can also bake the base on its own for 5 minutes, then add toppings and continue baking.

Cheese and Tomato Pizza ⓥ

This basic recipe can be embellished with almost anything you like (see the suggestions below). If the tomato sauce is very watery, drain in a sieve for 15 minutes before spreading on the base. For a lighter pie, you can use half the amount of Mozzarella.

Preparation time: 20 minutes
Cooking time: 25 minutes

1 large pizza base
150 ml (5 fl oz) thick tomato sauce, preferably homemade
175 g (6 oz) Mozzarella, drained and sliced or chopped thinly

Spread the sauce over the oiled pizza base then scatter on the cheese evenly. Add extra toppings if you wish and bake as in the Basic Pizza Dough recipe (see left) for about 25 minutes.

Variations

You can jazz up the pizza in numerous ways, including: spicy sausage, skinned, crumbled and lightly fried; Italian-style pepperoni or *pancetta* (bacon); green or red peppers, shredded; marinated mushrooms or artichoke hearts; anchovies, well drained; fresh or dried herbs, e.g. basil, oregano, sage; vegetables of your choice (e.g. peppers, aubergines, fennel, courgettes), fried or grilled with olive oil for 10 – 15 minutes.

Four Pizza Toppings ⓥ

All these will be sufficient for 1 pizza of around 30 – 35 cm (12 – 14 in) in diameter, or 8 – 10 smaller ones.

Sage and Goat's Cheese

Use a fairly soft, mild cheese; the mature varieties will be too salty.

15 – 20 fresh sage leaves
125 – 150 g (4 – 5 oz) goat's cheese, very thinly sliced

Shred the sage leaves if you wish or leave them whole. Brush the pizza base with some extra virgin olive oil then dot with the sage and top with the cheese, making sure the entire surface of the base (apart from a border of about 1.5 cm, ½ in) is covered. Use more cheese if you need to. Bake as in Basic Pizza Dough (see left), until the base is crisp and the cheese bubbling.

Rosemary and Garlic (Pizza Bianca) Ⓥ

This is based on a recipe in Carol Field's Italy in Small Bites.

3 garlic cloves, thinly sliced
45 ml (3 tablespoons) extra virgin olive oil
45 ml (3 tablespoons) fresh rosemary sprigs

Put the garlic and oil in a small pan and heat until the oil starts to sizzle then turn off the heat immediately and leave to infuse for at least 2 hours. When you're ready to bake, mix in the rosemary then spread the aromatic oil over the pizza base. It shouldn't need extra oil, but if the base seems dry, drizzle on a further tablespoon or so. Bake as in the Basic Pizza Dough recipe (see page 91).

Red and Purple Pizza Ⓥ

If you want to tone down the oniony flavour of this topping, toss the onions with the vinegar and leave for a couple of hours before baking.

2 small red onions, peeled
15 ml (1 tablespoon) red wine vinegar
15 – 30 ml (1 – 2 tablespoons) extra virgin olive oil
1 x 400 g (14 oz) tin Italian plum tomatoes

Cut the onions in half lengthwise, then slice as thinly as you can. Toss with the vinegar and oil (the vinegar helps them keep their colour).

Seed the tomatoes and cut into thickish shreds then drain in a sieve for a few minutes. Brush the pizza base with oil, scatter over the onions and tomatoes and bake as in Basic Pizza Dough (see page 91).

Pizza alla Puttanesca

This recipe is an adaptation of one of my favourite pasta sauces, a Roman classic whose name means 'whore's-style'. It is hot, pungent, and very serious – not a pizza to serve to children.

100 g (4 oz) black or green olives, pitted and coarsely chopped
1 – 2 garlic cloves, coarsely chopped
1 tin anchovies, drained and coarsely chopped
½ fresh green or red chilli, finely chopped
15 ml (1 tablespoon) extra virgin olive oil
1 x 400g (14oz) tin of Italian plum tomatoes, drained, seeded, and finely chopped
30 ml (2 tablespoons) capers

Scatter all the ingredients evenly over the pizza base and bake as Basic Pizza Dough (see page 91). Take care not to overcook this pizza: crunchy olives are unpleasant to eat.

Pizzas on the Hob Ⓥ

This is a great trick when you're pressed for time – no pre-heating required. The result isn't exactly like a baked pizza, but it's very good.

Preparation time: 5 minutes
Cooking time: 10 – 25 minutes

⅓ quantity **Basic Pizza Dough (see page 91)**
Topping of your choice

Roll out the dough to about 2.5 mm (⅛ in) thick and to a size that will fit snugly into the flat bottom of your largest non-stick frying pan. Heat the pan over a medium heat with just enough oil on the bottom to prevent the dough from sticking. When it's hot, slide in the pizza base; if you get any drips or folds, sort them out with a pair of tongs and a spatula. Cook this way until the bottom is crisp (around 5 – 10 minutes). Turn the dough and cook until the other side is crisp (another 3 – 10 minutes).

Meanwhile, pre-heat the grill to medium-hot and assemble your topping ingredients.

When the base is browned, scatter over the topping and put the pan under the grill. Cook it just long enough to heat the topping and melt the cheese (if using). This can be as short as a minute or as long as 5, if you're using a thick topping with tomato sauce. Carefully lift the pie onto a serving plate, then just dig in.

Variation

Another way with pan-fried pizzas is to sandwich the filling between 2 thin discs of dough, sealing the edges so nothing oozes out. From the outside it will just look like dough; but the interior will be delicious. Try this with Mozzarella or another cheese, serving tomato sauce on top of the slices.

Basic Shortcrust Pastry

This is a foolproof and very quick way to make shortcrust pastry. It's worth making it in large quantities and freezing in recipe-weight chunks to make a convenient basis for tarts and pies.

Preparation time: 10 minutes

275 g (10 oz) plain flour
2.5 ml (½ teaspoon) salt
A large pinch of sugar
225 g (8 oz) unsalted butter, cut into small pieces
About 120 ml (8 tablespoons) ice-cold water

Put the flour, salt, sugar and butter in a food processor. Blend quickly until the mixture resembles breadcrumbs (10 – 20 seconds). With the processor running, gradually add the water. Take care towards the end as too much water can make the mixture more doughy. When it's ready, gather the dough into a ball, wrap in cling-film, and refrigerate for 30 minutes before using.

Scarpaccia Viareggina

This savoury tart can be eaten warm or at room temperature.

**Preparation time: 30 minutes
Cooking time: 25 – 30 minutes**

225 g (8 oz) small courgettes, thinly sliced
1 medium onion, finely chopped
125 g (4 oz) plain white flour
300 ml (10 fl oz) milk
120 ml (8 tablespoons) extra virgin olive oil
1 egg, beaten
Salt and freshly ground black pepper

Toss the courgettes and onion with around 5 ml (1 teaspoon) fine salt and leave to drain in a colander for 30 minutes.

Meanwhile, pre-heat the oven to 230°C/450°F/Gas 8. Sieve the flour into a mixing bowl and whisk in the milk, half the oil, and the egg. Season with black pepper and set aside until needed. Use the remaining oil to grease 2 metal pie tins, each around 23 cm (9 in) in diameter; take special care to oil the sides of the tins as well as the base as this is where sticking is most likely to occur.

Wash the courgettes and onions and pat dry then mix into the batter. Divide between the pie tins then bake the tarts until set and lightly browned (around 25 – 30 minutes). Leave to cool, then cut into wedges.

Pissaladière

This great Provençal dish is a close relation of the pizza. This recipe is the traditional way of doing it.

**Preparation time: 30 minutes
Cooking time: 1 hour**

30 ml (2 tablespoons) extra virgin olive oil
800 g (1¾ lb) onions, thinly sliced
2.5 ml (½ teaspoon) herbes de Provence
½ quantity Basic Pizza Dough (see page 91)
1 tin anchovies, well drained
125 g (4 oz) black olives, pitted and halved or quartered

Heat the oil in a large frying pan and gently cook the onions, stirring occasionally, until the onions are well coloured and very soft (around 30 – 35 minutes). If they still seem too wet after that time, increase the heat and cook hard for a couple of minutes; you can't really overcook these onions. When they're done, mix in the herbs. The recipe can be prepared in advance up to this point.

Roll out the dough to make a large square or rectangle about 2.5 mm (⅛ in) thick. Spread over the onions in an even layer and top with the anchovies and olives. Drizzle with a little extra oil and bake in the top of the oven until the topping is hot (15 – 25 minutes).

Scarpaccia Viareggina

Onion Tart Ⓥ

The onions can be cooked well in advance and refrigerated.

Preparation time: 20 minutes
Cooking time: 1 hour

275 g (10 oz) Basic Shortcrust Pastry (see page 94)
30 ml (2 tablespoons) extra virgin olive oil
800 g (1¾ lb) onions, thinly sliced
1.25 ml (¼ teaspoon) sugar
2.5 ml (½ teaspoon) wine vinegar
1.25 ml (¼ teaspoon) herbes de Provence

Roll out the pastry into a circle about 30 cm (12 in) in diameter and 2.5 mm (⅛ in) thick. Place on a baking sheet, pinching the edges to make a raised border and refrigerate to firm up.

Meanwhile, heat half the oil in a large frying pan and gently cook the onions, sugar, vinegar and herbs, stirring occasionally, until the onions are well coloured and very soft (around 30 – 35 minutes).

Pre-heat oven to 200°C/400°F/Gas 6 and remove the pastry from the fridge. Prick the bottoms all over with a fork, line with aluminium foil, and weight down with dried beans. Bake blind on the middle shelf for 10 minutes, then remove the foil and bake again until the pastry is lightly coloured (around 10 minutes more).

Remove the foil, spread the onions over the pastry in an even layer, and bake on the top shelf for 15 – 20 minutes. If the rim of the base is getting too dark, cover it with aluminium foil.

The tart can either be eaten straight from the oven or served at room temperature.

Spinach and Feta Tart V

This tart gets its refreshing tang from the cheese. The tart will be pale on the surface (feta doesn't brown much) but a deep green inside.

Preparation time: 20 minutes
Cooking time: 1 hour

275 g (10 oz) Basic Shortcrust Pastry (see page 94)
30 ml (2 tablespoons) extra virgin olive oil, or half oil and butter
4 – 5 spring onions, green parts included, finely chopped
A pinch of freshly grated nutmeg
30 ml (2 tablespoons) dry white wine or vermouth
450 g (1 lb) frozen chopped spinach
3 eggs, size 1
100 ml (4 fl oz) double cream or crème fraîche
125 – 150 g (4 – 5 oz) feta cheese, thinly sliced or crumbled

Roll out the pastry until it is about 2.5 mm (⅛ in) thick and large enough to line a 25 cm (10 in) flan dish. Refrigerate for 30 minutes or so to firm up.

Meanwhile, heat the oil (or oil and butter) in a small pan and gently cook the spring onions, nutmeg and wine for a minute or so, just to soften slightly. In a separate pan (or, better still, the microwave), cook the spinach until it is just heated through. Squeeze out as much of the water from the spinach as you can, in either a sieve or a tea towel. Place in a bowl and add the spring onions.

Pre-heat the oven to 200°C/400°F/Gas 6 and remove the pastry from the fridge. Prick the bottom with a fork, line with aluminium foil, and weigh down with dried beans. Bake blind on the middle shelf for 15 minutes, then remove the foil and bake again until the pastry is lightly coloured (around 10 minutes more). Remove the foil and leave to cool. The recipe can be prepared in advance up to this point.

Beat the eggs thoroughly with the cream. Spread the spinach over the pastry and pour over the egg mixture. Add the cheese in an even layer and bake on the top shelf until the flan is set (around 35 minutes). If the rim of the base gets too dark, cover with aluminium foil.

The tart can be eaten straight from the oven or left to cool for 10 minutes or so.

Red Pepper Tart V

This is another tart where the filling is cooked in advance, so the tart needs nothing more than re-heating after assembly. It's pungent, tasty, and quick to make.

Preparation time: 20 minutes
Cooking time: 1 hour

3 – 4 large red peppers
3 garlic cloves, unpeeled
275 g (10 oz) Basic Shortcrust Pastry (see page 94)
15 ml (1 tablespoon) extra virgin olive oil
25 g (4 oz) red onion, finely chopped
3 sun-dried tomatoes, finely chopped
15 ml (1 tablespoon) wine vinegar
10 ml (2 teaspoons) tomato purée
Salt and freshly ground black pepper

Pre-heat oven to 200°C/400°F/Gas 6 and roast the peppers until they're blackened all over and very soft. Put in a bag for 10 minutes, then peel and seed leaving the peppers whole, if possible.

If you want to tone down the sting of the garlic, put it in a small pan with about 300 ml (10 fl oz) water. Bring to the boil, drain, discarding the water. Repeat the process, this time simmering the garlic vigorously for 5 minutes. Drain and leave to cool then chop finely.

Meanwhile, roll out the pastry until it is about 2.5 mm (⅛ in) thick and large enough to line a 25 cm (10 in) flan dish. Refrigerate for 30 minutes or so to firm up.

Heat the oil in a small pan and gently cook the onion, garlic, tomatoes, vinegar and tomato purée for 3 – 5 minutes, to soften slightly and blend their flavours. Leave to cool.

Remove the pastry from the fridge. Prick the bottom all over with a fork, line with aluminium foil and weight down with dried beans. Bake blind on the middle shelf of the oven for 15 minutes, then remove the foil and continue baking until the crust is a deep golden brown. Remove the foil and leave to cool. The recipe may be prepared in advance up to this point.

Spread the onion mixture evenly over the base of the pie crust, then lay on the pepper slices in as even a layer as you can manage. Brush with extra oil and bake until the peppers are warm (around 15 – 20 minutes). Serve immediately.

Aubergine and Olive Tart ⓥ

Another tart in which most of work's done in advance. Make the Green Olive Paste from the recipe on page 152 or buy a jar; if you don't have a griddle (grill pan), use your heaviest frying pan. This is a fairly rich tart and will serve 6 as a main course at lunch.

Preparation time: 20 minutes
Cooking time: 1 hour

3 medium aubergines, peeled (optional) and cut into 5 mm – 1.5 cm (¼ –½in) slices
275 g (10 oz) Basic Shortcrust Pastry (see page 94)
Vegetable oil, for frying
100 ml (4 fl oz) Green Olive Paste (see page 152)
Extra virgin olive oil, for brushing
Freshly grated Parmesan
Freshly ground black pepper

Pre-heat the griddle (grill pan) over a high heat and brush the aubergine slices as lightly as possible with oil; you want just enough to keep the slices from sticking. Slap onto the griddle and cook until they're done, turning once only (around 5 – 8 minutes). Remove to a large platter and leave to cool.

Meanwhile, roll out the pastry to about 2.5 mm (⅛ in) thick and large enough to line a 25 cm (10 in) flan dish. Refrigerate for 30 minutes or so to firm up.

Remove the pastry from the fridge. Prick the bottom all over with a fork, line with aluminium foil and weigh down with dried beans. Bake blind on the middle shelf for 15 minutes, then remove the foil and continue baking until the crust is a deep golden brown. Remove the foil and leave to cool. The tart can be prepared in advance to this point.

Arrange half the aubergine slices over the base of the pie crust, then spread on the Green Olive Paste in as even a layer as you can manage; season with pepper but no salt (the olive paste will be salty). Top with the remaining aubergines, brush with a little olive oil and sprinkle with Parmesan.

Bake until the aubergines are hot and the cheese a light golden brown (around 15 – 20 minutes). Serve hot or warm, but not cold.

Courgette Tart with Pesto ⓥ

Making perfect vegetable tarts can be a tricky business. In this easy version the crust and filling are cooked separately, then warmed through together. 450 g (1 lb) store-bought pastry can be used if you're pressed for time.

Preparation time: 20 minutes
Cooking time: 30 minutes.

1 quantity Basic Shortcrust Pastry (see page 94)
900 g (2 lb) small courgettes, sliced in 5 mm (¼ in) discs
30 ml (2 tablespoons) fine salt
15 ml (1 tablespoon) extra virgin olive oil
120 ml (8 tablespoons) pesto

Put the courgettes in a colander and toss with the salt. Leave to drain for 30 minutes or so, then rinse and dry well on a tea towel. Heat the oil in a large frying pan and stir-fry the courgettes briskly until soft (8 – 10 minutes). The tart may be prepared in advance up to this point.

Pre-heat the oven to 200°C/400°F/Gas 6. Divide the pastry into 2 equal pieces and roll out to around 2.5 mm (⅛ in) thick. Use to line 2 x 25 – 30 cm (10 – 12 in) pie tins; if the tins aren't non-stick, butter them lightly first. Prick the base of the pastry cases all over with a fork and bake blind for 15 minutes. Remove the foil and continue baking until the crust is a deep golden brown.

Mix together the pesto and courgettes and divide between the tarts. Bake for 10 – 20 minutes, until the tart is warm. Serve immediately.

Baked Spanish Omelette ⓥ

This oven-cooked version of the great tortilla española isn't authentic, but it can't be beat for sheer convenience.

Preparation time: 10 minutes
Cooking time: 1 hour

900 g (2 lb) potatoes, peeled and cut into 5 mm (¼ in) slices
1 – 2 medium onions, coarsely chopped
50 ml (2 fl oz) vegetable oil
12 eggs
50 ml (2 fl oz) extra virgin olive oil
Salt and freshly ground black pepper

Bring a large pan of well salted water to the boil and cook the potatoes until just done (around 10 minutes). Drain, rinse well under cold running water and place in a colander to cool.

Meanwhile, cook the onions in the vegetable oil until very soft (around 15 minutes). Beat the eggs with salt and freshly ground black pepper, and pre-heat oven to 200°C/400°F/Gas 6.

Use some of the olive oil to coat a large baking dish and arrange the potatoes in neat, overlapping layers. Drizzle over the oil, pour in the eggs and bake until the eggs are just set and slightly runny in the middle (around 40 minutes). Serve at any temperature from oven-hot to lukewarm but I think it's at its best around 10 minutes after leaving the oven.

Baked Spanish Omelette

Vegetables
& Salads

Gratin de Potiron (page 109), served here with Chicken Tajine with Dried Fruit (page 57)

Vegetables
& salads

While I can't imagine being a vegetarian, neither can I imagine a serious meal without vegetables. Meat, fish and poultry need a vegetable accompaniment of equal distinction or the meal is simply incomplete. Most of the recipes in this chapter are the kind of accompaniment I look for.

Cooking vegetables is easy. It involves two essential principles: buy good vegetables in the first place and then cook them in any way that preserves and enhances their innate goodness.

Sadly, the second principle can be easier to follow than the first. From personal experience and reports from others, I know that top-quality produce can be hard to find even at greengrocers regarded as the best in their area. At some shops I've been unable to spot a single piece of produce that was worth buying.

Supermarkets are not necessarily better: quality varies from shop to shop, area to area and day to day. But at least we can pick our own produce, without relying on the word of a greengrocer who might just be trying to get rid of last week's stock. The alternative to supermarkets is to persuade your greengrocer to let you choose for yourself. Better still, buy from a good farm shop if you have access to one.

Some of the recipes here can serve either as side dishes or as main courses. The gratins especially would make a perfect centrepiece for a weekend lunch or vegetarian dinner – and I wouldn't hesitate to serve them that way, even if everyone at the table were a meat-eater.

Then there are salads. Like most people, I adore salads. But when I talk about salad, I'm not just talking about leaves with a vinaigrette. I'm talking also about other vegetables, both raw and cooked; about olives, capers, croûtons, herbs and other well-flavoured items that give a maximum of flavour with a minimum of bulk; and about fish, cheese, ham and bacon to provide the substance needed in a main course or generous starter.

I hate giving recipes for salad: this should be an area for spontaneous improvisation. Go to the market and see what looks beautiful, then put it together with whatever larder items take your fancy. Just remember the basics: wash and dry the leaves very thoroughly, make your dressing from good oil and vinegar, and don't add dressing until the last moment. As long as you do that, using good, fresh ingredients, your salad will be delicious.

My favourite salad dressing is plain oil-and-vinegar, perhaps with a touch of garlic, mustard or herbs. But there's plenty of scope for experimentation, especially in combining oils and vinegars for maximum complexity of flavour: extra virgin olive, sesame, walnut or hazelnut oils; sherry, rice wine or balsamic vinegars. Lemon juice and balsamic vinegar make a particularly good combination and soy sauce and sesame oil can be blended for a Chinese accent. A syrupy reduction of the juices from a left-over chicken or joint can replace some of the oil, and Bio or Greek yoghurt used as a base. Try a mixture of dry vermouth and vinegar or, with very flavourful leaves, eliminate the vinegar altogether. As long as you use good ingredients, you can't go wrong.

Shredded Peppers with Double Onions Ⓥ

This would be worth making even if it weren't so beautiful. It's equally good served hot and at room temperature and it makes a perfect vegetable dish for a barbecue. Note that you should begin preparation 24 hours in advance.

Preparation time: 15 – 20 minutes
Cooking time: 25 – 30 minutes

1 medium red onion, halved and thinly sliced
45 ml (3 tablespoons) extra virgin olive oil
10 ml (2 teaspoons) red wine or sherry vinegar
1 small bay leaf
15 ml (1 tablespoon) vegetable oil
1 – 2 bunches spring onions, with green parts,
    cut into 7.5 cm (3 in) shreds
5 – 6 large peppers, preferably red and yellow, thickly sliced
30 – 45 ml (2 – 3 tablespoons) olive or vegetable oil
45 ml (3 tablespoons) dry white wine
Salt and freshly ground black pepper

Put the sliced red onion in a glass or ceramic bowl. Mix 15 ml (1 tablespoon) of olive oil with the vinegar, bay leaf and a large pinch of salt. Grind on some black pepper, toss with the onion, and refrigerate, covered tightly, for at least 8 hours. A full day is better. The onions can be kept in perfect condition for almost a week. Stir occasionally to make sure they're uniformly coated with the marinade.

Heat the vegetable oil in your largest frying pan (or a wok) and cook the spring onions and peppers over a gentle heat, stirring frequently, until they're done the way you like them, 5 – 10 minutes for very *al dente*, 20 – 25 minutes for fully cooked. Add the wine towards the end of the cooking time and let it boil away. The salad can be prepared in advance to this point.

When you're ready to serve, gently re-heat the peppers and spring onions (if necessary), toss with the remaining olive oil and arrange on a large serving platter. Scatter over the red onion, spreading out the shreds as evenly as possible.

Variations
To vary the dish, serve it on a bed of grilled aubergine slices or add fresh herbs to the peppers and onions just before serving. You could also use the dish as a pasta sauce or as a topping for grilled, roasted or barbecued chicken.

Grilled Summer Vegetables with Coriander Salsa Ⓥ

This salsa uses fresh coriander, one of the most seductive of summer flavours, to its full advantage. The recipe can be a vegetarian main course, but if you're serving it as a side dish you can use just 2 or 3 of the vegetables suggested here. The grilled vegetables make a great partner for any kind of grilled or barbecued meat or chicken.

Preparation time: 20 – 25 minutes
Cooking time: 30 – 40 minutes

1 – 2 garlic cloves, finely chopped
½ dried red chilli, seeded and finely chopped
100 – 150 ml (4 – 5 fl oz) extra virgin olive oil
Juice of 1 large lemon
A large handful of fresh parsley, preferably flat-leaf
A large handful of fresh coriander
675 g (1½ lb) mixed vegetables – aubergines, peppers,
    courgettes, flat mushrooms, fennel, potatoes
Salt and freshly ground black pepper
Lemon wedges, to garnish

Mix the garlic and chilli in a bowl then add the oil, lemon juice, and plenty of freshly ground black pepper. Leave to steep for at least 30 minutes. Meanwhile, wash and dry the parsley and coriander.

An hour or so before you want to eat, prepare the vegetables as necessary. Anything that needs slicing should be cut to about 1.5 cm (½ in) thick. Pre-heat the grill or a griddle (grill pan) to a medium heat, brush the vegetables lightly with oil and grill them, turning once, until they're cooked the way you like them. This can take anything from 5 – 15 minutes and it's easiest if you do one variety at a time. As the vegetables finish cooking, transfer them to a large serving platter.

When you're ready to serve, chop the parsley and coriander either coarsely or finely, as you prefer. Add to the salsa, taste for seasoning (you will probably need salt) and pass the sauce separately with the lemon wedges.

Variations
This dish can be varied almost endlessly, both in accompaniments and in dressings. Try a home-made herb-and-garlic mayonnaise or vinaigrette with honey. The vegetables can be served in layers, like a stack of pancakes, with the biggest on the bottom and the smallest on top.

Steam-fried Courgettes with Tomatoes and Basil Ⓥ

This vegetable dish utilizes one of my favourite methods for cooking small, top-notch courgettes. It's laughably simple, can be varied in many different ways, and looks nice to boot.

**Preparation time:
10 – 15 minutes
Cooking time:
around 5 minutes**

15 – 30 ml (1 – 2 tablespoons) **extra virgin olive oil**
Juice of 1 lime
15 – 30 ml (1 – 2 tablespoons) **vegetable oil**
675 g (1½ lb) **small courgettes, thinly sliced**
30 ml (2 tablespoons) **chicken stock or water**
225 g (8 oz) **red, ripe cherry tomatoes, halved**
10 – 15 **sprigs of basil**
Salt and freshly ground black pepper

Whisk the olive oil and lime juice with some salt and freshly ground black pepper. Heat the vegetable oil in a large, heavy frying pan, preferably non-stick. If it doesn't have a lid, get out a baking sheet (weighed down with something heavy to prevent buckling) or something similar and have it at the ready.

When the oil is really hot, add the courgettes. Don't stir them, but shake the pan to level them out. Cook at a real sizzle for 2 minutes, stepping back to avoid splashes of hot oil. Reduce the heat to low, pour in the stock or water and cover the pan. Cook for 5 minutes more. By that time, the courgettes on top should have cooked in the steam while those on the bottom will be nicely browned.

To serve, toss or top with the tomatoes and vinaigrette, and garnish with basil. Serve hot or at room temperature.

Variations

This dish can be varied by using large tomatoes, thinly sliced, instead of the cherry tomatoes. Vary the seasonings as you like, using different herbs and different vinaigrettes. Use the same technique with fennel or sliced red peppers. Try serving on pasta or good toast with grated Parmesan.

Griddled Vegetables with Goat's Cheese Vinaigrette Ⓥ

This takes some time to cook, but it's easy work – and can all be done well in advance. Use a selection of summery vegetables, 2 at least and preferably 4. If you don't have a griddle (grill pan), use your heaviest frying pan.

**Preparation time:
5 – 10 minutes
Cooking time: up to 40 minutes**

900 g (2 lb) **mixed vegetables – aubergines, courgettes, fennel, squash, carrots, mushrooms, onions, peppers**
Vegetable oil, for frying
150 ml (5 fl oz) **extra virgin olive oil**
60 ml (4 tablespoons) **fromage frais**
25 ml (1½ tablespoons) **wine or sherry vinegar**
75 g (3 oz) **young, mild goat's cheese**
Juice of ½ lemon
Salt and freshly ground black pepper

Pre-heat the griddle (grill pan) over a high heat and prepare the vegetables as necessary: they should be trimmed and sliced anything from 5 mm – 1.5 cm (¼ – ½ in) thick. Working with 1 vegetable at a time, brush the slices very lightly with oil and slap onto the griddle. Cook until they're done then remove to a large platter, and proceed with the next batch; the cooking can take from 1 minute (for mushrooms or onions) to 6 – 8 minutes for aubergines. When they all are done, leave to cool and cover loosely with aluminium foil.

Meanwhile, whisk the olive oil, fromage frais and vinegar with salt and pepper to taste. Crumble in the cheese and whisk until the dressing is perfectly smooth; this is almost instant in a blender or food processor. The salad and dressing can be prepared in advance to this point.

When you're getting ready to serve, core and halve the radicchio and shred finely. Squeeze the lemon juice into the vinaigrette. Scatter the radicchio over the vegetables and drizzle on some of the dressing. Serve with the remaining dressing passed separately.

Baked Vegetables with Herbs and Onions Ⓥ

This recipe is based on Deborah Madison's Greens Cookbook, *the best vegetarian cookbook ever written. Madison uses aubergines only, but I prefer a combination. The dish is a meal in itself.*

Preparation time: 20 – 25 minutes
Cooking time: 45 – 50 minutes

2 ripe beef tomatoes
80 – 100 ml (3 – 4 fl oz) extra virgin olive oil
3 – 4 garlic cloves, thinly sliced
450 g (1 lb) onions, red if you can find them, thinly sliced
5 ml (1 teaspoon) fennel seeds
5 ml (1 teaspoon) dried mixed herbs, e.g. *herbes de Provence*
3 bay leaves
6 – 8 sprigs of fresh thyme
4 small aubergines each about 7.5 – 10 cm (3 – 4in long),
   halved lengthwise
2 large red peppers, seeded and halved
2 large yellow peppers, seeded and halved
4 medium courgettes, halved lengthwise
125 g (4 oz) olives, black or green
75 ml (5 tablespoons) dry white wine
Salt and freshly ground black pepper

Plunge the tomatoes into boiling water for 10 seconds, then core, skin, seed and cut into 1.5 cm (½ in) strips.

Gently heat 45 ml (3 tablespoons) of the oil in a large frying pan. Add the garlic, onions, fennel seeds and dried herbs. Cook without colouring until the onions just start to soften (5 – 10 minutes). Put half this mixture in a very large baking dish with the tomatoes, bay leaves and half the thyme.

Meanwhile, pre-heat the oven to 200°C/400°F/Gas 6. Arrange the aubergines, peppers and courgettes over the onions and drizzle with the remaining oil, taking special care to get a good sprinkling on the aubergines; use more if you need to. Tuck the olives in between the vegetables and top with the remaining onion mixture and the thyme. Drizzle over the wine, cover with aluminium foil and bake until all vegetables are soft. The peppers will probably be done after 30 – 35 minutes and should be removed to the serving platter; the courgettes and aubergines will need another 10 minutes or so.

Serve either hot or warm, with good bread and perhaps a green salad.

Variations

To vary the recipe, fry some minced anchovy fillets, sun-dried tomatoes and a little chilli powder or fresh chilli with the onions and garlic.

Grilled Leeks with Goat's Cheese Glaze Ⓥ

Nearly all the work in this recipe is done well in advance, with just a few minutes of work when your guests are at the table. The glaze is based on a goat's cheese 'mayonnaise' I found in Maddalena Bonino's Fast & Fresh Entertaining. *It is essential that you buy fairly small leeks which are all about the same size.*

Preparation time: 10 – 15 minutes
Cooking time: 5 – 10 minutes, plus a few minutes just before serving

18 small leeks, 2.5 cm (1 in) in diameter, trimmed
   and cut into 7.5 – 10 cm (3 – 4 in) lengths

For the glaze
150 g (5 oz) soft goat's cheese
15 ml (1 tablespoon) wholegrain mustard
15 ml (1 tablespoon) wine vinegar
15 ml (1 tablespoon) vegetable oil
30 ml (2 tablespoons) extra virgin olive oil
Juice and grated rind of ½ small lemon
A good handful of herbs (chives, parsley, dill, mint), finely
   chopped

Bring a very large pot of well salted water to the boil and cook the leeks briskly until they're just cooked (around 10 minutes). Drain well then refresh under cold running water and leave until needed.

Meanwhile, make the glaze. Crumble the cheese and blend in the food processor with the mustard and vinegar. When it's well mixed, pour in the oils in a thin, steady stream. Remove to a bowl and mix in the lemon juice and rind. Chop the herbs finely and mix them in. Refrigerate until needed.

Around 15 minutes before you want to eat, pre-heat the grill and lay the leeks in a flat-bottomed ovenproof dish. Spoon over the glaze, using as much as you need to coat the leeks thoroughly. (The leftovers are good hot or cold.) Put the dish under the grill and cook until the glaze is brown and bubbling. Serve from the dish with crusty bread.

Potatoes, Bacon and Cheese

This dish is perfect for guests whose arrival time is unknown. The potatoes and bacon are pre-cooked and then re-heated at the last minute.

Preparation time: 10 minutes
Cooking time: 35 minutes

900 g (2 lb) small waxy or new potatoes
Oil, for frying
125 g (4 oz) streaky bacon, rinds removed, thinly sliced
125 g (4 oz) any good melting cheese – Gruyère, mozzarella,
    Emmental, Cheddar
Fresh herbs, to garnish, optional

Boil the potatoes, unpeeled, until they're just done; overcooking would
complicate matters at the second stage of cooking. Meanwhile, heat

a little oil in a very large frying pan, using more oil if the pan isn't non-
stick. Cook the bacon until slightly crisp but not crunchy (around
5 – 10 minutes). If there's a lot of fat in the pan, spoon some of it out.

When the potatoes are cooked, halve or quarter them and add to
the pan with the bacon. Cook over a low heat, turning the spuds frequently, until they're very lightly coloured. The dish can be prepared
in advance to this point.

When you're ready to eat, re-heat the bacon and potatoes, if necessary. Let them cook, with occasional stirring, while you slice the cheese
thinly. When the potatoes are sizzling, distribute the cheese evenly over
them and cover the pan. Let the cheese melt for a couple of minutes,
then serve quickly with a sprinkling of fresh herbs, if you like.

Roulade of Peppers and Aubergines ⓥ

This exquisite recipe, created by a chef in Sydney, comes from Roast Chicken and Other Stories, *by Simon Hopkinson with Lindsey Bareham. It's great for dinner parties (or even a vegetarian Christmas) because all the work is done a day in advance.*

**Preparation time: 30 – 40 minutes
plus overnight refrigeration
Cooking time: 25 – 30 minutes**

4 large red peppers
2 large aubergines, stalks removed
100 ml (4 fl oz) extra virgin olive oil
30 basil leaves, torn into small pieces
2 – 3 garlic cloves, peeled and thinly sliced
15 ml (1 tablespoon) balsamic vinegar, or to taste
Salt and freshly ground black pepper

Grill or roast the peppers at a medium heat until they're blackened all over and very soft. Put in a bag for 10 minutes, then peel and seed leaving the peppers whole, if possible. Meanwhile, slice the aubergines as thinly as possible and heat the oil in a large pan until it's almost smoking. Fry the aubergine slices until golden brown on both sides, draining them on kitchen towels as they're done.

Clear your work surface and lay down a very large piece of cling film – 60 cm (24 in) should be about right. In the centre, make a rectangle of the aubergine slices with the edges overlapping slightly. Season with salt and pepper, then scatter the basil and garlic evenly over the surface. Sprinkle with vinegar and finally lay the peppers on top.

Carefully lifting a long edge of the cling film, roll up the peppers and aubergines so they form a shape like a Swiss roll. Be sure not to get the film caught up inside. Tuck the other long edge underneath the roll, then twist the ends like Christmas crackers and turn them tightly in opposite directions. This will tighten the roll and firm it up. Refrigerate overnight.

To serve, cut the roll into 5 cm (2 in) sections with the cling film still in place. A serrated knife is best for this purpose. Transfer the slices to plates or a serving platter and, finally, remove the collars of cling film. You can serve it with a tomato sauce or something similar, but I think it's great on its own.

Moroccan-style Sprouts ⓥ

This recipe is based on one using carrots, which can either be combined with the sprouts or used instead.

**Preparation time: 10 minutes
Cooking time: 10 – 15 minutes**

900 g (2 lb) Brussels sprouts, trimmed
1 – 2 garlic cloves, minced
1.25 ml (¼ teaspoon) ground cumin
1.25 ml (¼ teaspoon) paprika
1.25 ml (¼ teaspoon) cayenne pepper
Extra virgin olive oil or unsalted butter to taste
Salt and freshly ground black pepper

Steam the sprouts or boil them in plenty of well salted water until they're not quite cooked (i.e., a little harder than *al dente*). When you're getting ready to serve, toss with the remaining ingredients and re-heat over a gentle heat for 3 – 5 minutes, stirring occasionally. Once they're fully cooked they can be served immediately or left for up to 10 minutes.

NB: If this dish seems too spicy for the children, set aside a bowlful of carrots for them and toss with butter, salt and pepper. Left-overs can be used in a vegetable soup.

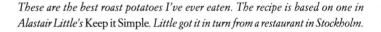

Hasselback Potatoes ⓥ

These are the best roast potatoes I've ever eaten. The recipe is based on one in Alastair Little's Keep it Simple. *Little got it in turn from a restaurant in Stockholm.*

**Preparation time: 15 minutes
Cooking time: 50 – 60 minutes**

4 large baking potatoes, each weighing around 350 g (12 oz)
100 ml (4 fl oz) extra virgin olive oil
Coarse salt

Pre-heat the oven to 200°C/400°F/Gas 6. Peel the potatoes, dropping them in a bowl of cold water as you go. When they are all peeled, drain and then dry and halve them. Put them on your chopping board with the flat surface of the potato down and, using a very sharp, thin-bladed knife, make a series of parallel incisions at 1.5 cm (½ in) intervals. The knife should go just over half way into the potato, not all the way through. Return each piece to a fresh bowl of water as you go.

When the potatoes are all scored, drain and dry them and put in a roasting tin, flat side down; if it's not a non-stick pan, oil it lightly first. Brush the potatoes with oil, sprinkle with coarse salt and roast until soft inside and well browned outside (50 – 60 minutes). Baste with oil every 15 minutes or so. The potatoes will open up slightly where you've cut them, allowing more of the surface to brown.

Verdure Affogate

Verdure Affogate

This is based on a recipe in Carol Field's Italy in Small Bites.

Preparation time: 15 minutes
Cooking time: 40 minutes

45 ml (3 tablespoons) olive oil
50 – 75 g (2 – 3 oz) pancetta or streaky bacon, shredded
2 small leeks, whites only, cut into approximately 5 mm (¼ in) slices
2 red, ripe beef tomatoes, chopped
1 kg (2.2 lb) Savoy cabbage, broccoli or spring greens, washed and cut into fairly large pieces
225 ml (8 fl oz) white wine
Salt and freshly ground pepper

Heat the oil in a large saucepan and gently cook the bacon and leeks until they're good and soft (around 20 minutes). Add the tomatoes, greens and wine, plus salt and plenty of pepper. Cover the pot and simmer gently, stirring every few minutes, until the vegetables are soft (around 20 minutes). This can be seasoned with garlic or chillis, if you wish.

Roasted Peppers

Roasted Red Peppers Ⓥ

This is one of those recipes that can be varied endlessly: add anchovies, sun-dried tomatoes, spring onions, chillis and a bit of Parmesan.

Preparation time: 5 minutes
Cooking time: 30 minutes

4 red peppers
15 ml (1 tablespoon) capers
A small handful of fresh herbs, e.g. basil, tarragon or dill
30 ml (2 tablespoons) extra virgin olive oil
Freshly ground black pepper

Pre-heat the oven to 200°C/400°F/Gas 6. Cut the tops off the peppers, halve them lengthwise, and remove all the seeds and pith. Chop the capers and herbs, season with freshly ground black pepper and mix with the oil. Divide this mixture between the peppers and bake on a baking sheet or roasting tin until the peppers are soft and deeply coloured but not blackened (around 30 minutes). Serve either hot, warm, or at room temperature.

Gratin de Potiron Ⓥ

This pumpkin recipe is based on a recipe in Raymond Blanc's Cooking for Friends, *though the method itself is classic. Tinned pumpkin is much easier than fresh, and gives excellent results.*

Preparation time: 15 minutes
Cooking time: around 20 minutes

1 x 400g (14 oz) tin pumpkin purée
2 eggs, separated
10ml (2 teaspoons) caster sugar
Around 25g (1 oz) unsalted butter
50g (2 oz) Gruyère or Emmental cheese, finely grated
Juice of ¼ lemon
Salt and freshly ground black pepper

Cook the pumpkin in a saucepan until it has the consistency of fairly dry mashed potatoes, and leave to cool. Meanwhile, beat the egg yolks and sugar. Pre-heat the oven to 180°C/350°F/Gas 4, and butter a medium-sized gratin dish.

Mix the cooled pumpkin into the egg yolks with around ⅔ of the cheese. Season with pepper and a little salt.

Whisk the egg whites until they form soft peaks, and add the lemon juice with a little more pepper. Beat a few spoonfuls into the pumpkin, then gently fold in the remaining whites. Pour this mixture into the gratin dish, dot with the remaining butter and sprinkle on the remaining cheese. Bake until lightly browned (around 20 minutes), and serve.

Easy Potato Gratin

This alternative to roast potatoes (perfect for Christmas) is much easier than a classic gratin such as gratin Dauphinois. Adjust the cooking time if you're cooking other dishes in the oven at the same time.

Preparation time: 15 minutes
Cooking time: 1 ½ – 2 hours

1.25 kg (2½ lb) potatoes, cut into approximately 1.5 cm (½ in) chunks or slices
225 ml (8 fl oz) single cream
2 large onions, coarsely chopped
2 large dessert apples, peeled, cored and coarsely chopped
2.5 ml (½ teaspoon) freshly grated nutmeg
225 ml (8 fl oz) chicken, beef or turkey stock
Salt and freshly ground black pepper

Pre-heat the oven to 200°C/400°F/Gas 6. Toss the potatoes in a large bowl with the cream, onions and apples. Add the nutmeg, salt and pepper, and toss everything thoroughly.

Put into 1 or 2 large ovenproof dishes and pour over the stock. Bake near the top of oven until potatoes are soft and the top nicely browned (1½ – 2 hours). You can speed things up slightly by covering the dish(es) with aluminium foil for the first 45 minutes of cooking.

Aubergine and Tomato Layer Cake Ⓥ

This beautiful dish is substantial enough to serve as a main course for vegetarians. Preparation and cooking can be done in advance, but the cake should be assembled just before serving.

Preparation time: 5 minutes
Cooking time: 20 – 30 minutes

4 medium aubergines weighing about
  1 kg (2.2 lb)
Olive oil, for frying
450 g (1 lb) red, ripe tomatoes
A hunk of Parmesan
15 ml (1 tablespoon) balsamic vinegar
Salt and freshly ground black pepper

Top and tail the aubergines and slice lengthwise around 5 mm (¼ in) thick. If you like, you can sprinkle them with salt and leave in a colander for 30 minutes; I generally skip this step. If you salt them, rinse and dry the slices very well on paper towels.

In a large frying pan, heat enough oil to film the bottom generously. When hot, put in a few slices and turn them instantly; this enables you to use less oil. Fry them on both sides until nicely browned and soft throughout. Drain on paper towels and cook the remaining slices, using more oil as needed.

When you're getting ready to serve, core and thinly slice the tomatoes. Using a thin-bladed knife or a vegetable peeler, cut 10 – 12 thin shavings from the Parmesan and crumble into pieces about the size of a 20p coin. Put a layer of aubergine slices into a loose-bottomed cake tin and top with a layer of tomatoes. Sprinkle over some cheese and season with salt and pepper. Repeat until all ingredients are used, making sure the top layer is tomato. Using a plate, press down firmly on the 'cake'; this will make serving easier. Dribble on the vinegar and add extra cheese if you wish. Lift from the tin. To serve, cut into wedges with a very sharp knife.

Aubergine and Tomato Layer Cake

Leek and Potato Gratin

Leek and Potato Gratin ✔

This gratin is somewhat lighter than the recipe for Easy Potato Gratin (page 110), as it contains no cream, and is eminently comforting on a cold winter's night. Skip the mushrooms if you prefer – they're not strictly necessary.

Preparation time: 15 minutes
Cooking time: around 1 hour

Unsalted butter
675 g (1½ lb) old potatoes, cut into approximately 1.5 cm (½ in) slices
500 g (1 lb 2 oz) leeks, whites only, cut into approximately 1.5 cm (½ in) slices
A pinch of cayenne pepper
300 ml (10 fl oz) milk
175 g (6 oz) mushrooms, thickly sliced
Freshly grated Parmesan
Salt and freshly ground black pepper

Pre-heat the oven to 230°C/450°F/Gas 8. Generously butter a medium-sized gratin dish then add the potatoes and leeks. Season with salt, pepper and cayenne. Pour in the milk and dot generously with butter. Cover with aluminium foil and bake in the centre of the oven until the vegetables are soft (around 1 hour).

Meanwhile, briskly fry the mushrooms (if using) in more butter until barely soft. Drain off the juices and save for a soup. When the gratin is cooked, pre-heat the grill and add the mushrooms with a good quantity of grated Parmesan. Grill just long enough to get a light-golden crust of cheese. Leave for a couple of minutes before serving. This goes particularly well with pork or lamb.

Braised Chicory

Most people use this expensive leaf in salads. I prefer it when cooked to a melting consistency in the oven. Chicory should be tightly closed, with no traces of brown or green in the leaves.

Preparation time: 5 minutes
Cooking time: 1 – 2 hours

12 heads chicory
50 g (2 oz) unsalted butter
450 ml (15 fl oz) chicken or turkey stock
Freshly ground black pepper
Toasted breadcrumbs, to garnish, optional

Pre-heat the oven to 200°C/400°F/Gas 6. Trim the base off each head of chicory, avoid removing too much or the head will fall apart. Grease a baking or gratin dish just large enough to hold the chicory in a single layer with as much butter as needed. Put in the heads and pour over the stock, leaving the heads covered by around half. (You can use more or less stock as needed.)

Season well with pepper, cover loosely with aluminium foil and bake near the bottom of the oven until browned and very soft (around 1½ hours). If it seems to be cooking too fast or too slowly, it can be moved around in the oven or even taken out for a time.

Incidentally, this dish cooks well and very quickly in the microwave. Cover with cling film and cook at full power, turning once, for around 20 minutes.

To serve, leave whole or halve lengthways and sprinkle with toasted breadcrumbs if you wish.

Leeks in Mustard Vinaigrette ✔

Choose firm new-season leeks with a minimum of green, which barely need cleaning. This dish can be served hot or cold.

Preparation time: 10 minutes
Cooking time: 45 – 50 minutes

2 kg (4.4 lb) small leeks, white parts only, washed and trimmed
30 ml (2 tablespoons) salt
100 ml (4 fl oz) plus 15 ml (1 tablespoon) vegetable oil
100 ml (4 fl oz) extra virgin olive oil
100 (4 fl oz) dry white wine
60 ml (4 tablespoons) red wine vinegar
45 ml (3 tablespoons) Dijon mustard
10 ml (2 teaspoons) caster sugar
5 ml (1 teaspoon) dried thyme
A small handful of parsley, chopped, optional
Salt and freshly ground black pepper

Pre-heat the oven to 170°C/325°F/Gas 3 and boil a kettle. Lay the leeks neatly in a large roasting tin. Dissolve the salt in a little boiled water, then mix with 1 tablespoon of vegetable oil and pour over the leeks. Add more water until the leeks are half covered. (You may need to boil another kettle.)

Cover loosely with aluminium foil and cook in the oven until the vegetables are easily pierced with a knife (around 45 – 50 minutes).

Meanwhile, make the vinaigrette by mixing all the remaining ingredients except the parsley with a wire whisk; season well with salt and pepper and leave to infuse for at least 20 minutes.

When the leeks are done, remove from the oven and drain. Leave to cool if you're not serving them hot. Just before serving, pour over the vinaigrette and top with parsley (if using).

Serve immediately.

Mashed Potatoes and Celeriac ⓥ

This makes a very classy accompaniment for a good banger, but also goes well with any game dish. Slicing the vegetables cuts the cooking time to almost nothing.

Preparation time: 5 – 10 minutes
Cooking time: 12 – 15 minutes

800 g (1¾ lb) potatoes, peeled and cut into 5 mm (¼ in) slices
1 large celeriac weighing about 800 g (1¾ lb), peeled and cut into 5mm (¼ in) slices
3 large garlic cloves, peeled and thinly sliced
100 ml (4 fl oz) milk
A large knob of unsalted butter

Bring a large pot of well salted water to the boil. Add the vegetables and garlic, bring back to the boil, then reduce the heat and simmer until they're soft but not disintegrating. This should not take more than 12 – 15 minutes, but start checking them after 8 minutes.

Drain the vegetables and return to the pot over a low heat to evaporate any remaining water. (Celeriac has quite a lot of it, so this may take a few minutes.) Mash well, adding the milk gradually. The final mixture should be creamy but not too wet. Finish off with the butter, using more or less (or none at all) as you please. With the lid on, the mash can be kept warm for a good couple of hours.

Sautéed Wild Mushrooms V

Use any wild mushrooms for this dish, even the cultivated type. Try to use a variety, e.g. chanterelles, oyster, brown cap.

Preparation time: 15 minutes
Cooking time: 5 – 15 minutes

450 g (1 lb) wild mushrooms
50 ml (2 fl oz) extra virgin olive oil
3 shallots or 2 spring onions, finely chopped
A small handful of fresh parsley, preferably flat-leaf, coarsely chopped
15 – 30 ml (1 – 2 tablespoons) lemon or lime juice
Salt and freshly ground black pepper

Clean and trim the mushrooms. You may either leave them whole or slice them (both caps and stems) to whatever thickness you like.

Heat the oil in a large frying pan until it's medium-hot and add the mushrooms, shallots or spring onions and a good dose of salt and pepper. Cook, stirring continuously, for anything from 5 – 15 minutes. Softer varieties like oyster mushrooms and chanterelles take less time. You can spoon out the liquid midway through cooking and save it for soups and sauces.

Just before the mushrooms are ready, add the parsley and lemon or lime juice, and cook for another 1 – 2 minutes. This can be served immediately or left to cool to room temperature; it also makes a great sauce for pasta or rice.

Baked Root Vegetables with Ginger and Red Chilli V

If you're using parsnips, cut out the hard woody cores. Potatoes can be cooked in the same way.

Preparation time: 15 minutes
Cooking time: 1 hour

900 g (2 lb) mixed root vegetables, e.g. parsnips, turnips, swede, peeled if necessary and cut into chunks
5 ml (1 teaspoon) turmeric
7.5 ml (1½ teaspoons) dry mustard
60 ml (4 tablespoons) vegetable oil
30 ml (2 tablespoons) wine vinegar
6 thin slices peeled ginger, thinly shredded
1 long red chilli, seeded and thinly sliced
30 ml (2 tablespoons) sunflower seeds, optional
Salt and freshly ground pepper

Pre-heat the oven to 200°C/400°F/Gas 6 and put the vegetables in a large baking dish. Whisk the turmeric and mustard with 3 tablespoons of the oil and the vinegar, and a good dose of salt and pepper. Pour over the vegetables and toss to coat thoroughly, then cover with aluminium foil and bake in the centre of the oven until the vegetables are soft (50 – 60 minutes).

When you're ready to serve, put the remaining oil in a small frying pan over a medium heat. Add the ginger, chilli and sunflower seeds (if using), and stir-fry briskly for 1 – 2 minutes or just long enough for the ginger to get slightly crisp. Sprinkle over the vegetables and serve.

Sweet Potatoes with Ginger and Sherry Vinegar V

I love sweet potatoes, especially when their flavour is balanced out by something sharp. Here the sharpness comes from sherry vinegar, one of my favourite flavourings. This makes a great side dish for any game bird, or for the Christmas turkey.

Preparation time: 2 minutes
Cooking time: 15 – 60 minutes

2 kg (4 lb) sweet potatoes
A large knob of unsalted butter
6 – 8 slices fresh ginger, finely chopped
175 ml (6 fl oz) milk or chicken stock
45 ml (3 tablespoons) sherry vinegar
Salt and freshly ground black pepper

Boil, bake or microwave the potatoes until just soft. This will take about 1 hour in the oven and 30 – 45 minutes in water. The microwave is fastest by far: prick each potato a dozen times with a sharp knife, place on a large plate and cook uncovered at full power (750 watts) for around 12 – 15 minutes. Leave until they're cool enough to handle, then peel, slice lengthwise and turn out into a large saucepan with the butter and ginger.

Heat gently while you mash and mix well with a good dose of salt and pepper. Add the milk or stock a splash at a time, stirring constantly to blend well. Since sweet potatoes vary so much in the amount of water and starch they contain, some will need much more liquid and others (possibly) a bit less. The final consistency should be the same you would aim for with ordinary mashed potatoes: neither too wet nor too dry. The recipe can be prepared in advance to this point.

When you're ready to serve, re-heat the mash gently, if necessary, adding more milk or stock if the potatoes have dried out. Add the sherry and stir well, using more if you like a stronger flavour. Serve immediately.

Spicy Vegetable Stew ⓥ

Vegetable stews must be cooked carefully to preserve texture. This version achieves that aim by cooking some of the vegetables whole. It's perfect for serving with couscous (see page 145). The ingredients list may be varied according to the availability of the vegetables, but the aubergines mustn't be huge or they will not cook satisfactorily.

Preparation time: 10 minutes
Cooking time: 1 hour

30 ml (2 tablespoons) vegetable oil
5 ml (1 teaspoon) paprika
5 ml (1 teaspoon) chilli powder or
　cayenne pepper
3 – 4 garlic cloves, thinly sliced
1 – 2 large onions, thinly sliced
30 ml (2 tablespoons) tomato purée
400 g (14 oz) okra, washed but left
　whole

225 g (8 oz) small courgettes,
　washed but left whole
225 g (8 oz) small aubergines,
　washed but left whole
225 g (8 oz) French beans or
　mangetouts, topped and tailed
15 ml (1 tablespoon) extra virgin olive
　oil, optional
Salt and freshly ground black pepper

Heat the vegetable oil in a heavy-based pan or casserole and cook the spices gently for 1 minute. Add the garlic, onions and tomato purée, and season with salt and pepper. Continue cooking gently until the onions are just soft. Add the okra with a splash of water and cook, covered, for 10 minutes. Now add the courgettes and aubergines, plus a little more water, and put the lid back on.

Continue cooking until the courgettes and aubergines are soft but retain a hint of resistance to the touch (around 10 minutes for the courgettes, 15 – 20 for the aubergines). As they are done, remove the courgettes and aubergines to a chopping board. Continue cooking the okra until it is done; it should take around 45 – 50 minutes from start to finish. The stew can be prepared in advance to this point.

When you're getting ready to serve, stir in the beans and cook for at least 5 minutes, or longer if you want them very soft. Meanwhile, cut the aubergines and courgettes into bite-sized pieces. Return to the pot just long enough to heat through, then add the olive oil if using. Stir well and serve immediately.

New Potatoes and Mangetouts with a Creamy Wild Mushroom Sauce ⓥ

This recipe is unashamedly rich. For the dried mushrooms use morels (wildly expensive), porcini or Chinese black mushrooms. The potatoes can also be served on their own.

Preparation time: 10 minutes
Cooking time: 15 minutes

450 g (1 lb) new potatoes
450 g (1 lb) mangetouts

For the sauce
25 g (1 oz) dried wild mushrooms
A good knob of butter
1 large spring onion, finely chopped
15 ml (1 tablespoon) dry white wine or
　vermouth
225 ml (8 fl oz) double cream
Salt and freshly ground black pepper

Put the mushrooms in a small bowl and pour in about 100 ml (4 fl oz) of hot (but not boiling) water. Leave for 10 minutes or so, until the mushrooms are soft. Rinse quickly under the cold tap and chop finely. Strain the water through a fine sieve and reserve.

Melt the butter in a small pan and cook the onion gently for a minute or until it starts to sizzle slightly. Add the wine and soaking water. Boil rapidly to reduce to a few tablespoons, then add 200 ml (7 fl oz) of the cream with a bit of salt and pepper. Reduce for around 5 minutes, then stir in the mushrooms and the remaining cream. The dish can be prepared in advance to this point.

Meanwhile, cook the potatoes and mangetouts (separately) by steaming, microwaving or boiling them in plenty of well salted water. Spread the peas out on a serving platter with the potatoes arranged on top. Spoon over the sauce and serve immediately.

New Potatoes and Mangetouts with a Creamy Wild Mushroom Sauce

Flat-cap Mushrooms with Gremolata ⓥ

I adore mushrooms, especially when they're very simply cooked either fried on top of the stove in olive oil or cooked in the microwave. This recipe, using large, flavourful flat-cap mushrooms, makes a simple but impressive starter.

Preparation time: 5 minutes
Cooking time: 10 – 15 minutes

30 ml (2 tablespoons) extra virgin olive oil, for frying
4 – 8 large flat-cap mushrooms, stems trimmed
60 ml (4 tablespoons) Gremolata (see page 71)
Chopped herbs, optional
Salt and freshly ground black pepper

To cook the mushrooms on the hob, heat the oil in a large lidded frying pan which will hold the fungi in 1 layer. When the oil is hot, put in the mushrooms with stalks facing up and cover the pan. Cook until they're barely softened, taking care not to overcook (3 – 5 minutes).

To microwave the mushrooms (this method works even better than frying on the hob), put the mushrooms 2 at a time on a large plate, cover with a second plate and cook for 2 – 3 minutes at full power. If they're not done, cover them again with the plate and give them 30 seconds more. The aim is to heat them thoroughly and soften them but retain a good hint of 'bite'.

Whichever method you use, either serve the mushrooms immediately or leave to cool to room temperature. Put 1 – 2 mushrooms on each of 4 serving plates and top with a little pile of Gremolata, plus a sprinkling of salt and pepper. Extra chopped herbs may be added if you like.

Rich Tomato Salad

This turns a bacon and tomato sandwich into a luxurious salad. It's served with a vinaigrette based on Boursin cheese, one of my favourite all-purpose ingredients – as useful in cooking as it is when served with toast or biscuits.

Preparation time: around 20 minutes
Cooking time: 5 – 6 minutes

125 g (4 oz) green streaky bacon
4 – 5 thick slices good white bread
60 ml (4 tablespoons) extra virgin olive oil
25 g (1 oz) Boursin with garlic and herbs
45 ml (3 tablespoons) low-fat or Bio yoghurt
10 ml (2 teaspoons) wine vinegar or lemon juice
Chopped fresh herbs, optional
450 g (1 lb) red, ripe tomatoes
8 – 10 sprigs of fresh herbs – basil, tarragon, parsley, to garnish

Cut the rinds off the bacon, then slice the meat into thin shreds. Refrigerate until needed. Cut the bread into 1.25 cm (½ in) square pieces – you don't need to cut the crusts off. Heat the oil in a heavy-based frying pan and fry the croûtons, stirring constantly, until they're a light golden brown. Place on paper towels and leave to drain for at least 10 minutes.

Make the dressing by mashing the cheese and yoghurt together, then whisking thoroughly with the vinegar and some fresh herbs (if desired). Core the tomatoes and slice thickly.

A few minutes before you want to eat, arrange the tomatoes on 4 large serving plates, forming a ring with a 7.5 – 10 cm (3 – 4 in) 'hole' in the middle. Heat the frying pan until it is medium-hot and fry the bacon shreds until they're brown and crisp. Drain on paper towels, then toss with the croûtons. Put a pile in the centre of each plate, dress the tomatoes with the vinaigrette and garnish with the herbs. Serve immediately.

Variations
Use a herby oil-based vinaigrette instead of the creamy version here.

Add shreds of sun-dried tomatoes to the bacon and croûtons, or substitute smoked haddock or canned tuna for the bacon.

Salade Baussenque Ⓥ

This is adapted from a dish I once ate at London's Auberge de Provence. There the salad is assembled inside a hollow ring, which is lifted to leave a neat circle of greenery. Follow their example if you have the right kind of ring (15 cm/6 in diameter), or use the method described below.

Preparation time: 20 minutes
Cooking time: 3 minutes

125 g (4 oz) French beans
4 artichoke hearts in oil
125 g (4 oz) button mushrooms
8 small radishes
A few large handfuls of mixed lettuce leaves,
   e.g. oak leaf, frisée, radicchio, curly endive
4 large or 8 small tomatoes

For the dressing

45 ml (3 tablespoons) extra virgin olive oil
10 ml (2 teaspoons) wine vinegar
A small bunch of tarragon and/or basil, optional
A pinch of mustard powder, optional
30 ml (2 tablespoons) pine nuts
Salt and freshly ground black pepper

Top and tail the beans and blanch in well salted water until just cooked (around 3 minutes). Drain, refresh under cold running water and pat dry. Slice the artichoke hearts, mushrooms, radishes and beans in thin slices. Prepare the lettuces and mix. Slice or dice the tomatoes.

Make vinaigrette by mixing together the oil, vinegar, salt and freshly ground black pepper. Mince the tarragon and/or basil and add with the pinch of mustard (if using).

To assemble the salad, lay the tomatoes on 4 plates and top with the heavier ingredients – artichoke hearts, radishes and mushrooms in that order. Now add the lettuce leaves, spreading them evenly over the top. When you're ready to serve, heat a small, dry frying pan and toast the pine nuts for 1 – 2minutes until they turn a light golden brown. Sprinkle over the salad, pour on a little vinaigrette and serve.

Variations

You can substitute other vegetables, such as fennel, kohl rabi or par-boiled mangetouts.

Use coarse breadcrumbs, lightly toasted or fried in olive oil, instead of the pine nuts.

Top the salad with edible flowers for a colourful effect. Lavender and nasturtiums are popular choices, though I prefer the flowers from herbs such as thyme, rosemary and chives.

Burghal Salad with Peppers and Herbs ⓥ

This recipe couldn't be easier to make – or more enjoyable to eat. Use mint instead of basil, if you have some around.

Preparation time: 10 minutes

300 g (11 oz) burghal (bulgar wheat)
2 lemons
60 ml (4 tablespoons) extra virgin olive oil
4 – 5 spring onions
85 g (3 oz) bunch fresh parsley,
    preferably flat-leaf
50 g (2 oz) bunch basil
1 large red pepper
1 large yellow pepper
Salt and freshly ground black pepper

Soften the burghal by soaking it in plenty of cold water for 30 minutes; if that doesn't work, bring to the boil for a couple of minutes and then leave to cool until soft. Meanwhile, squeeze the juice from the lemons and mix with the oil. (You need around 80 ml/3 fl oz of juice.) Top and tail the spring onions and chop into shreds or discs.

When the wheat is soft, put it in a strainer and leave for at least 5 minutes to drain. Mix while still warm, boiled, with the onions, lemon juice and oil. Season with salt and plenty of freshly ground black pepper. Pinch the parsley and basil leaves off the stems and chop coarsely. Core and seed the peppers then chop into 5 mm (¼ in) dice. Just before serving, mix the herbs and peppers into the burghal. The salad can be eaten warm or at room temperature.

Variations
Roast the peppers and peel them.

Use other vegetables in addition to (or instead of) the peppers: diced tomatoes, courgettes or fennel would all be great.

Scoop the insides out of large beef tomatoes and serve the salad inside them.

Cucumbers with Herb Yoghurt ⓥ

Though similar to an Indian raita, this recipe uses Western flavourings. It should be prepared only when you're ready to serve, but the work involved is minimal.

Preparation time: 5 – 10 minutes

A large handful of parsley, preferably flat-leaf
10 – 12 leaves fresh mint
5 – 6 fresh sage leaves
225 ml (8 fl oz) Bio yoghurt
3 – 4 large cucumbers, cut into thick chunks or slices
Juice of ½ large lemon
Salt and freshly ground black pepper

Chop the herbs and mix with the yoghurt, then season with salt and pepper. Taste the mixture and if it is too sharp, add more yoghurt. Pour the yoghurt onto the cucumbers or toss together in a bowl. Add the lemon juice and serve immediately.

Cucumber Salad with Feta Cheese ⓥ

The colours in this salad are lovely and the sharp flavour is a perfect accompaniment to grilled or barbecued meat or poultry.

Preparation time: 10 minutes

2 medium cucumbers
175 g (6 oz) feta cheese
45 ml (3 tablespoons) extra virgin olive oil
15 ml (1 tablespoon) red wine vinegar
125 – 175 g (4 – 6 oz) green olives, preferably with herbs and/or garlic
1 bunch radishes, with leaves on if possible
A small handful of fresh herbs – basil, chervil, parsley, coriander
Salt and freshly ground black pepper

Top and tail the cucumbers and peel them if you wish; I prefer to leave the skin on for extra colour. Alternatively, only partially peel them, leaving contrasting stripes of skin and flesh.

Halve lengthwise and scoop out the seeds using a small, sharp knife and a teaspoon. Blot dry with paper towels and cut on the bias into slices about 5 mm (¼ in) thick. Crumble or thinly slice the cheese.

Whisk the oil and vinegar with a little salt (the cheese is quite salty) and a lot of freshly ground black pepper. Pit the olives if you wish and wash the radishes; if they're very fresh, the leaves are delicious and can be cut off and served with the salad. Chop the herbs coarsely.

Arrange the cucumbers on a fairly small serving platter or put them in a bowl. Dot with the olives, radishes, and finally, the cheese. Dribble over the vinaigrette and toss, if you're using a bowl. Sprinkle over the herbs and serve immediately.

Variations
To vary the recipe, use tomatoes instead of cucumber for a more traditional-style Greek salad.

Substitute a fairly mild (i.e., young) French or British goat's cheese for the feta.

Pit and chop the olives and slice the radishes very thinly.

Lay the cucumber slices on a large piece of good toast, top with the remaining ingredients and serve as an open sandwich.

Mixed Asparagus Salad Ⓥ

Preparation time: 5 minutes
Cooking time: 20 – 30 minutes

250 g (9 oz) baby sweetcorn, halved lengthwise
450 g (1 lb) asparagus, cut into 7.5 cm (3 in) lengths
300 g (11 oz) fennel, thinly sliced and fronds coarsely chopped
15 ml (1 tablespoon) extra virgin olive oil
10 ml (2 teaspoons) vegetable oil
10 ml (2 teaspoons) balsamic vinegar
2.5 ml (½ teaspoon) lemon juice
Salt and freshly ground black pepper

Bring 7.5 cm (3 in) well salted water to the boil in a large frying pan. Cook the sweetcorn until softened but still very firm (around 5 minutes). Remove and drain in a colander. Cook the asparagus in the same way for around 5 – 10 minutes. Drain well and leave to cool for 10 minutes or so. Meanwhile, make a vinaigrette from the oils, vinegar and lemon juice, adding a good dose of salt and pepper. Put all the vegetables on a serving plate, pour over the dressing and serve immediately.

Warm Bean Salad

This is one of my favourite vegetable dishes. The recipe is based on a dish that my mother makes. It's perfect for using up cheap, abundant green beans in August. Although it's delicious at any temperature, I prefer it warm.

Preparation time: 5 minutes
Cooking time: 10 minutes

450 g (1 lb) French or runner beans
1 small red onion, or 3 shallots or 3 spring onions
1 lemon
15 – 20 ml (1 – 2 tablespoons) extra virgin olive oil
1 small sprig of fresh rosemary
Salt and freshly ground black pepper

Bring a large pan of water to the boil while you top and tail the beans. When the water reaches boiling point, salt it well and add the beans. Bring back to the boil and boil for 1 minute (French beans) or 2 minutes (runner beans). Drain in a colander and refresh under cold running water. Leave to drain, but don't worry about drying.

Peel the onions (if necessary) and slice them paper-thin. Peel the lemon and cut off the rinds. Make 15 ml (1 tablespoon) finely diced lemon zest.

Heat the oil gently in a large frying pan and add the rosemary needles. Toss in the oil for a minute with some salt and freshly ground black pepper, then add the beans and toss again. Cook until the beans seem to be about half cooked (around 3 – 5 minutes). Add the onions and zest and cook for a few more minutes, longer if you want the beans to be very soft. When the beans are cooked, turn off the heat. Slice the lemon thinly, removing any seeds then toss with the beans. Leave until you're ready to eat – 5 seconds minimum, 2 hours maximum.

Celery Salad with Red Pepper Dressing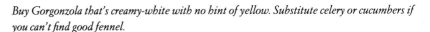

The peppers aren't strictly necessary to this salad but they do add a welcome note of colour.

Preparation time: 10 minutes
Cooking time: 3 – 4 minutes

2 heads celery
15 ml (1 tablespoon) extra virgin olive oil
5 ml (1 teaspoon) soy sauce
5 ml (1 teaspoon) red wine vinegar
2 red peppers, seeded and cut into 2.5 mm (⅛ in) dice
Salt and freshly ground black pepper

Bring a large pan of well salted water to the boil. Wash the celery and slice, on the bias, into 1.5 cm (½ in) thick pieces. Add to the pan, bring the water back to the boil and cook for 1 minute exactly. Drain well and toss while hot with the oil, soy sauce, vinegar and salt and pepper.

Just before serving, add the diced peppers to the celery and toss the salad at the table. Serve either hot or at room temperature.

Variations

The celery can also be cooked in the microwave with a little olive oil or water for around 10 minutes in an 850 – watt oven. Stir 4 or 5 times. Toss with vinaigrette as above.

Fennel Salad with Gorgonzola

Buy Gorgonzola that's creamy-white with no hint of yellow. Substitute celery or cucumbers if you can't find good fennel.

Preparation time: 10 minutes

125 g (4 oz) Gorgonzola
100 ml (4 fl oz) Bio yoghurt
5 ml (1 teaspoon) wine vinegar
2 spring onions
4 – 5 leaves fresh basil
4 medium bulbs fennel
Salt and freshly ground black pepper

Mash the cheese and blend with the yoghurt and vinegar. Mince the onions and mix in well. This can be done up to 4 hours in advance.

When you're ready to serve, chop or tear the basil into small pieces and mix into the dressing. Trim the fennel and chop into 1.5 cm (½ in) chunks. Dress with the cheese mixture, season with plenty of pepper and taste for salt; the cheese is fairly salty so you may not need any. Serve immediately.

Potato Salad with Sesame Vinaigrette Ⓥ

This is best made with Jersey Royals, those tiny delicacies that start appearing in shops during May. But it can be made equally well with any small new potato.

Preparation time: 5 minutes
Cooking time: 20 – 30 minutes

2 large red or yellow peppers, seeded and cut into small chunks
450 g (1 lb) small new potatoes
25 ml (1½ tablespoons) low-fat yoghurt
2.5 ml (½ teaspoon) wine or balsamic vinegar
2.5 ml (½ teaspoon) sesame oil
1 bunch spring onions, finely shredded and cut into 7.5 cm
   (3 in) lengths
30 ml (2 tablespoons) sesame seeds
Salt and freshly ground black pepper

Bring some water to the boil in a steamer and cook the peppers until softened but still firm (around 10 minutes). Remove and steam the potatoes until just cooked (around 10 – 20 minutes). Meanwhile, mix together the yoghurt, vinegar and oil and season with salt and pepper.

When the potatoes are cooked, leave to cool for around 5 minutes then toss with the peppers and top with the onions. Heat the sesame seeds in a dry frying pan until they're lightly browned. Pour over the dressing, sprinkle on the sesame seeds and serve immediately.

Pasta,
grains & pulses

Borlotti Bean Salad (page 137)

Pasta,
grains & dried pulses

Pasta is many people's favourite food nowadays. And it is remarkably versatile stuff. It can be a hearty meal for a cold winter evening or a light dish suitable for summer lunch; a starter or a main course; an instant meal for weekday dinners or a long-cooked extravaganza stretching over hours.

Most of the pasta recipes here concentrate on quick sauces. There are few things better than a long-cooked ragú, the classic tomato sauce of Bologna, but it takes time to make properly. Simpler sauces with fewer ingredients often fit better into busy schedules.

I rarely use fresh pasta, one of the trendy foods of recent years. When the trend first took off, commercial fresh pastas were pretty awful. Manufacturers have made great progress in quality since then, but I still prefer Italian dried pasta, one of the greatest mass-produced foods in the world.

Serving sizes for pasta are a contentious point. Most recipes specify 85 – 125 g (3 – 4 oz) of dried pasta per person and some go as low as 65 g (2 ½ oz) per person. In my experience, that's not enough. I make 150 – 175 g (5 – 6 oz) per person and use any left-overs the next day. Most pasta dishes re-heat well in a double boiler or microwave.

Among the other grain-based foods, polenta is a particular favourite of mine. Traditional recipes give forbidding cooking methods, calling for at least 40 minutes of constant stirring. I have found that 20 minutes will suffice, with vigorous stirring using a wire whisk or an electric whisk set at medium speed.

You can avoid the hard beating altogether by using my version of Anna Del Conte's baking technique. Easier and faster still is microwaved polenta, which requires just one stir midway through cooking. Quick-cooking polenta is sold in some delicatessens and good supermarkets.

Polenta can be served immediately or cooled and re-cooked by grilling, baking or frying. When re-cooked it has a crunchy exterior which most people adore. It's cooled in a tin or on a large board. Then you cut any shape you like. But whichever way you make it, make lots: cooked polenta keeps in the fridge for a week.

Rice is another personal favourite, partly because it's absurdly easy to tart up with extra ingredients. My favourites include chicken stock and a chopped onion; whole spices such as fennel seeds, cardamom, cumin, coriander and fenugreek; dried thyme and a clove of garlic.

Pulses are another distinctive vehicle for rich flavours from any of the world's great cuisines. The recipes here derive inspiration from a wide range of culinary traditions.

Most dried beans must be soaked before use, usually overnight, and even those that don't need it will, if soaked, take less time to cook. If you're pressed for time, the process can be speeded up. On the hob, boil beans in unsalted water for 5 minutes, then leave (covered) for 1 hour. In the microwave, cook in a large bowl with twice the volume of water, covered, for 12 – 15 minutes. Leave for 10 minutes, then pour in a cup of hot water and leave (covered) for 1 hour.

I generally cook pulses on their own before adding other flavours. Simmer the beans (don't boil) if you want them to keep their skins. You can get extra flavour by putting a quartered onion, a bay leaf, and a halved clove of garlic in the water, and by draining when nearly done and completing the cooking in stock.

Penne with Peppers and Bacon

The bacon here is optional but it does add an extra dimension to the flavour. Use pancetta (Italian bacon) if possible.

Preparation time: 5 – 10 minutes
Cooking time: 20 minutes

45 ml (3 tablespoons) extra virgin olive oil

3 large red, orange or yellow peppers (or 1 of each), seeded and
  cut into approximately 5 mm (¼ in) slices

2 garlic cloves, finely chopped

500 g (1 lb 2 oz) penne

175 g (6 oz) thick-cut green bacon or pancetta, rinds removed,
  cut in thin shreds

Salt and freshly ground black pepper

Freshly grated Parmesan, to serve

Heat the oil in a large frying pan and fry the peppers and garlic very gently, stirring frequently. Grind in some black pepper. Cook the peppers until they are soft but with a good hint of crunch (around 15 minutes). The sauce can be prepared in advance to this point.

Bring a large pan of salted water to the boil and add the pasta gradually so that the water retains a rolling boil. Cook until firm but tender.

Heat a frying pan over a fairly high heat and stir-fry the bacon or *pancetta* (with a little extra oil if necessary) until it's fairly crunchy (around 5 minutes). Re-heat the peppers (if necessary) over a low heat. Drain the cooked pasta, toss with the hot bacon, then pour on the peppers and take the bowl to the table. Serve with grated Parmesan.

Pasta Salad with Prosciutto, Shaved Parmesan and Cherry Tomatoes

This salad gets maximum mileage out of prosciutto, one of the world's greatest (and priciest) foods.

Preparation time: 10 minutes
Cooking time: 10 – 12 minutes

500 g (1 lb 2 oz) penne or fusilli

60 ml (4 tablespoons) extra virgin olive oil

2 green peppers, seeded and finely chopped

2 spring onions, finely chopped

A small handful of fresh dill, mint or fresh parsley
  (preferably flat-leaf), finely chopped

12 – 16 paper-thin slices prosciutto di Parma

25 ml (1½ tablespoons) balsamic vinegar

12 – 16 paper-thin slices Parmesan

Cook the pasta in plenty of salted boiling water, then drain and refresh it immediately under cold running water. Shake out as much water as possible and toss immediately with the oil. Spread out on a large platter so it cools quickly.

When the pasta is cool, toss with the peppers, onions and herbs in a large bowl. You can do this in advance, but no more than a couple of hours. Cover and keep cool without refrigerating.

When you're ready to serve, cut the *prosciutto* into shreds and toss with the vinegar. Add a little more oil if the pasta seems too dry. Put a generous mound of pasta on each plate, top with the *prosciutto*, and finally a few slices of Parmesan. Serve immediately with a green salad.

Spaghetti with Prawns and Asparagus

This is based on a recipe in Giuliano Hazan's Classic Pasta Cookbook. *If you can't get raw prawns, use the cooked variety instead and just heat them through in the sauce.*

Preparation time: 10 – 15 minutes
Cooking time: 15 – 20 minutes

350 g (12 oz) asparagus
350 g (12 oz) prawns, raw if possible
60 ml (4 tablespoons) extra virgin olive oil
2 large garlic cloves

500 g (1 lb 2 oz) spaghetti
A good knob of butter
Salt and freshly ground black pepper

Boil several inches of water in a large frying pan or roasting tin. Add lots of salt. Trim and wash the asparagus then boil in the water until barely tender (anything from 5 – 10 minutes). Drain well, reserving the cooking water. When cool enough to handle, cut into 2.5 cm (1 in) lengths.

Shell and remove the veins from the prawns (if necessary). Cut into 1.5 cm (½ in) pieces. Save the shells to make stock or prawn butter. Heat the oil in a frying pan and chop the garlic finely. Fry in the oil until it starts to become fragrant, then add the asparagus and stir-fry for a couple of minutes. Add 120 ml (8 tablespoons) of the cooking water and boil rapidly until reduced by about half. Add the prawns, season well with pepper and cook until they have all turned pink (2 – 3 minutes). The sauce should be slightly runny; if it is too dry, add a little more asparagus water. Check the seasoning and remove from the heat.

Cook and drain the pasta, then toss with the butter and top with the sauce (which should be re-heated very gently if cooked more than 10 minutes in advance). I don't think cheese is needed with this dish.

Pasta with Triple Tomato Sauce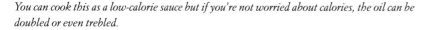

You can cook this as a low-calorie sauce but if you're not worried about calories, the oil can be doubled or even trebled.

Preparation time: 10 minutes
Cooking time: 45 minutes minimum

10 ml (2 teaspoons) extra virgin olive oil
1 small onion, finely chopped
1 garlic clove, finely chopped
1 sun-dried tomato, finely chopped
1 x 400 g (14 oz) tin plum tomatoes
10 ml (2 teaspoons) tomato purée
1 small carrot, finely chopped
1 celery stick, finely chopped

45 ml (3 tablespoons) red wine
5 ml (1 teaspoon) dried mixed herbs
500 g (1 lb 2 oz) dried pasta
A small handful of fresh parsley, preferably flat-leaf, coarsely chopped
Salt and freshly ground black pepper
Freshly grated Parmesan, to serve

Heat the oil in a pan and cook the onion and garlic slowly until deeply browned (around 20 minutes). Add the tomatoes and tomato purée, carrot, celery, wine and herbs, and season with salt and pepper. Continue cooking, stirring occasionally, for at least 30 minutes. Cook the pasta in plenty of boiling salted water and drain. Mix with the sauce and parsley, and serve with grated Parmesan passed separately.

Linguine with Vegetables and Prosciutto

The vegetables in this dish are cooked fairly gently, then jazzed up with shreds of prosciutto di Parma (Parma ham). Some people like prosciutto with a bit of crispness. I think its inimitable (and expensive) character is better preserved by cooking just long enough to heat it through.

Preparation time:
10 – 15 minutes
Cooking time: 15 minutes

15 ml (1 tablespoon) vegetable oil
2 garlic cloves, finely chopped
1 medium onion, thinly sliced
450 g (1 lb) mixed green vegetables, all thinly sliced or cut into small pieces
125 g (4 oz) mushrooms, thickly sliced
85 g (3 oz) prosciutto, cut or torn in small pieces
500 g (1 lb 2 oz) linguine or another long, flat pasta
30 – 45 ml (2 – 3 tablespoons) extra virgin olive oil
15 ml (1 tablespoon) wine vinegar
15 ml (1 tablespoon) dry white wine or vermouth
Salt and freshly ground black pepper
Freshly grated Parmesan, to serve

Heat the oil until it is moderately hot in a large frying pan and cook the garlic and onion for 1 minute or so, just to get them sizzling a little. Add the vegetables, plus a splash of water and some salt and pepper and toss well. Turn down the heat, cover the pan part-way, and leave to cook with frequent stirring, until the vegetables are tender but firm (around 5 – 8 minutes). Add the *prosciutto* towards the end of the cooking time allowing it to warm through for between 30 – 60 seconds, if you want it crisper, leave for 2 – 3 minutes. The sauce can be prepared in advance up to this point.

Cook the pasta in plenty of boiling, salted water. When it's nearly done, gently re-heat the vegetables (if necessary) and add the olive oil, vinegar and wine. Mix well and stir into the cooked pasta. Serve with the cheese passed separately.

Linguine with Vegetables and Prosciutto

Penne alla Romana

This dish is time consuming but well worth it. If you can't get ripe beef tomatoes, use red peppers instead.

Preparation time: 20 – 30 minutes
Cooking time: 25 minutes

6 beef tomatoes or 6 large red peppers
60 ml (4 tablespoons) extra virgin olive oil
2 garlic cloves, finely chopped
675 g (1½ lb) aubergines
150 g (6 oz) ricotta cheese
500 g (1 lb 2 oz) penne
10 – 12 leaves fresh basil, torn into small pieces
Freshly grated Parmesan cheese, to serve

If using tomatoes, plunge each one into rapidly boiling water for 10 seconds. Peel, seed and cut into 5 mm (¼ in) dice. If using peppers, grill or roast in a hot oven until the skins are blackened, then peel, seed and cut into 5 mm (¼in) dice.

Heat 15 ml (1 tablespoon) of the oil in a large frying pan and add the garlic and tomatoes or peppers. Cook rapidly, stirring a few times, for 3 minutes. Remove to a strainer placed over a bowl and set aside. Top and tail the aubergines and cut into 5 mm (¼ in) dice. In the same pan, heat the remaining oil and cook the aubergines, stirring frequently, until they're just soft (around 10 – 15 minutes). Return the aubergines and tomatoes to the pan and re-heat for a few minutes, with the ricotta mixed in towards the end of the cooking time.

Cook the penne in plenty of well salted water until tender but firm to the bite. Drain then pour into a large serving bowl. Mix in the sauce, top with the basil and serve immediately with the Parmesan passed separately. If there are left-overs, save them for lunch the next day: this is almost as good cold as it is hot.

Pasta Sauce from Left-over Beef

This is a good way of using left-over meat, whether from a braise or a roast. It will sauce 500 g (1 lb 2 oz) of pasta.

Preparation time: 10 minutes
Cooking time: 30 minutes

30 ml (2 tablespoons) extra virgin olive oil
75 g (3 oz) celery, finely chopped
100 g (4 oz) onion, finely chopped
2 garlic cloves, finely chopped
50 g (2 oz) carrot, finely chopped
Salt and freshly ground black pepper
1 small chilli, seeded and finely chopped
5 ml (1 teaspoon) ground cumin
2.5 ml (½ teaspoon) ground coriander

2 x 400 g (14 oz) tins plum tomatoes
100 ml (4 fl oz) red wine
15 ml (1 tablespoon) tomato purée
500g (1 lb 2 oz pasta)
300 g (11 oz) cooked beef, pork or lamb, coarsely chopped
A large handful of parsley, finely chopped
Freshly grated Parmesan, to serve

Heat the oil over a low heat in a medium-sized pan and gently cook the celery, onions, garlic and carrot until they start to sizzle slightly (about 3 minutes). Season with salt and pepper then add the spices and simmer for 5 minutes more. Add the tomatoes, wine and purée and simmer for at least 30 minutes more.

Cook the pasta in plenty of boiling salted water. Add the meat to the sauce and cook for 10 minutes, just to heat it through and take up some of the sauce flavours. When the pasta is cooked, mix in the sauce and the parsley. Serve with grated Parmesan passed separately.

Fusilli with Fennel Cream Sauce

Fennel is one of my favourite vegetables, whether raw or cooked. Here it's combined with garlic and double cream to make a quick, luxurious pasta sauce (or a side dish on its own, if you prefer).

Preparation time: 10 minutes
Cooking time: 30 minutes

30 ml (2 tablespoons) extra virgin olive oil
3 fennel bulbs, weighing 350 g (12 oz), coarsely chopped
2 garlic cloves, finely chopped
30 ml (2 tablespoons) dry white wine or vermouth

100 ml (4 fl oz) double cream or crème fraîche
500 g (1 lb 2 oz) fusilli or another short pasta
A small knob of butter
Salt and freshly ground black pepper
Freshly grated Parmesan, to serve

Heat 5 ml (1 teaspoon) of the oil in a large frying pan over a low heat. Gently cook the fennel and garlic, stirring frequently. Add salt and pepper and cook until everything's soft but still has a hint of bite (around 20 minutes). Add the wine or vermouth and the cream, and cook hard to reduce by around half. The sauce can be prepared in advance up to this point.

Cook the pasta in plenty of boiling salted water. Just before it's done, add the remaining olive oil and the butter to the sauce. Drain the cooked pasta and toss in the sauce and serve with the Parmesan passed separately.

Pasta with Creamed Onion 'Salad' Ⓥ

This is two dishes in one: pasta with a creamy sauce and a topping of crisp green vegetables. The cooking method allows for separate timing of each of the vegetables, ensuring that they're all done perfectly. Vary the vegetables according to seasonal availability – or just serve the sauce on its own.

Preparation time: 20 minutes
Cooking time: 20 – 25 minutes

500 g (1 lb 2 oz) mixed green vegetables –
   broccoli, courgettes, green beans, peas – trimmed and
   cut into bite-sized pieces as necessary
45 ml (3 tablespoons) extra virgin olive oil
2 garlic cloves, finely chopped
250 g (9 oz) mixed onions – red onions, spring onions,
   shallots – thinly sliced
4 spring onions, finely shredded
80 ml (3 fl oz) Bio yoghurt or crème fraîche
350 g (12 oz) tagliatelle or linguini
A small handful of fresh parsley, preferably flat-leaf,
   coarsely chopped
Freshly grated Parmesan, to serve

Bring a large pan of well salted water to the boil and cook the vegetables one at a time until they're barely done – they should retain a good hint of bite (anything from 2 – 5 minutes). Remove as they're done and leave to drain in a colander as you cook the remainder. Asparagus (if using) should be cooked last.

Meanwhile, heat the oil in a large frying pan and cook the garlic gently, without browning, until slightly soft and fragrant (around 3 minutes). Add the onions and spring onions and cook for another few minutes, just long enough to soften them. Add the rinds plus the yoghurt or cream, mix well and turn off the heat. The sauce can be prepared in advance to this point.

Boil the pasta in plenty of boiling salted water. When the pasta is a couple of minutes from being done, gently re-heat the onion mixture (if necessary). Drain the pasta, toss with the sauce, then top with the vegetables and parsley. Serve immediately with grated Parmesan passed separately.

Chunky Pasta Salad Ⓥ

This is both a salad and a main course.

Preparation time: 10 minutes plus 30 minutes draining time
Cooking time: 10 – 12 minutes

500 g (1 lb 2 oz) pasta lumache (snails) or shells
60 ml (4 tablespoons) extra virgin olive oil
1 large cucumber
2 Italian mozzarella cheeses
15 ml (1 tablespoon) capers
350 g (12 oz) cherry tomatoes
Salt and freshly ground black pepper
Lemon wedges, to serve

Cook the pasta in plenty of boiling salted water, then drain and re-fresh immediately under cold running water. Shake out as much excess water as possible and toss immediately with the oil. Spread out on a large platter to cool quickly.

Halve the cucumber lengthwise and peel if you wish. Scoop out the seeds with a small spoon. Dry the cucumber, then cut into 1.5 cm (½ in) chunks. Toss in a colander with around 7.5 ml (1½ teaspoons) salt and leave for 30 minutes. Rinse under cold running water then dry thoroughly with a clean tea towel. Refrigerate until needed. Meanwhile, drain the cheeses and cut into chunks around the same size as the cucumber. Chop the capers finely.

When you're ready to serve, mix all the ingredients including the tomatoes in a large bowl and season with salt and plenty of freshly ground black pepper. Add a little more oil if the salad seems too dry. Give each eater a big plateful with a lemon wedge for squeezing on.

Variations
Optional extras include fresh herbs (basil, parsley, coriander, dill), olives and drained, chopped anchovies. This is the sort of dish you can jazz up with whatever catches your eye at the supermarket.

Fusilli with Tomato Cream Ⓥ

This dish, named by my daughter Alice, couldn't be quicker or easier. But it's very tasty and a great standby when hungry children need instant feeding. Passata, a useful larder-and-fridge standby, is just sieved tomato pulp. Note the variation for adult eaters.

Preparation time: 30 seconds
Cooking time: 10 minutes

150 ml (5 fl oz) passata
30 ml (2 tablespoons) single or 15 ml (1 tablespoon) double cream
2.5 ml (½ teaspoon) sugar
Salt and freshly ground black pepper
Freshly grated Parmesan, to serve

Begin cooking the pasta in plenty of boiling salted water.

Meanwhile, put the passata in a large frying pan. Heat it vigorously until it starts to bubble enthusiastically, then swirl in the cream and sugar. Cook fairly hard for 2 minutes and then reduce to a gentle simmer.

Drain the cooked pasta and add it to the sauce. Cook gently for 1 – 2 minutes to blend the flavours then serve immediately with plenty of grated Parmesan.

To accompany the pasta you need nothing more than a mixed salad or a platter of crudités, served, if you like, with 1 or 2 dips. A loaf of crusty bread wouldn't go amiss, either.

Variation

If you want to make the adults' sauce a little more exciting, seed and finely chop a green or red chilli. Soften it in a little butter while the sauce is cooking. Serve the pasta in 2 bowls and mix the chilli into the bowl for the grown-ups.

Cinnamon Fried Rice with Summer Vegetables Ⓥ

Preparation time: 10 – 15 minutes
Cooking time: 20 – 25 minutes

225 g (8 oz) long-grain rice
3 small courgettes
2 red or yellow peppers
2 celery sticks
125 g (4 oz) mangetouts
2 spring onions
30 ml (2 tablespoons) extra virgin olive
  oil
1.25 ml (¼ teaspoon) ground cinnamon
50 ml (2 fl oz) dry white wine
ablespoon) lemon or lime juice
reshly ground black pepper

good pinch of salt. Bring to the
the rice is just cooked but is still
ld running water until the rice is

ery and mangetouts and cut into
ions and cut into fine shreds (in-

cinnamon, garlic and chilli then
black pepper. Stir-fry over a me-
e frying until most of the liquid
e the heat a little and stir-fry for
iately with Instant Yoghurt Sauce

and Lemon Ⓥ

ther green vegetables.

ve, thinly sliced
2 oz) rigatoni (or penne)
lespoons) extra virgin olive oil
emon
shly ground black pepper

oli into small pieces then blanch
- 4 minutes). Drain then refresh
at least.
heat and stir-fry the fennel until
i and garlic after 1 – 2 minutes.
stir-frying for a couple of min-
be left in the pan, with the heat

well, re-heating the sauce in the
nd finally the lemon juice. Toss

Rice Mould with Herbs Ⓥ

This technique, which I learned from my old friend Dorothy Pace, can be used with well flavoured rice of any description. It makes a great side dish for meat dishes.

Preparation time: 5 minutes
Cooking time: 45 minutes

250 g (9 oz) long-grain rice
3 spring onions, finely chopped
15 ml (1 tablespoon) extra virgin olive oil
2.5 ml (½ teaspoon) dried thyme
A small handful of parsley or dill,
  finely chopped
10 ml (2 teaspoons) pine nuts
Salt and freshly ground black pepper

Bring a large pan of salted water to the boil. Add the rice, stirring well for 30 seconds or so then boil until well cooked (around 20 minutes). Drain in a colander, then rinse under cold running water. Leave to drain for at least 5 minutes.

Meanwhile, gently fry the onions in the oil until soft but not browned. In a separate pan, combine with the remaining ingredients and mix with the rice, then pack the mixture firmly into an ovenproof dish which will fit in your roasting tin. The dish can be prepared in advance to this point.

When you're ready to cook, pre-heat the oven to 180°C/350°F/Gas 4. Half-fill the roasting tin with hot water and place the rice dish in it. Cover the dish with foil then bake until the rice is hot all the way through (around 30 minutes). Remove the dish from the oven and cover with a serving platter. Holding the platter and dish firmly with pot holders or a tea towel, quickly invert the dish. The rice should come out cleanly. If not, neaten up any stray bits by hand.

Variations

The seasonings here can be varied endlessly, with flavours from either eastern or western cooking. You can also use Fragrant or Basmati rice, left-over rice and smaller dishes (e.g. ramekins) instead of a large mould.

Wild Rice Salad ✔

This is adapted from a recipe in Annie Bell's Evergreen. *The vegetables can be varied according to availability and personal preference.*

Preparation time: 15 minutes
Cooking time: 45 minutes

For the dressing
3 thin slices fresh ginger, minced
1 garlic clove, minced
30 ml (2 tablespoons) lemon juice or wine vinegar
45 ml (3 tablespoons) extra virgin olive oil
45 ml (3 tablespoons) vegetable oil

For the rice
85 g (3 oz) wild rice
125 g (4 oz) plain white rice
85 g (3 oz) fennel
85 g (3 oz) sugar snap or mangetout peas
85 g (3 oz) baby sweetcorn
45 ml (3 tablespoons) flaked almonds
2 spring onions
1 small head radicchio
A small handful of fresh coriander

Mix the dressing ingredients and set aside. Cook the 2 rices in separate pans of salted water, allowing 30 – 45 minutes for the wild and around 15 for the plain. Drain in a colander, rinse under cold running water and drain for at least 5 minutes before combining in a large bowl.

While the rice is cooking, prepare the vegetables. Slice the fennel into thin rings, top and tail the peas and halve the sweetcorn lengthwise. Cook the peas and corn in a large pot of well salted water for 1 minute, then drain and refresh under cold running water. Fry the almonds in a dry pan, stirring frequently, until lightly browned. Allow to cool. The dish can be prepared in advance to this point.

To serve, finely slice the spring onions and radicchio, and chop the coriander. Mix the rice with the vegetables and heap onto a small serving platter. Scatter on the spring onions, radicchio and coriander, then strain the dressing and drizzle over. Eat immediately.

Baked Basmati Rice with Saffron ✔

Vary the vegetables according to your preference.

Preparation time: 20 minutes
Cooking time: 20 – 25 minutes

250 g (9 oz) Basmati rice
1 large red pepper, diced
1 large onion, coarsely chopped
30 ml (2 tablespoons) vegetable oil
A pinch of saffron
50 ml (2 fl oz) chicken stock or water
A small handful of fresh mint, chopped

Wash the rice in 4 – 5 changes of cold water, until the water runs nearly clear, then add fresh water and leave to soak for at least 30 minutes.

Meanwhile, bring a large pan of salted water to the boil. Add the rice, stir well for 30 seconds or so, then boil until just cooked (around 5 minutes). Drain in a colander, rinse under cold running water and drain again. The dish can be prepared in advance up to this point and even left overnight in the fridge if well drained and tightly covered.

Pre-heat the oven to 200°C/400°F/Gas 6. Quickly fry the pepper and onion in half the oil until the onion is lightly browned and both are very fragrant. Meanwhile, toss the rice in a shallow baking dish with the remaining oil, then spread it out evenly over the whole area of the dish. Rub the saffron to a powder and sprinkle over the rice with the stock or water. Top with the vegetables, cover with foil and bake until the rice is hot (around 20 – 25 minutes). To serve, sprinkle the mint on top. This dish is good with Instant Yoghurt Sauce (see page 164).

Variation
The dish can also be re-heated successfully in the microwave: use half the stock or water, cover tightly with cling film and cook at medium power for 6 – 7 minutes. Stir once to ensure even heating.

Basmati Rice with Whole Spices ✔

You can throw in a handful of cooked wild rice for extra colour.

Preparation time: 5 minutes
(plus 30 minutes' soaking time)
Cooking time: 20 – 25 minutes

225 g (8 oz) Basmati rice
7.5 ml (1½ teaspoons) vegetable oil
1 small onion, finely chopped
2.5 ml (½ teaspoon) whole cumin seeds
2.5 ml (½ teaspoon) whole coriander seeds
2.5 ml (½ teaspoon) whole fenugreek
350 ml (12 fl oz) chicken or vegetable stock

Put the rice in a bowl and wash it several times in cold water until the water runs nearly clear. Cover again with water and soak for 30 minutes, then drain in a sieve.

Heat the oil in a heavy-based pan and add the onion. Cook over a brisk heat for 1 minute then add the spices and stir-fry for 1 minute. Add the rice then pour in the stock and bring to a boil. Reduce the heat to a simmer and cook, uncovered, for 2 minutes. Turn the heat down to its lowest point, cover the pan and cook gently for 15 minutes. If the rice is still crunchy, cook it for another 3 – 5 minutes. As soon as it's done, fluff it by stirring with a fork. It is at its best when served immediately, but can be left, off the heat and covered, for up to 20 minutes.

Basmati Rice with Whole Spices

Beans and Rice Ⓥ

Basic Beans (see opposite) can be cooked with rice to make a south-western American concoction. This is highly nutritious, as the beans and rice combine to make a complete protein, and it's also delicious. Use red beans for a prettier effect.

**Preparation time:
10 minutes
Cooking time:
around 30 minutes**

250 g (9 oz) long-grain rice
15 – 30 ml (1 – 2 tablespoons)
    vegetable oil
3 small onions, finely chopped
2 garlic cloves, finely chopped
2.5 ml (½ teaspoon) ground cumin
2.5 ml (½ teaspoon) ground
    coriander
2.5 ml (½ teaspoon) cayenne pepper
1 x 400 g (14 oz) tin plum tomatoes,
    drained and coarsely chopped
225 – 250 g (8 – 9 oz) cooked beans
(see Basic Beans opposite)
A small handful of fresh parsley or
    coriander
Salt and freshly ground black pepper

Cook the rice in plenty of boiling, well salted water until barely done (around 15 minutes), then drain well and stir with a fork to separate the grains. Meanwhile, heat the oil in a pan and cook the onions, garlic and spices over a medium heat for about 5 minutes. Add the tomatoes plus a good grinding of black pepper and cook briskly for a further 5 minutes or so.

Now add the beans, stirring them in thoroughly and cooking until they've absorbed some of the flavour from the sauce (10 – 15 minutes). Finally, add the rice and cook until the flavours are well blended. Stir in the herbs and serve immediately.

Spanish Rice

This recipe can be varied endlessly, but you must use Spanish or Italian short-grain rice, such as arborio. Add half-cooked meat, poultry or shellfish before it goes into the oven for a one-dish meal of rare excellence. This cooking method leaves the grains soft but not mushy.

**Preparation time: 10 minutes
Cooking time: 40 minutes.**

5 ml (1 teaspoon) plain vegetable oil
5 ml (1 teaspoon) extra virgin olive oil
5 rashers streaky bacon, rinds removed, shredded
2 small red peppers, finely chopped
2 large garlic cloves, finely chopped
2 small onions, finely chopped
1.2 litres (2 pints) chicken stock
1 or 2 ripe beef tomatoes, seeded and diced
1 large pinch of saffron threads
450 g (1 lb) short-grain rice
Salt and freshly ground black pepper

Pre-heat the oven to 180°C/350°F/Gas 4. Heat the oils in a wide, shallow casserole (or heavy frying pan which can go in the oven). Gently fry the bacon for a couple of minutes, then add the peppers, garlic and onions. Fry, stirring every minute or so for 10 minutes. The dish can be prepared in advance up to this point.

Heat the stock in a pan. Add the tomatoes, saffron and rice to the frying pan, season well, and stir thoroughly for 1 – 2 minutes. Pour on the hot stock and increase the heat. Cook, stirring constantly, until the liquid turns thick and sludgy (around 5 minutes). Reduce the heat and cook for another 5 minutes, then cover the pan (with aluminium foil if it doesn't have a lid) and bake for 10 minutes. Remove from the oven and leave for 5 minutes with the lid on. Serve immediately.

Frijoles Refritos Ⓥ

The name of this famous dish, often translated as 'refried beans', actually means 'well cooked beans'. Beans cooked from scratch with onions and garlic are cheaper, but tinned beans do just fine.

**Preparation time: 3 minutes
Cooking time: 40 minutes**

2 tins red kidney beans
2 small onions
2 – 3 garlic cloves
30 – 45 ml (2 – 3 tablespoons) bacon fat or vegetable oil
Salt and freshly ground black pepper

Drain the beans and place in a pan with enough water to cover them generously. Add 1 onion and 1 garlic clove, both coarsely chopped. Bring to a boil and simmer, uncovered, until everything is very soft (around 30 minutes). In the meantime, heat the oil or fat in a small frying pan. Chop the remaining onion and garlic and fry gently until lightly browned (around 10 minutes).

When the beans are ready, purée them in the food processor or mash in the pan with a potato masher. Mix in the contents of the frying pan and continue cooking until the mixture is fairly dry (around 10 minutes). This can be done a day in advance – or more, if the beans are then frozen. When ready to serve, re-heat gently.

Basic Beans Ⓥ

This recipe makes a lot of beans, but the left-overs freeze well so it's worth making extra. Soak the beans the night before you want to cook them.

Preparation time: 15 minutes
Cooking time: 1 hour

500 g (1 lb 2 oz) dried cannellini or kidney beans, soaked overnight
1 clove
1 bay leaf
3 small onions, quartered
2 garlic cloves, halved
Water or chicken stock
Salt and freshly ground black pepper

Drain the soaked beans then place in a large pan with the clove, bay leaf, onions and garlic. Add enough water or chicken stock to cover the beans by about 2.5 cm (1 in). Bring to the boil, skim, then reduce the heat and simmer.

When the beans are done, remove the clove and bay leaf. Season to taste with salt and pepper. If they're still very watery, boil down rapidly to reduce. The beans may be prepared up to 24 hours in advance.

Borlotti Bean Salad Ⓥ

This was inspired by a recipe in Marcella Hazan's Classic Italian Cookbook. *The brown borlotti beans contrast well with the onion and peppers. Serve with fish, chicken or a selection of grilled or roasted vegetables.*

Preparation time: 15 minutes
Cooking time: 1 hour

400 g (14 oz) borlotti beans, soaked
1 onion, optional
1 bay leaf, optional
2 medium red onions, chopped or sliced
30 ml (2 tablespoons) lemon juice
45 ml (3 tablespoons) extra virgin olive oil
1 red pepper, diced or sliced
1 yellow pepper, diced or sliced
10 ml (2 teaspoons) balsamic vinegar
A few large sprigs of fresh parsley, preferably flat-leaf
Salt and freshly ground black pepper

Put the beans in a pan with enough water to cover them by at least 5 cm (2 in). Add the onion and bay leaf (if using). Bring to a simmer and cook until the beans are soft all the way through; this will probably take about an hour, but start testing after 45 minutes. It is particularly important not to let the beans overcook because they'll be served in a salad.

Meanwhile, put the red onions in a large bowl with the lemon juice, oil, and lots of salt and pepper. Toss well and leave to infuse while the beans are cooking. (This also helps take some of the sting out of the onions.)

When the beans are cooked, drain well and toss with the onions in the bowl. Add the peppers and toss again thoroughly. The salad can be served hot or left to cool to room temperature. Just before serving, add the vinegar and sprinkle on the parsley.

Spicy Black Kidney Beans

This is a pungent and beautiful dish with a deep glossy colour. Serve with any red meat, especially venison or pork.

**Preparation time: 10 minutes
Cooking time: 1 hour**

400 g (14 oz) black kidney beans, soaked
1 onion, optional
1 bay leaf, optional
10 ml (2 teaspoons) vegetable oil
4 slices streaky bacon, rinds removed, cut
  into shreds
2 small onions, roughly chopped
5 ml (1 teaspoon) paprika
5 ml (1 teaspoon) chilli powder
5 ml (1 teaspoon) ground cinnamon
2.5 ml (½ teaspoon) ground cumin
2.5 ml (½ teaspoon) dried thyme
2.5 ml (½ teaspoon) dried oregano
150 ml (5 fl oz) chicken, beef or
  vegetable stock
Fresh herbs, chopped, to serve
1 large green chilli, seeded and finely
  shredded, to serve, optional
Salt and freshly ground black pepper

Put the beans in a pan and add enough water to cover by at least 5 cm (2 in). Add the onion and bay leaf (if using). Bring to a simmer and cook the beans until they're barely done; this will take about an hour, but watch towards the end to prevent overcooking.

Meanwhile, heat the oil in a large non-stick frying pan and gently cook the bacon and onions until the onions start turning translucent and the bacon fat starts to run (around 5 – 10 minutes). Add the spices and dried herbs, plenty of pepper and a little salt, and stir until everything is well blended. Pour in the stock and simmer gently, covered at first, until most of the stock has cooked away and the onions are completely soft.

When the beans are done, scoop out a cupful of cooking water and reserve. Drain the beans well. Return them to the pot with the reserved cupful of cooking water, add the bacon and onion mixture and simmer, with frequent stirring, until the flavours are well blended (around 10 minutes). Serve with herbs sprinkled on top and – if you like your food really hot – with chilli shreds.

Cannellini Gratin ⓥ

I love beans with anything creamy – cheese, milk, cream, crème fraîche or yoghurt. This substantial dish can be a meal in itself or an accompaniment for chicken or grilled meat. It can also be made with haricot beans.

**Preparation time: 20 minutes
Cooking time: 1 hour**

350 g (12 oz) cannellini beans, soaked
1 onion, optional
1 bay leaf, optional
30 ml (2 tablespoons) softened butter
30 ml (2 tablespoons) plain white flour
1 chicken or vegetable stock cube
2.5 ml (½ teaspoon) dried tarragon or
  mixed herbs
600 ml (1 pint) whole milk
125 g (4 oz) grated cheese, e.g. Gruyère,
  Emmental, mature Cheddar
Salt and freshly ground black pepper

Put the beans in a pan with enough water to cover them by at least 5 cm (2 in). Add the onion and bay leaf (if using). Bring to a simmer and cook until the beans are barely done; this should take around 40 minutes, but watch at the end to prevent overcooking.

Melt the butter in a pan over a low heat and stir in the flour. Cook, stirring constantly with a wooden spoon, for 2 – 3 minutes; the mixture should froth and bubble, but not brown. Add the stock cube, breaking it up with the spoon, then add the tarragon or mixed herbs. Gradually incorporate the milk a splash at a time, stirring vigorously using a wire whisk if lumps form. Season with salt and pepper and simmer for 20 – 30 minutes, stirring every few minutes and scraping the bottom to prevent sticking. When the sauce is thick enough to coat the back of the spoon, put in a little bit of cheese and mix with the cooked beans.

Pre-heat the oven to 180°C/350°F/Gas 4. Put the beans in a lightly buttered gratin dish and top with the remaining cheese. Bake in the centre of the oven until the beans are bubbling and the top browned (about 1 hour).

Lentilles de Puy with Parsley Pesto (page 141)

Mung Beans with Spinach (page 141)

Lentilles de Puy with Parsley Pesto Ⓥ

Serve with any fish or chicken dish. Lentilles de Puy, small green lentils from the Puy region of France, are available from most large supermarkets.

Preparation time: 20 minutes
Cooking time: 30 minutes

400 g (14 oz) lentilles de Puy
1 onion, optional
1 bay leaf, optional
2 garlic cloves, finely chopped
4 small carrots, finely diced
45 ml (3 tablespoons) extra virgin olive oil
3 large spring onions (green bits included), finely chopped
A large handful of fresh parsley, preferably flat-leaf, finely chopped
45 ml (3 tablespoons) freshly grated Parmesan
45 ml (3 tablespoons) pine nuts
Salt and freshly ground black pepper

Put the lentils in a saucepan with enough water to cover them by at least 5 cm (2 in). Add the onion and bay leaf (if using). Bring to a simmer and cook gently until done (around 30 minutes).

Meanwhile, place the garlic and carrots in a small pan with 15 ml (1 tablespoon) of the oil. Heat until it is sizzling lightly, then turn down the heat and cook, stirring frequently, until the carrots are soft (around 10 minutes).

To make the pesto, mix the onions, parsley and Parmesan with the remaining oil. Put the pine nuts in a small frying pan without any oil and heat gently for a few minutes until the nuts are lightly browned and shiny. Leave to cool, then chop very finely and mix with the other ingredients.

Re-heat the lentils if necessary and stir in the carrot and garlic mixture. A little cooking water (or stock) can be added if they seem dry. Season with salt and pepper, and serve with a blob of pesto on top. Left-over pesto can be saved for up to 48 hours and used on pasta, potatoes, rice or chicken.

Mung Beans with Spinach Ⓥ

Mung beans don't need soaking, but if you do it shortens the cooking time and keeps them from falling apart in the pan. Amchoor is powdered green mango. Serve on rice as a one-dish vegetarian meal, or with fish, chicken, or a meat dish.

Preparation time: 15 minutes
Cooking time: 30 minutes

400 g (14 oz) mung beans, soaked
1 onion, optional
1 bay leaf, optional
15 ml (1 tablespoon) vegetable oil
1 x 1.5 cm (½ in) piece ginger, finely chopped
2 garlic cloves, finely chopped
1 medium onion, finely chopped
2.5 ml (½ teaspoon) whole cumin seeds
2.5 ml (½ teaspoon) whole coriander seeds
2.5 ml (½ teaspoon) fenugreek
2.5 ml (½ teaspoon) amchoor, optional
1 or 2 x 450 g (1 lb) packets frozen spinach, defrosted
Salt and freshly ground black pepper
Greek or Bio yoghurt, to garnish
Fresh mint and/or coriander, to garnish

Put the beans in a pan with enough water to cover them by at least 5 cm (2 in). Add the onion and bay leaf (if using). Bring to a simmer and cook until the beans are barely done; this will probably take around 25 – 30 minutes, but watch towards the end to prevent overcooking.

Meanwhile, heat the oil in a frying pan or saucepan and gently cook the ginger, garlic and onion with some salt and pepper until they turn soft and fragrant (around 15 minutes). Add the spices and amchoor and cook for another minute, then stir in the spinach and cook until the spinach is just done. When the beans are ready, drain well and toss over a low heat with the spinach.

This dish can be kept warm for an hour or so and re-heated just before serving, but it's better if eaten straightaway. Top each serving with a dollop of yoghurt and some of the herbs, either chopped or whole.

Lentils with Smoked Haddock

The combination of pulses and fish is a memorable one. This quick, simple dish can also be made with smoked cod.

Preparation time: 10 minutes
Cooking time: 20 – 30 minutes

450 g (1 lb) red lentils
15 ml (1 tablespoon) extra virgin olive oil
1 large onion, finely chopped
2 garlic cloves, finely chopped
1 medium carrot, finely chopped
1 bay leaf
5 ml (1 teaspoon) oregano
5 ml (1 teaspoon) mild curry powder
225 g (8 oz) smoked haddock, skinned, boned and cut into thin shreds
Salt and freshly ground black pepper

Wash the lentils and pick them over to remove stones, etc. then drain well. Heat the oil in a pan and gently cook the vegetables and all the remaining ingredients except the haddock for 5 minutes or so, then add the lentils with just enough water to cover them by around 2.5 cm (1 in). Simmer until the lentils are just soft; this can take anything from 15 – 25 minutes, depending on the age of the lentils. Add more water as necessary. The dish can be prepared in advance up to this point.

When you're ready to eat, carefully stir the fish into the lentil mixture and cook for 1 – 2 minutes or just long enough to heat the fish through. Add more curry powder, some cayenne pepper or a dried red chilli to make the dish spicier.

Baked Chick Peas with Red-hot Salsa

Baked Chick Peas with Red-hot Salsa Ⓥ

This dish is fiery and pungent so you might want to serve some of the salsa separately.

Preparation time: 10 minutes, plus soaking time for the chick peas
Cooking time: 1 hour

350 g (12 oz) dried chick peas,
    soaked overnight
25 ml (1½ tablespoons) dried oregano
2 medium red onions, thinly sliced
3 garlic cloves, finely chopped
2 – 3 red chillis, seeded and thinly sliced
    lengthwise
100 ml (4 fl oz) extra virgin olive oil
Salt and freshly ground black pepper

Drain the soaked chick peas and place in a flameproof casserole with enough water to cover them by 5 cm (2 in). Bring to a boil, skim, sprinkle on half the oregano, and simmer until very soft (anything from 1 – 3½ hours, depending on the age of the peas). Strain, reserving the water and mash some of the chick peas with a few spoonfuls of their water. The dish can be prepared in advance to this point.

Re-heat the peas if necessary and add enough liquid to moisten them slightly. Just before serving, stir in the onions, garlic, chillis and remaining oregano (or add only half the amount, with the rest passed separately) and toss well with salt and pepper.

Basic Polenta Ⓥ

I have given here both the traditional method and a baking method adapted from Anna Del Conte's Entertaining all'Italiana. *This quantity serves 6 – 8 as a side dish, with plenty of left-overs which are intended for re-cooking. For serving immediately, proceed in the same way but use an extra 100 ml (4 fl oz) of water.*

Cooking time: 18 – 25 minutes

300 g (11 oz) medium or coarse cornmeal
1.75 litres (3 pints) water
10 ml (2 teaspoons) salt

The traditional method

Put the cornmeal in a jug with a good pouring spout. Bring the water to the boil in a large pan and add the salt, then reduce the heat bringing the water to a simmer. Holding a wire whisk in your stronger hand, pour in a few spoonfuls of cornmeal and start stirring as soon as the first grains hit the water. When all the lumps are gone, pour in more and keep whisking. If lumps seem to be forming, stop pouring and whisk as if your life depended on it.

When the cornmeal has been added, whisk hard to eliminate any lingering lumps, then settle down to a constant, moderate stir. If you like, you can switch to an electric whisk (low or medium speed); but make sure it's plugged in before you start so you don't have to interrupt the stirring.

After 20 minutes or so the polenta should be coming away easily from the sides of the pot. This means it is done and should be served immediately or poured into a buttered or non-stick baking dish. The polenta can be anything from 1.25 – 2.5 cm (½ – 1 in) deep. Leave to cool for 10 minutes, then cover with cling film or foil to prevent a skin from forming. Skin-formation can also be prevented by brushing on some extra virgin olive oil or butter.

The baking method

Pre-heat the oven to 190°C/375°F/Gas 5. Generously butter or oil a heavy baking dish around 12.5 x 20 cm (5 x 8 in) in size. Proceed as in the recipe above but stir/whisk the polenta in the pan for 2 – 3 minutes only before pouring it into the baking dish. Smooth down the top and cover with aluminium foil. Bake in the centre of the oven for 40 – 60 minutes. Anna Del Conte says that 60 is the right timing, but I find that it cooks faster than this. Check to be on the safe side.

When the polenta is cooked it can be served immediately or cooled and re-cooked as in any of the following recipes. Strictly speaking, it should be transferred to another dish for cooling; but leaving it in the baking dish works well enough.

Re-cooking polenta

This can be done by frying, grilling or baking. The aim is to produce a crisp, golden-brown exterior, and by the time you've done that the inside should be hot, too.

Frying should be done in a hot pan, generously oiled (or lightly oiled if the pan is non-stick). It will take anything from 5 – 10 minutes per side. I think this is the best method, producing a crispy-brown exterior while leaving the inside creamily moist.

Grilling needs a medium-high heat and will take longer than frying. The plus side to grilling is that it requires less oil.

Baking is incredibly flexible and ideal when you're serving large crowds. The oven temperature can be anything from 180°–230°C/350°–450°F/Gas 4–8, so it can cook alongside other dishes. And the timing can be varied to suit your own schedule. You can heat the polenta fairly gently in the oven for up to an hour at a lower heat and then brown it under the grill, or blast it for a shorter time (around 25 minutes) at high heat. For a maximum of crispy surface when baking, cut the polenta into fat 'chips'.

Polenta with Peppers and Onions

Polenta with Peppers and Onions Ⓥ

Cooked vegetables other than the ones given here can also be used, as long as they're not too watery and are cut into small pieces. A good vegetarian main course all on its own, this also works well as a side dish to chicken or grilled meat.

**Preparation time:
1 – 5 minutes plus cooking time for polenta
Cooking time: 30 – 40 minutes**

1 large green pepper
1 large red pepper
1 medium Spanish onion,
   coarsely chopped
1 large garlic clove, finely chopped
25 ml (1½ tablespoons) extra
   virgin olive oil
1 quantity Basic Polenta
   (see page 143)
Salt and freshly ground black
   pepper

Before you cook the polenta, cook the vegetables. The peppers should be grilled until soft and blackened all over (around 15 – 20 minutes) and then put in a paper or plastic bag. Leave for a few minutes, then slip off the skins, cut them open and discard the seeds and stem. Cut into pieces around 2.5 cm (1 in) square. Meanwhile, gently cook the onion and garlic in the oil until soft and fragrant (around 15 – 20 minutes). The recipe can be prepared in advance up to this point.

When the polenta is cooked, mix with the vegetables and spread out in a baking dish or tin. It can now be re-cooked immediately or left to cool and be cooked later on. This works best in the oven, though a final grilling will produce some nicely charred bits of vegetable.

Polenta Fingers with Roasted Asparagus Ⓥ

450 g (1 lb) asparagus
45 ml (3 tablespoons) extra virgin olive oil
Coarse salt
½ quantity Basic Polenta (see page 143),
   cooled and cut into 2.5 cm (1 in) x 15 cm (6 in) fingers

Pre-heat the oven to 230°C/450°F/Gas 8. Wash the asparagus and trim the ends off then shake as dry as you can get it. Put the spears in a roasting pan and drizzle on half the oil, shaking the pan for a minute or so to coat the spears evenly. Scatter over the salt in a fine, even layer; you will probably need around 5 ml (1 teaspoon).

Put the polenta fingers on a separate tray and brush with the remaining oil. Place the asparagus on a shelf in the centre of the oven and the polenta at the top. Roast for around 10 minutes, testing the asparagus after 5 minutes, and proceed cautiously, so you don't overcook the stuff. The polenta may take as much as 20 – 25 minutes, but don't worry: the asparagus is good hot, warm or at room temperature. This recipe makes the perfect accompaniment to any meat or poultry dish and can also be eaten on its own.

Couscous Ⓥ

Couscous is semolina processed into flour-coated pellets. It has a reputation for being laborious to make and that reputation is justified if you demand absolutely perfect results. If you're satisfied with something that's 95 per cent perfect, these methods will do just fine.

**Preparation time: 5 minutes.
Cooking time: 10 – 20 minutes**

450 g (1 lb) couscous
Butter or extra virgin olive oil

Put the couscous in a large, fine-meshed sieve or in a colander lined with a clean tea towel or J-cloth. Bring some water to boiling point in a large pan which will hold the sieve or colander comfortably. Fill a small bowl with cold water and flick some at the couscous. Mix it in with one hand while you continue flicking water. Repeat this process until the couscous is lightly but thoroughly dampened.

Place the sieve or colander over the pan of boiling water, checking to make sure that the bottom doesn't touch the water. Cover with aluminium foil or another tea towel. Steam over a medium heat until the grains are softened and swollen (around 20 – 25 minutes). It's advisable to stir the grains once or twice during cooking, either with a wire whisk or a fork.

The couscous is now ready for eating. Give it a thorough stir with a fork or whisk and toss with a little butter or oil.

If you prefer, you can cook the couscous in advance and re-heat just before serving. Spread out the cooled couscous in a thin layer on a large plate or baking sheet and work out any lumps with your hand and add the butter or oil before re-heating.

The re-heating may be done either by steaming or in the microwave. In the steamer it will take 10 – 15 minutes. The microwave will do the job beautifully in around 8 minutes, cooking at full power for 2 minutes at a time and then fluffing up with a fork or whisk.

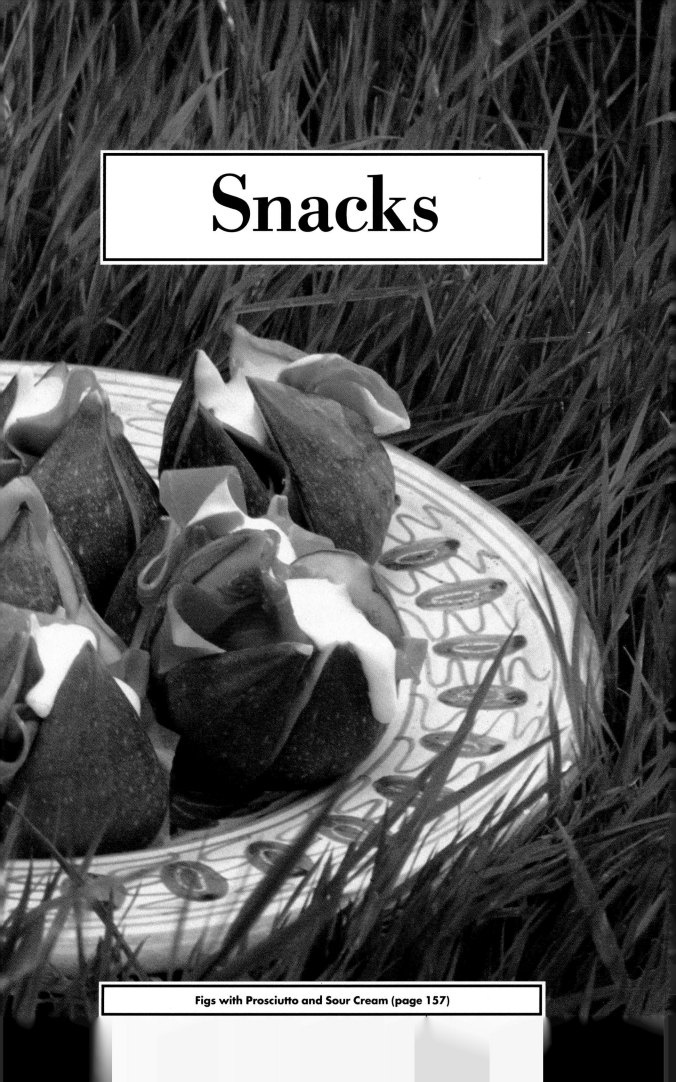

Snacks

Figs with Prosciutto and Sour Cream (page 157)

Snacks

The recipes in this chapter are a miscellany of delicious things and well worth the small trouble they take to make. There are a few sandwiches of distinction, excellent ideas for a weekend or weekday lunch; a few nibbles for serving with drinks; and a few side dishes for special meals.

But even if the dishes are accessories rather than complete outfits, what applies in clothing applies in meal planning as well: the right touches can make anything look great. Take the recipe for *Duxelles* (see page 151) as an example. This classic French mushroom recipe can serve as the base for a sauce, but it's even better served on its own, re-heated on toast as canapés for a preprandial nibble. It should do nothing more than whet the appetite, yet it's so delicious that everyone remembers it when the dinner party's over.

And sometimes, little nibbles can be turned into a meal of their own. This is certainly the case with the four toppings for crostini or bruschetta – Italian toasts. These can be served as part of a *merenda* feast, which is probably what I would ask for if I had to choose my desert island meal. *Merenda* (plural *merende*) means snack in Italian and it refers to the Italian habit of nibbling on delicious things throughout the day – a little sandwich with morning coffee, crostini before lunch, a cake in the afternoon. I can't think of a better way to eat.

That's one approach to *merende*, and you won't hear me complaining about it. But those little snacks can also be used to make the most fantastic lunch or dinner parties, with a profusion of small dishes replacing the conventional three-course starter, main course and pudding. Instead of getting large helpings of a few dishes, you get a generous taste of many. There's no better way to avoid palate-fatigue halfway through the meal.

The key to a *merenda* feast is variety: make as many dishes as you have time and energy for. Olives are a must, on their own or combined with cheese, anchovies, sun-dried tomatoes and artichoke hearts. If you can't get good olives, buy ordinary brined olives and make your own using the recipe on page 154. Mozzarella cheese is another essential, raw or cooked. Serve it in chunks with a wrapping of *prosciutto* or marinated red peppers. Or marinate it in olive oil with fresh herbs and perhaps a chilli pepper.

The centrepiece of the meal is made up of two dishes, both for serving at room temperature. One is *Scarpaccia Viareggina*, a courgette and onion tart from Tuscany (see page 94). I learned this recipe from Carol Field's *Italy in Small Bites*, and it's a real winner. The other is a seafood salad with a pungent dressing (page 35), not exactly Italian but close enough to qualify as a *merenda*.

Many of the other recipes could be used in the same way for an informal drinks-with-food party. If you make enough of everything, and have sufficient variety, your guests might go away feeling – rightly – that they'd had a full meal and not just a collection of nibbles.

There are two recipes here for cheese biscuits, a small dish that I find incredibly useful. They take no time to prepare and cook, and you can make them with any cheese you happen to have around. And everyone falls on them, including children who might turn their noses up at the cheese if I served it on its own.

Tomato Tonnato

This is a delicious low-calorie snack or lunch for 1 person. Unripe tomatoes can be improved with a few days in a brown paper bag, unrefrigerated.

Preparation time: 5 – 10 minutes.

50 g (2 oz) tinned tuna, well drained of oil or brine
5 ml (1 teaspoon) capers, finely chopped
15 ml (1 tablespoon) low-fat cottage cheese
3 slices cucumber, seeded and finely chopped
2.5 ml (½ teaspoon) wine, sherry or balsamic vinegar
1 large beef tomato, top removed and insides scooped out

Mix the filling ingredients, season with pepper, and stuff into the tomato. Eat any excess on toast or crispbread.

Grilled Aubergine in Pitta Bread ⓥ

1 small aubergine
15 ml (1 tablespoon) extra virgin olive oil
2.5 ml (½ teaspoon) balsamic or sherry vinegar
1 medium beef tomato
3 – 4 leaves fresh basil, or sprigs of fresh coriander
2 pitta breads

Peel the aubergine and slice into rounds about 5 mm (¼ in) thick. Brush with some of the oil and grill at a medium heat until the slices are well browned outside and perfectly soft inside (around 5 minutes each side). Leave to cool, then dress with the remaining oil and the vinegar.

When you're ready to eat, and not a moment before, slice the tomato, chop the herbs finely and lightly toast the 2 pitta breads. (Pitta should just be warmed through, rather than fully toasted.) Cut them open along 1 side and fill with slices of aubergine and tomato. Sprinkle on the herbs and eat immediately.

Smoked Fish 'Paste'

This is simple to make in the food processor, and thus well suited for use as a nibble at large parties. If you're feeling extravagant, use proper smoked salmon. If not, use smoked salmon pieces, mackerel, trout, cod or haddock.

Preparation time: 4 – 5 minutes

1 – 2 shallots, or a spring onion, cut into chunks
1 pickled green chilli, cut into chunks
350 g (12 oz) smoked fish, skinned, boned if necessary, and cut into chunks
225 g (8 oz) cottage cheese
15 ml (1 tablespoon) double cream
A small handful of parsley, finely chopped

Put the shallots or onion and chilli in the food processor and process to a fine mince. Add the fish and process until smooth. Then add the cheese and cream and process again until well blended. Refrigerate, covered, until needed.

Just before serving, add the parsley and blend in. Serve with toast or breadsticks.

Piadine

Piadine Ⓥ

These delicious unleavened breads, a speciality of Romagna, are cooked very quickly in a frying pan. They make a perfect accompaniment for Italian-style finger food.

Preparation time: around 15 minutes
Cooking time: around 20 minutes

500 g (1 lb 2 oz) plain flour
7.5 ml (1½ teaspoons) salt
2.5 ml (½ teaspoon) baking soda (bicarbonate of soda)
80 ml (3 fl oz) extra virgin olive oil
100 ml (4 fl oz) water
120 ml (8 tablespoons) milk
A little oil, for frying

Put the flour, salt and soda in the bowl of your food processor. Process briefly, then add the olive oil followed by water and milk. Mix to a rough dough, then remove to a lightly floured work surface and knead for a few minutes until smooth and elastic. It can rest for a while if you wish.

Heat a heavy frying pan over a fairly high heat. Tear or cut off pieces of dough about the size of a golf ball and roll them out into circles of about 20 cm (8 in) in diameter and 2.5 mm (⅛ in) thick; thickness is more important than size.

When the pan is hot enough to make a drop of water sizzle away almost immediately, brush it with oil and fry the *piadine* one at a time until lightly coloured on both sides (around 1 minute per side). Resist the temptation to overcook them.

Though they are at their best when served immediately, wrapped in a clean towel, they can also be wrapped in foil and re-heated in a moderate oven for 15 minutes or so.

Courgette and Spring Onion Sandwich Ⓥ

Cooking time: 5 – 8 minutes

1 small courgette
1 spring onion
5 ml (1 teaspoon) extra virgin olive oil
A few drops of lemon juice
Salt and freshly ground black pepper

Steam the courgette and onion whole (not even topped and tailed) until they're just cooked (around 5 – 8 minutes). Leave to cool, then trim and slice thinly into discs or strips. Toss with the oil and lemon juice and some salt and pepper. Serve within 5 minutes on focaccia or ciabatta bread.

Duxelles Ⓥ

Duxelles – minced mushrooms sautéed in butter – make a peerless freezer emergency-pack. They can be used for soups, sauces, casseroles, stuffings, or (as here) one of the most delicious canapés imaginable. This quantity makes enough to serve 8 – 10 people with other canapés. I would make double the quantity and freeze the rest for another occasion.

Preparation time: 15 – 20 minutes
Cooking time: 5 – 10 minutes

225 g (8 oz) cultivated mushrooms, cleaned and trimmed
15 ml (1 tablespoon) extra virgin olive oil
A good knob of butter
2 shallots or ½ small onion, minced
8 – 10 leaves fresh parsley, preferably flat-leaf, finely chopped
15 – 30 ml (1 – 2 tablespoons) dry breadcrumbs, optional
30 – 45 ml (2 – 3 tablespoons) double cream, optional
15 – 30 ml (1 – 2 tablespoons) freshly grated Parmesan

Chop the mushrooms finely in the food processor. Put them, in 2 batches, in a clean towel and squeeze out as much moisture as you can. This is hard work, but it saves cooking time. When both batches are ready, heat the oil and butter in a very large frying pan (preferably non-stick) until it is just short of sizzling.

Add the mushrooms and cook briskly for 2 minutes, then add the shallots or onion. Continue to cook, with regular tossing and turning, until the mushrooms stop giving off moisture (around 5 – 10 minutes). Add the parsley and cook for another 30 seconds. If you wish, you can ensure complete dryness by mixing in the breadcrumbs. Leave to cool in the pan, then freeze or refrigerate until needed.

To serve, mix the duxelles with the cream, if using, and spread a little on small pieces of bread (a baguette would be perfect) and sprinkle with a little cheese. Bake in the top of the oven until the bread is toasted, the cheese melted, and the duxelles hot. Serve.

Port Wine Jelly

This is a nice thing to make with the remains of the festive bottle; if not using that, buy ruby or perhaps a cheap LBV. The jelly can be eaten with cream, for a pudding, or with leftover turkey, goose or gammon.

Preparation time: 2 minutes
Cooking time: 4 – 5 minutes

2 sachets gelatine (2 tablespoons)
225 ml (8 fl oz) sugar
100 ml (4 fl oz) orange juice
45 ml (2 tablespoons) lemon juice
225 ml (8 fl oz) port

Mix together the gelatine and sugar and pour on 450 ml (15 fl oz) of boiling water. Stir until everything dissolves, then add the remaining ingredients and stir. Pour into a mould (or several smaller ones) and refrigerate until set.

Feta Biscuits

The pastry can be made in advance and then frozen.

Preparation time:
15 – 20 minutes
Cooking time: 8 – 10 minutes

85 g (3 oz) unsalted butter, softened
85 g (3 oz) full-fat feta cheese, crumbled
175 g (6 oz) plain flour
2.5 ml (½ teaspoon) dried oregano

Mash the butter and cheese together with a fork and gradually mix in the flour. When thoroughly blended, add the oregano and knead briefly. Form into a ball and refrigerate for at least 30 minutes.

Pre-heat the oven to 200°C/400°F/Gas 6. Pinch off marble-sized pieces of pastry and flatten out to make very thin circles or ovals. Put them on a lightly buttered baking sheet (or a non-stick sheet without butter) and bake for 8 – 10 minutes, until the pastry is golden brown. Leave for 2 – 3 minutes before serving.

Four Toppings for Crostini or Bruschetta

Each of these will suffice for 5 – 10 pieces of bread.

Green Olive Paste

This recipe is endlessly flexible and can be quickly adjusted by simply altering the seasonings. If the olives are already well flavoured, no further seasoning will be necessary. The crumbs help prevent separation.

Preparation time: 2 minutes

1 small garlic clove, quartered
1 small dried red chilli, seeded
1.25 ml (¼ teaspoon) dried
  mixed herbs
225 g (8 oz) pitted green olives
50 ml (2 fl oz) extra virgin olive oil
15 ml (1 tablespoon) dry
  breadcrumbs, optional
Freshly ground black pepper

Put the garlic, chilli and herbs in the food processor and blend until finely chopped. Add the olives and chop finely, scraping down the sides of the bowl a few times to mix everything in. With the motor running, add the oil and then the breadcrumbs (if using). Season with black pepper and refrigerate for at least 1 hour so the flavours can develop.

Parmesan, Anchovies, Sun-dried Tomato

Preparation time: 2 minutes

5 large (or 10 small) sun-dried
  tomatoes in oil
10 anchovy fillets, well drained
10 – 20 shavings from a good hunk
  of Parmesan

Halve the tomatoes if they're large and put them on the toasts. The anchovies too can be halved to suit your numbers and should be curled up on the tomatoes. Finally add 1 or 2 shavings of cheese and serve immediately.

Tuna with Herbs and Olives

You could use mayonnaise (preferably home-made) instead of olive oil for this recipe.

Preparation time: 3 minutes

1 x 200 g (7 oz) tin tuna in brine
A small handful of fresh dill or
  parsley, or 4 sage leaves,
  finely chopped
30 ml (2 tablespoons) extra virgin
  olive oil
50 – 85 g (2 – 3 oz) pitted black
  olives, sliced
Salt and freshly ground black pepper

Drain the tuna thoroughly and mash with a fork, then mix with the herbs and dribble in a little oil to bind the mixture lightly. Season with salt and black pepper to taste, and mix in the olives.

Eggs, Brown Mushrooms and Rocket

Rocket is hideously expensive at most supermarkets. If you can't bear the expense, substitute watercress.

Preparation time: 5 minutes
Cooking time: 10 – 12 minutes

175 g (6 oz) brown mushrooms,
  thinly sliced
25 ml (1 ½ tablespoons) extra virgin
  olive oil
Juice of ¼ lemon
4 hard-boiled eggs, sliced or chopped
20 – 25 leaves rocket
Salt and freshly ground black pepper

Toss the mushrooms with the lemon juice, vinegar, and a little salt and pepper. Marinate for 15 minutes, then pile on the toasts with the eggs and rocket leaves. Serve immediately.

Four Toppings for Crostini or Bruschetta

Marinated Olives Ⓥ

This recipe is adapted from Annie Bell's A Feast of Flavours, one of the best vegetarian cookbooks of recent years.

Preparation time: 5 minutes
Marinating time: 2 days

450 g (1lb) olives, green or black
300ml (10 fl 0z) extra virgin olive oil
1 small onion, cut into 8 pieces
3 – 4 garlic cloves, peeled and halved
2 bay leaves
2.5 ml (½ teaspoon) fennel seeds
2 sprigs of fresh thyme or 2.5 ml (½ teaspoon) dried
5 cm (2 in) strip of orange peel
2.5 ml (½ teaspoon) whole coriander seeds

Combine all the ingredients in a glass jar and refrigerate for at least 48 hours.

Marinated Artichokes Ⓥ

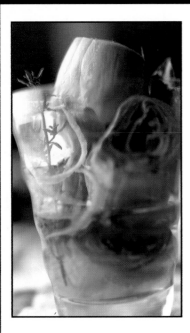

When I can only get hold of bland artichoke hearts in boring vegetable oil, I give them the following treatment.

Preparation time: 3 minutes
Marinating time: at least 4 hours

8 – 10 artichoke hearts
100 ml (4 fl oz) extra virgin olive oil
Juice and shredded rind of ½ lemon

Drain the artichoke hearts, reserve the oil and pat them dry. Halve, if they are large, and put in a glass or ceramic bowl. Season with salt and pepper, pour on the oil, add the lemon juice and rind, and leave for at least 4 hours or preferably overnight. Turn occasionally if they're not completely covered and serve with a little of the reserved artichoke oil.

Marinated Mozzarella Ⓥ

Mozzarella is made just about everywhere nowadays, but the best comes from Italy.

Preparation time: 5 minutes
Marinating time: 4 hours minimum

2 x 150 – 175 g (5 – 6 oz) packets Italian mozzarella
100 ml (4 fl oz) extra virgin olive oil
1 dried red chilli, seeded and crumbled, optional
1 garlic clove, thinly sliced or chopped
8 peppercorns, crushed
A small handful of fresh herbs, e.g. rosemary, basil, marjoram, tarragon

Drain the cheese, pat dry with paper towels and prick lightly with a fork to allow the oil to penetrate. Put in a strong plastic bag or a glass or ceramic bowl with the other ingredients. Seal tightly and chill in the fridge overnight, or at room temperature for 4 – 5 hours. Turn occasionally if the cheeses are not completely covered. To serve, cut into chunks and return to the marinade. Delicious on toast, or on its own.

Barbecued Ciabatta Ⓥ

This is a nice addition to a barbecued meal.

Preparation time: 1 minute
Cooking time: 4 – 6 minutes

1 loaf ciabatta bread
15 ml (1 tablespoon) extra virgin olive oil

Brush the bread all over with the oil, using a little more if you need to. Cook on the barbecue for around 2 – 3 minutes each side, until it feels just hot and is colouring lightly. Slice and serve.

Marinated Mozzarella

Cheshire Cheese Biscuits

Cheshire Cheese Biscuits (V)

These are so impressive that your guests will never guess how easy they are to make. They'll stay fresh for a few days in a tightly sealed container, but are much better served straight from the oven. Serve with drinks.

Preparation time: 15 minutes
plus 30 minutes chilling time
Cooking time: 8 – 12 minutes

100 g (4 oz) plain flour, or a mixture of light and strong flours
100 g (4 oz) unsalted butter, cut into small pieces
100 g (4 oz) Cheshire cheese, grated
2 tablespoons cold water
Sesame seeds, optional

Put the flour and butter in the food processor and process until the mixture resembles breadcrumbs. Add the cheese and mix briefly, then add the water and process until the mixture looks like a crumbly dough (10 – 15 seconds). Form into a ball and refrigerate for at least 30 minutes.

Pre-heat the oven to 200°C/400°F/Gas 6. Roll out the dough to a thickness of around 2.5 mm (⅛ in) and cut into rounds with a biscuit cutter or 5 cm (2 in) square squares with a knife.

Place on a non-stick baking sheet and cook near the top of the oven until the biscuits are a light golden brown (8 – 12 minutes). If you like, sprinkle each biscuit with a pinch of sesame seeds before baking.

Egg Parcels (V)

This method of cooking eggs makes a nice addition to dinner or lunch parties. The important thing is the method – the fillings can be varied endlessly and some suggestions are given below. Serve with drinks.

Preparation time: 1 minute
Cooking time: 5 – 10 minutes

6 eggs, size 1
10 ml (2 teaspoons) vegetable oil, plus a little extra for cooking
Salt and freshly ground black pepper

Beat the eggs thoroughly with the 2 teaspoons of oil, seasoning with salt and pepper. Heat a non-stick pan over a medium-low heat and add a tiny bit of oil. Fill a 15 ml (1 tablespoon) measuring spoon with beaten egg and pour into the pan. Swirl it around to make a circle and cook until the top is just slightly liquid (20 – 30 seconds). Remove to a plate and repeat the process with the remaining egg.

This number of eggs will yield around 20 pancakes, which should be left to cool (and refrigerated if you're cooking more than 1 hour in advance).

To fill them, use any or all of the following: a small blob of pesto, olive paste, tapenade, or any other paste/sauce sold in jars; stir-fried shreds of spring onion, courgette, or aubergine; shredded *prosciutto* or a hard cheese such as Parmesan; finely chopped sun-dried tomatoes and/or olives; thin shreds of smoked cod, haddock or salmon. Roll the 'omelettes' around the filling or fold the edges in and then roll to make a parcel.

Pitta Bread with an Italianate Filling (V)

One of the great lunches of all time. Makes one serving.

Preparation time: 5 minutes

1 pitta bread, white or wholemeal
1 hunk of Parmesan
1 small beef tomato or ½ large one
1 – 2 green olives, pitted and thinly sliced
4 – 5 capers, finely chopped
Fresh herbs of your choice
A few drops of oil and/or vinegar, optional
Salt and freshly ground black pepper

Lightly toast the pitta bread, making sure it doesn't get so crisp as to be unmanageable. Meanwhile, shave off a few slices of Parmesan, seed the tomato, and cut into fine dice. Mix all the ingredients. Slit open the bread, stuff it with the filling and eat.

Figs with Prosciutto and Sour Cream

This is closely modelled on a recipe in Richard Olney's Simple French Food. It can be served as a snack or a light lunch dish and it is absolutely delicious.

Preparation time: 15 minutes
Chilling time: 1 hour

12 ripe figs
3 – 4 paper-thin slices prosciutto, fat removed
12 sprigs fresh mint
3 – 4 chives, optional
Juice of ½ lemon
150 ml (5 fl oz) soured cream

Peel the figs, if you wish, and slice into the tops to make 2 crossed cuts extending around halfway into the fruit. Squeeze the sides to open up slightly, as you would with a baked potato. Put the figs on a large plate and chill for 1 hour to firm them up.

Meanwhile, cut each slice of *prosciutto* into shreds or quarters. Remove the stems from the mint and finely chop the chives (if using).

When you're ready to serve, squeeze a few drops of lemon juice into each fig with a tiny bit of salt and pepper. Put some of the ham in each one, then top with a dab of sour cream and finally the herbs. The figs should be eaten as soon as possible, using your fingers.

Sauces

Yellow Pepper Sauce (page 167)

Sauces

Once upon a time, sauces were considered the very heart and soul of fine cooking. That was when French cuisine was regarded as the pinnacle of the culinary landscape, and no dish could be complete without an elaborate mask of butter, reduced stock, wine and aromatic vegetables. Flour played a major role, and so did cream.

Those days are gone, outside old-fashioned French restaurants. Which is a shame in a way, as some of the classic sauces are wonderful – and adventurous home cooks could do worse than experiment with them once in a while. But nowadays the emphasis is on speed and lightness and on an approach to cooking which emphasizes the flavours of the main ingredients.

That approach is certainly embodied in salsas, one of the most useful ideas in modern cookery and a major part of this chapter. Often translated as sauce, salsa is actually a kind of relish, with chopped bits (either fresh or preserved) in liquid and/or oil. There are more bits than wet stuff, making salsa a spooning sauce rather than a pouring sauce.

In all its forms, it is remarkably versatile. A salsa can be made with just oil, something oniony, something acidic and a handful of fresh parsley. But that's just the beginning. Matters can be delightfully complicated with anchovies, capers, beetroot, cucumber, celery, lime, garlic, tomato, peppers, chillis, any form of onion. Instead of parsley you can use other herbs: coriander, dill, tarragon, mint, basil, chervil.

The key to salsa is harmony and balance. No ingredient should overpower the others: you should be able to taste everything, in just the right proportions. But those proportions are generously flexible. You can add a little more of this or a little less of that. You can chop everything fine or chunky or in thin strips. Whatever you do, you're certain to end up with something delicious.

And you can use the results on just about anything, hot or cold: simply cooked fish, chicken or meat; pasta, pulses or rice; or as a stuffing or garnish for vegetables such as tomatoes, courgettes or aubergines. I serve salsas regularly with almost every kind of dish, and no one ever complains. Indeed, the only problem is making enough: people always want more of a salsa.

Avocado Dressing ⓥ

This can be made well in advance, as the acidity of the yoghurt and citrus keeps the avocado from turning brown. Goes well with cold chicken, any green vegetable, or just a mixed salad.

Preparation time: 5 – 10 minutes.

200 ml (7 fl oz) Greek or Bio yoghurt
Juice of 1 lemon or 2 limes, about 60 ml (4 tablespoons)
4 – 5 spring onions, finely chopped
1 small garlic clove, finely chopped
2 avocados, preferably the Hass variety
A small handful of fresh coriander, coarsely chopped
Salt and freshly ground black pepper

Put the yoghurt in your blender or food processor with the citrus juice, onions, garlic and a little salt and pepper. Blend to a fine purée, then halve the avocados, scoop out the flesh and add to the blender. Blend again until the avocados are completely amalgamated.

This will produce a fairly thick dressing; if you want a thinner one, add more yoghurt, to taste. The dressing can be prepared in advance to this point. When you're ready to serve, mix in the coriander and taste for seasoning.

Basic Tomato Sauce ⓥ

2 garlic cloves, finely chopped
1 medium onion, finely chopped
1 small carrot, finely chopped
1 celery stick, finely chopped
1 bay leaf
45 ml (3 tablespoons) extra virgin olive oil
2 x 400 g tins plum tomatoes, drained and coarsely chopped
7.5 ml (1½ teaspoons) dried mixed herbs
A pinch of sugar
15 ml (1 tablespoon) sherry vinegar
Salt and freshly ground black pepper

Put the garlic, onion, carrot, celery, bay leaf and oil in a pan. Season with salt and pepper, and cook over a gentle heat until soft (around 15 minutes). Add the remaining ingredients and simmer gently, stirring occasionally, for at least 30 minutes and preferably for an hour or more. Longer cooking concentrates the sauce, making it better for pizza toppings. Remove the bay leaf before using the sauce.

Parsley Butter Sauce ⓥ

This is similar to a French beurre blanc, but much easier because the cornflour give stability.

**Preparation time: 1 minute
Cooking time: 10 minutes**

1 shallot or spring onion, finely chopped
100 ml (4 fl oz) dry white wine or vermouth
2.5 ml (½ teaspoon) cornflour
85 g (3 oz) butter
Juice of ½ lemon
A small handful of parsley, leaves only
Salt and freshly ground black pepper

Put the shallot or onion in a small pan with the wine, cornflour and a little salt and pepper. Whisking steadily, boil down to reduce the sauce by about half. Add the butter a little at a time, whisking constantly, and finally add the lemon juice. Set aside until needed.

Just before you're ready to serve, re-heat the sauce, whisking again to remove any lumps. Add the parsley. Stir just long enough to let the parsley get hot, then serve immediately.

Classic Salsa Verde ⓥ

This recipe comes from Culinary Classics and Improvisations *by Michael Field, a great American cookery writer whose books have never been published in the UK. Follow the measurements given here the first time you attempt salsa verde, just to sample a perfect specimen. Then do your own variations. Great on cold beef, simply cooked fish, or even potatoes.*

**Preparation time: 10 – 15 minutes
Resting time: 5 – 30 minutes**

30 ml (2 tablespoons) finely chopped shallots or spring onions
5 ml (1 teaspoon) finely chopped garlic
4 anchovy fillets, drained well and finely chopped
30 ml (2 tablespoons) capers, drained and finely chopped
45 ml (3 tablespoons) finely chopped parsley, preferably flat-leaf
45 ml (3 tablespoons) lemon juice
60 ml (4 tablespoons) extra virgin olive oil

Combine all the solid ingredients and moisten with the lemon juice and oil. If you've chopped everything very finely, the mixture should resemble a purée in which no one flavour predominates. Coarser chopping will produce not only a chunkier texture but a bolder taste. Once made, the sauce can be served immediately or left for up to 30 minutes.

Red, Green and Spicy Salsa ⓥ

The ferocious heat of the chillis is tamed – somewhat – by the cooling effect of cucumber and peppers. Especially good with any kind of chicken or lamb cooked on the grill or barbecue.

Preparation time: 15 minutes
Resting time: 1 hour

2 small green chillis, seeded and finely chopped
2 small red chillis, seeded and finely chopped
2 large or 4 small spring onions, green parts included, finely chopped
60 ml (4 tablespoons) extra virgin olive oil
30 ml (2 tablespoons) red wine vinegar
Salt and freshly ground black pepper
A bunch of coriander, coarsely chopped
15 cm (6 in) length cucumber, peeled and finely diced
2 small red peppers, finely diced

Mix the chillis with the spring onions, oil and vinegar. Season with salt and pepper, and leave for an hour or so. No more than 15 minutes before you plan to eat, add the coriander. Just before serving, add the cucumber and red peppers. Mix well and serve within 5 minutes.

Tomato and Tarragon Salsa Cruda ⓥ

This is based on a Mexican standby, a regular feature of almost any Mexican meal. It can be eaten on its own, as a salad or with vegetables or chicken.

Preparation time: 10 minutes
Resting time: 30 minutes maximum

400 g (14 oz) red, ripe tomatoes, seeded, dried and coarsely diced
2 large spring onions, coarsely chopped
15 ml (1 tablespoon) capers, coarsely chopped
15 ml (1 tablespoon) balsamic vinegar
10 – 15 sprigs of fresh tarragon, torn in half
Salt and freshly ground black pepper

Mix together all the ingredients, including salt and pepper and serve within 30 minutes of preparation.

Garlic, Ginger and Spring Onion Salsa ⓥ

This salsa uses the three basic flavourings of Chinese cooking along with sesame oil. A little chilli sauce may be added if you wish. Use on noodles or chicken, or with any red meat.

Preparation time: 5 minutes
Resting time: 30 minutes

2 – 3 garlic cloves, finely chopped
3 – 4 spring onions, finely chopped
10 thin slices ginger, peeled and shredded
90 ml (6 tablespoons) rice or red wine vinegar
10 ml (2 teaspoons) vegetable oil
60 ml (4 tablespoons) sesame oil
15 ml (1 tablespoon) soy sauce
2 medium celery sticks, finely chopped
A large handful of fresh coriander, coarsely chopped
Salt and freshly ground black pepper

Put the garlic, spring onions and ginger in a medium-sized mixing bowl and toss with the vinegar. Leave for around 30 minutes so the flavours can blend and soften, then add the oils, soy sauce and celery. The salsa may be left for another 15 – 20 minutes at this point. Just before serving, add the coriander and a good grinding of black pepper, plus a little salt if you wish.

Black Bean Salsa ⓥ

This salsa from the south-western USA is chunky enough to serve as a side dish. Eat with rice or with anything cooked on the barbecue.

Preparation time: 5 minutes
Resting time: 2 hours minimum

1 x 340 g tin sweetcorn
1 x 400 g (14 oz) tin kidney beans, rinsed and drained
2 spring onions, coarsely chopped
1 medium red onion, coarsely chopped
1 – 2 fresh chillis, finely chopped
75 ml (5 tablespoons) red wine vinegar
15 ml (1 tablespoon) extra virgin olive oil, optional
A small handful of fresh coriander, finely chopped
Chilli sauce, optional
Salt and freshly ground black pepper

Put the sweetcorn, beans, onions and chillis in a glass bowl. Whisk the vinegar and oil (if using) with salt and black pepper, then pour over the corn mixture and toss well. Leave for 2 hours to allow the flavours to blend and mix in the coriander just before serving. If you want the salsa hotter, add a few drops of chilli sauce.

Pickled Walnut Salsa Ⓥ

The name is a joke: the recipe contains not walnuts but walnut oil and two pickled ingredients. Increase the quantity of pickled chillis for a racier effect and get the best French cornichons you can find. Serve with fish or burgers.

Preparation time: 5 minutes
Resting time: 3 hours

1 small onion, coarsely chopped
2 small pickled chillis, coarsely chopped
6 – 8 small cornichon-style pickles, coarsely chopped
15 ml (1 tablespoon) extra virgin olive oil
1.25 ml (¼ teaspoon) balsamic vinegar
5 ml (1 teaspoon) walnut oil
1 large green pepper, coarsely chopped (see method)
A small handful of fresh herbs (parsley or dill), finely chopped, optional
Freshly ground black pepper

Thoroughly mix all the ingredients except the green pepper and herbs in a medium-sized mixing bowl. Season with black pepper but no salt. Refrigerate for a few hours to allow the flavours to develop, then add the green pepper (which should be chopped at last moment) and the herbs.

Salsa Niçoise

This takes some of the classic ingredients of salade Niçoise and turns them into a salsa. Use on hard-boiled eggs, fish, roasted or grilled vegetables – or even a green salad.

Preparation time: 15 minutes
Resting time: 1 hour or more

2 garlic cloves, finely chopped
30 ml (2 tablespoons) extra virgin olive oil
4 spring onions, coarsely chopped
4 anchovy fillets, finely chopped
1 small bulb fennel, finely chopped
125 g (4 oz) black olives, preferably the Niçoise type, pitted and coarsely chopped
1 bunch purple radishes, quartered
A small handful of fresh basil or mint leaves
Salt and freshly ground black pepper

Mix together all the ingredients, except the radishes and herbs, in a medium-sized mixing bowl with a little salt and plenty of pepper; leave for at least 1 hour to reduce the pungency of the garlic. Five minutes before eating, top with the radishes and herbs.

Pico de Gallo Ⓥ

This Mexican recipe is adapted from one in W. Park Kerr and Norma Kerr's El Paso Chile Company's Texas Border Cookbook. The name (meaning 'rooster's beak') may refer to the sharpness of the salsa. Long green Anaheim chillis, with their relatively mild flavour, are available from some supermarkets and from Asian food shops.

Preparation time: 20 minutes
Resting time: 1 hour

6 long green chillis
Juice of 2 limes
2 red, ripe beef tomatoes, cored, seeded and coarsely chopped
2 medium onions, coarsely chopped
2 – 3 small green chillis, seeded and finely shredded
Freshly ground black pepper

Cook the long chillis under a pre-heated grill, turning several times, until they're blackened all over. Place in a plastic or paper bag and leave to cool, then peel, seed, and coarsely chop them. Meanwhile, heat the limes briefly in boiling water or the microwave (around 30 seconds) and leave to cool.

Combine all the solid ingredients in a glass or ceramic bowl and squeeze over the lime juice. Toss well, adding a little pepper if you wish, and chill for 1 hour.

Avocado Salsa Ⓥ

The avocado mustn't be chopped and mixed in until the very last moment. It must also be perfectly ripe, though not squishy. Eat with chicken or meat and add a diced beef tomato if you wish.

Preparation time: 15 minutes
Resting time: around 2 hours

2 medium red onions, coarsely chopped
2 – 3 spring onions, coarsely chopped
1 large green chilli, seeded and finely chopped, or a few good dashes of chilli sauce
45 ml (3 tablespoons) lime juice
30 ml (2 tablespoons) extra virgin olive oil
A large handful of fresh coriander or parsley
2 ripe avocados
Salt and freshly ground black pepper

Combine all ingredients, except the avocados, in a medium-sized mixing bowl with a little salt and pepper. Leave to stand for 2 hours or so to let the flavours blend. Just before serving, peel the avocados and chop into dice about the same size as the onions. Stir in well but gently and serve immediately.

Salsa Cruda con dos Chiles ⓥ

This salsa combines fresh chillis with pickled vegetables for a complex and medium-hot effect. The quantities can be increased or decreased, as you like.

Preparation time: 10 minutes

450g (1 lb) red, ripe beef tomatoes
1 small green or Scotch Bonnet chilli
1 pickled jalapeño or guindilla chilli
1 small onion
Juice of ½ lime
1 small handful of fresh coriander
Salt and freshly ground black pepper

Seed the tomatoes and chop coarsely. Mince the chillis and onion, seeding the chillis if you wish, and mix with the tomato and lime juice. If you want a smoother texture, you can chop the ingredients in a food processor. Season with salt and pepper then leave to stand at room temperature for 2 hours. At the last moment, chop the coriander and stir in.

Mango Salsa ⓥ

This is based on a recipe in Julee Rosso's Great Good Food. *I can never get mangoes to slice easily if they're very soft, so I use fruit that's just showing the first signs of ripeness. Especially good on burgers or pork.*

Preparation time: 20 minutes
Resting time: 2 hours

4 limes or 2 lemons
1 mango, not too ripe, fairly finely diced
1 ripe beef tomato, coarsely chopped
2 red peppers, seeded and coarsely chopped
2 red onions, coarsely chopped
2 garlic cloves, finely chopped
1 green chilli, seeded and finely chopped
5 ml (1 teaspoon) whole cumin seeds
5 ml (1 teaspoon) whole coriander seeds
15 ml (1 tablespoon) extra virgin olive oil, optional
30 ml (2 tablespoons) red wine or sherry vinegar
Salt and freshly ground black pepper

Peel the rind from the limes or lemons and cut into fine shreds. Squeeze the juice to obtain around 50 ml (2 fl oz) in all, and mix with the remaining ingredients including a bit of salt and pepper. Refrigerate for 2 hours before serving.

Salsa 'Girondine' ⓥ

This delicate, refined salsa is based on the recipe for Sauce Verte Girondine in Bruno Loubet's Cuisine Courante. *Use it with fish or chicken.*

Preparation time: 10 minutes
Resting time: 15 – 30 minutes

85 g (3 oz) shallots, preferably pink ones, finely chopped
1 small garlic clove, finely chopped
50 ml (2 fl oz) red wine vinegar
100 ml (4 fl oz) extra virgin olive oil
15 ml (1 tablespoon) finely chopped tarragon
15 ml (1 tablespoon) finely chopped parsley
15 ml (1 tablespoon) finely chopped chervil
15 ml (1 tablespoon) finely chopped basil
Salt and freshly ground black pepper

Mix the shallots and garlic with the vinegar and leave for 15 – 30 minutes so the flavours have time to blend. Add the remaining ingredients just before serving.

Instant Yoghurt Sauce ⓥ

This is another of my favourite ways of adding low-calorie pizzazz to almost any dish. The herbs can be varied as you please – try dill, chervil or sorrel instead of the coriander.

Preparation time: 5 minutes

1 small red onion or 2 spring onions, finely chopped
2 – 3 slices fresh ginger, finely chopped
½ small green chilli, seeded and finely chopped
A small handful of fresh coriander, finely chopped
Juice of ½ lemon
100 ml (4 fl oz) Greek or Bio yoghurt
Salt and freshly ground black pepper

Mix together all the ingredients with salt and pepper to taste. Leave for 15 minutes, with a final stir before serving.

Instant Yoghurt Sauce

Yellow Pepper Sauce

Yellow Pepper Sauce Ⓥ

I adore the great French emulsified sauces: Béarnaise, Hollandaise, mayonnaise. Unfortunately, they're as calorie-rich as ice cream. Here is a substitute inspired by a recipe in Sally Schneider's The Art of Low-Calorie Cooking. *Use it on vegetables, fish or any other dish that might be served with Hollandaise.*

**Preparation time:
5 minutes
Cooking time:
30 minutes**

2 large yellow peppers
1 garlic clove, finely chopped,
    optional
½ small green chilli, seeded
10 ml (2 teaspoons) white wine
    vinegar
15 ml (1 tablespoon) soured cream
30 ml (2 tablespoons) extra virgin
    olive oil, optional
Salt and freshly ground black
    pepper

Grill or roast the peppers (see page 109) until they're blackened all over, then put in a plastic bag and leave for 10 minutes so they'll be easy to peel. Remove the stems and skins, seed, and chop roughly.

Put the garlic and chilli in the food processor and chop. Season with salt and pepper, add the peppers and purée very thoroughly. Add the vinegar and process again to blend. If you don't have a food processor, chop the peppers by hand and finish in the blender. The sauce may be sieved to get a really fine texture, but I don't bother with the extra work.

Just before serving, whisk in the cream and drizzle on the oil. Run a spoon through it a few times, to mix in without amalgamating.

Melted Vegetable Sauce Ⓥ

The inspiration for this recipe is an Italian pasta sauce in which the onions are cooked slowly until meltingly soft. Here the principle is applied to peppers, celery and onions, the 'holy trinity' of Cajun cooking. The result can top pasta, rice, pulses, chicken or baked potatoes.

**Preparation time: 10 – 15 minutes
Cooking time: 2 hours**

30 ml (2 tablespoons) extra virgin olive oil
2 large peppers, 1 green and 1 red, seeded and thinly sliced
4 celery sticks, thinly sliced
2 large onions, thinly sliced
15 ml (1 tablespoon) fresh herbs, e.g. basil, dill, or sage
Lots of freshly grated Parmesan

Heat the oil over the lowest heat in a large pan and stir in the vegetables. Cook, partly covered, very slowly; stir every 10 – 15 minutes and add a little water if it seems to be 'catching' on the bottom of the pot. The sauce will take 1 – 1½ hours to reach true melting point, but if you're pressed for time you can eat it a bit crunchier. Put in the herbs for the last 5 minutes of cooking. The sauce can be prepared in advance and re-heated for serving. Pass the Parmesan separately.

Berry Sauce Ⓥ

This is designed for serving with fresh berries (dusted with sugar, if you like) and the almond biscuits on page 183. Use jam made with the same kind of fresh berry you are using.

Preparation time: 10 minutes

2 small punnets (around 500 g/1 lb 2 oz) fresh berries
15 – 30ml (1 – 2 tablespoons) sugar
15 – 30ml (1 – 2 tablespoons) jam

Wash the berries well and remove the leaves and hulls. Put the sugar and jam in a blender or food processor and process quickly, then add the berries a few at a time and blend. They will break up easily because of their high water content. When they're all in, blend for at least 30 seconds to dissolve the sugar and get a fine purée.

Put the purée into a fine sieve and press through the mesh gently with a spoon, reserving the sauce in a glass or ceramic bowl. The liquid should pass through fairly easily, leaving the seeds in the sieve. Cover tightly and refrigerate until needed.

Puddings

Orange Juice Whip (page 179)

Puddings

The world can be divided into sweet tooths and savoury tooths. Some people attack a starter and main course with gusto, then lose interest when the pudding arrives. Others merely toy with the first courses, saving their heavy artillery for an assault on the sweet stuff. This type of eater believes that dessert is the only part of the meal that really counts.

I'm a savoury tooth myself. Sweetness, to me, is a one-dimensional taste. And because pudding is the course that interests me least, it's the one I spend least time making. But I subscribe to the belief that pleasing one's guests is a sacred duty. Since some will be pudding-lovers, I've developed a small repertoire of recipes which usually succeed in making them happy.

Most of my favourite puddings call for fruit in some form, usually fresh but dried where appropriate. The choice should be dictated by season and quality, and most of the recipes here can be made with a substitute if the fruit specified is low in quality or high in price. This is a vital point for harried home cooks. And if you're feeling truly harried, fresh fruit on its own, with cheese, or in one of the simple salads in this chapter, never fails to win plaudits. To jazz up fruit salad with almost no extra work you can make a flavoured cream, plain or whipped, using liqueurs, cinnamon, vanilla essence or grated citrus zest.

I love bananas above all as a dessert fruit for their natural sweetness and adaptability. Other adaptable fruits include apples, pears, pineapple, mango, peaches and apricots. Fresh is always best, but tinned peaches can be perfectly acceptable if used properly.

My other favourite pudding ingredient is chocolate, which never fails to win murmurs (or something stronger) of satisfaction. When you're using it for cooking, there's no point in buying anything but the best – semi-sweet or unsweetened chocolate with a high cocoa content. The best tend to come from Europe – France, Switzerland or Belgium.

Again, my absolute favourite pudding ingredient is speed. Most of the recipes here reflect this, being quick both to prepare and to cook. On the other hand, elaborate puddings do have their place. Steamed puddings are classic, and invariably popular with guests. Sweet tarts are another sure-fire winner, and the work involved can be minimal. (If I have a single favourite recipe in this chapter, it's probably the *Cream Cheese Tart with a Prune Compôte* on page 183.) And *Bread and Butter Pudding* is an easy dish that can be prepared well in advance for last-minute cooking. If the other dishes for a dinner party are on the simple side, I am perfectly happy to go overboard for the sweet course.

No-cook Citrus Cheesecake

This isn't a proper cheesecake, but it's dead easy and very good. While a home-made shortcrust pastry shell is best, a bought shell will give excellent results. See the alternative serving suggestions.

Preparation time: 15 minutes
Cooking time: 10 minutes plus 3 hours setting time

60 ml (4 tablespoons) caster sugar
1 sachet (about 7.5 ml/1½ teaspoons) gelatine
1 – 2 oranges
½ lemon
150 ml (5 fl oz) single cream
225 g (8 oz) cottage cheese
1 x 24 cm (9½ in) pre-baked pastry shell

Dissolve the sugar in a small pan over a low heat with 100 ml (4 fl oz) of water. Sprinkle on the gelatine and stir until the gelatine has dissolved. Leave to cool until the syrup is barely warm (around 10 minutes). Meanwhile, peel the rind from 1 orange, chop into fine dice and add to the syrup. Squeeze the juice from the lemon and peeled orange and measure; if there's much less than 175 ml (6 fl oz) in all, add more orange juice.

Put the syrup, cream and citrus juices in your blender and add half the cottage cheese. Blend until smooth, then add the remaining cheese and blend again. It can take as long as 1 minute of blending to get a perfectly smooth mixture. Pour into the pastry shell and refrigerate until set (around 3 hours).

If you prefer, you can serve the cheesecake mixture in ramekins, individual pastry shells or the scooped out hollows of halved oranges. You will not need extra cream to serve with this dish.

Apple Brown Betty

This classic American dish, similar to crumble, is adapted from the venerable Fannie Farmer Cookbook. *Pears can be used instead of apples.*

Preparation time: 25 minutes
Cooking time: 45 minutes

1 lemon
1 kg (2 lb 2 oz) apples
200 g (7 oz) breadcrumbs
150 g (5 oz) butter, plus extra for greasing
85 g (3 oz) sugar
5 ml (1 teaspoon) ground cinnamon

Pre-heat the oven to 180°C/350°F/Gas 4. Grate the rind of the lemon and squeeze the juice into a mixing bowl. Core and peel the apples, then slice into thin wedges. Add the wedges to the lemon juice as you go, to prevent discolouration. Melt the butter and mix with the breadcrumbs. Mix the sugar with the cinnamon and grated lemon rind.

Generously grease a 30 x15 x 7.5 cm (12 x 6 x 3 in) baking dish with butter. Sprinkle on about 30 ml (2 tablespoons) of the breadcrumbs and shake the dish to spread them evenly. Put in half the apples, then half the sugar mixture.

Top with the remaining apples, then the remaining sugar and finally 100 ml (4 fl oz) of hot water. Sprinkle on the rest of the crumbs and cover loosely with aluminium foil. Bake for 15 minutes, then remove the foil and continue baking until the fruit is soft and the topping well browned (around 45 minutes in all). Serve hot, warm or at room temperature, with any form of cream.

Chocolate Brownie Cake

Chocolate Brownie Cake

This gooey, immorally rich concoction appeals equally to children and adults. Make it for a dinner party, then let the children fall on the left-overs (there will be some) the next day. If you don't have a spring-form tin, use an ordinary cake tin lined with greaseproof paper.

**Preparation time:
30 minutes
Cooking time:
35 – 40 minutes**

175 g (6 oz) unsalted butter, plus
    extra for greasing
175 g (6 oz) good dark chocolate
200 g (7 oz) sugar
3 eggs, size 1
65 g (2½ oz) flour
25 g (1 oz) chopped almonds,
    walnuts or pistachios, optional

Pre-heat the oven to 180°C/350°F/ Gas 4. Generously butter the sides and base of a 20 – 25 cm (8 – 10 in) spring-form cake tin, then dust lightly with flour. Melt the chocolate, 175 g (6 oz) butter and sugar over a gentle heat. Leave to cool.

Separate the eggs, making sure there is no trace of yolk in the whites. Beat the whites until they form soft but stiff peaks. Whisk the yolks into the chocolate mixture, then add the flour and nuts (if using). Fold in the whites thoroughly and gently, so they don't lose their airiness, and pour the mixture into the tin. Bake in the centre of the oven until a knife inserted at the centre comes out hot and clean (35 – 40 minutes). Don't worry if it doesn't rise: it's not supposed to.

Leave to cool completely, then run a knife round the sides, release the clip, and remove. The cake needs no icing but you could sprinkle over icing sugar to decorate.

Browned Bananas With Apricots

If you can only find apricots in syrup, omit the sugar from the first step.

**Preparation time: 5 minutes
Cooking time: 6 – 8 minutes**

1 x 400 g (14 oz) tin apricots in pear juice, drained
Juice of ¼ lemon
A large pinch of ground cinnamon
15 ml (1 tablespoon) Crème de Cassis, optional
30 – 45 ml (1 – 2 tablespoons) sugar, preferably unrefined
6 small bananas
25 – 50 g (1 – 2 oz) unsalted butter
45 ml (3 tablespoons) Grand Marnier or orange juice

Put the apricots in a glass bowl with the lemon juice, cinnamon, Crème de Cassis, if using, and 15 ml (1 tablespoon) sugar. Toss well and set aside until needed. The dessert can be prepared in advance to this point.

When you're ready to cook, spoon the apricots into the centre of the serving plates and halve the bananas lengthwise. Melt the butter in a large non-stick frying pan until it just starts to sizzle. Add the bananas, cut side down, and cook over a medium heat until lightly browned (around 3 minutes). Turn them over and cook for another 2 minutes or so, until they're barely softened all the way through. Sprinkle on the remaining sugar and then the Grand Marnier or orange juice, plus a splash of water. Swirl the pan around until the sugar has dissolved and the liquid is reduced to a light syrup.

To serve, put the bananas around the sides of the plates and pour over the syrup. Serve immediately with cream or whipped cream, if you wish.

Chocolate Pots with Cointreau

This unbelievably simple pudding is based on a recipe in The Carved Angel Cookery Book *by Joyce Molyneux with Sophie Grigson. They use brandy, but Cointreau adds a lovely hint of orange. Use the best chocolate you can find, such as Menier or Lindt Excellence.*

**Preparation time: 10 minutes
Cooking time: 5 minutes**

300 ml (10 fl oz) single cream
200 g (7 oz) plain chocolate
1 egg
15 ml (1 tablespoon) Cointreau

Put the cream in a pan and bring to the boil. Break the chocolate into squares and put in the food processor or blender. Add the boiling cream and process until smooth. Add the egg and the Cointreau and process until well blended. Pour into 6 ramekins and leave in the fridge overnight to set.

Chocolate Pots with Muscat and Pistachios

Another chocolate pot, this time flavoured with Muscat de Rivesaltes or Beaumes-de-Venise. This recipe produces a mildly bitter result; if you want it sweeter, use more sugar.

**Preparation time: 5 minutes
Cooking time: 30 minutes plus at least 4 hours setting time**

50 g (2 oz) dark chocolate
40 g (1½ oz) sugar
75 ml (5 tablespoons) Muscat-based dessert wine
Juice of 1 lime or ½ lemon
100 ml (4 fl oz) double cream
6 – 8 pistachios

Break the chocolate into small pieces. Put the sugar, wine and lime or lemon juice in a heavy pan over a gentle heat and cook, stirring steadily, until the sugar has dissolved. Stir in the cream and continue stirring until hot and well blended. Add the chocolate and stir until completely melted. Bring quickly to a boil, then reduce the heat and simmer very gently for 15 – 20 minutes or until the mixture is very dark and thick enough to coat a spoon. Pour into little pots, leave to cool completely, then cover with cling film and refrigerate for at least 4 hours.

Before serving, shell the nuts and remove the husks. Chop into tiny pieces or sandwich between 2 sheets of cling film and crush with a rolling pin. Sprinkle over the chocolate and serve.

Miniature Fruit Tarts

You can buy pre-baked pastry bases, but home-made shortcrust is even better: just make sure it's cool before you fill it. The lower quantity of sugar gives a slightly sour flavour which I love; some will want it sweeter.

Preparation time: 5 minutes

50 g (2 oz) Philadelphia cream cheese
15 – 45 ml (1 – 3 tablespoons) caster sugar
100 ml (4 fl oz) Bio yoghurt (3.5% fat)
7.5 ml (1½ teaspoons) Cointreau, optional
4 x 7 – 10 cm (3 – 4 in) pre-cooked pastry bases
Soft fruit, e.g. raspberries, strawberries, blueberries, ripe bananas, kiwi fruit
Ground cinnamon or good cocoa powder, optional
Icing sugar, for dusting

Put the cream cheese and sugar in a blender or food processor and blend quickly. Add the yoghurt and Cointreau (if using) and blend again until perfectly smooth. If using a food processor, give a final whisk by hand.

Spoon the cream mixture into the pastry bases, to a level just below the rim (around 45 ml/3 tablespoons per pastry). Refrigerate, uncovered, until the mixture has set (at least 2 hours).

Just before serving, slice the fruit and arrange on top in neat, overlapping layers. Whip up any remaining cream mixture and spoon it around the edges of small serving plates (dust with cinnamon or good cocoa powder if you wish). Put a tart at the centre of each plate, dust with icing sugar and serve immediately.

Miniature Fruit Tarts

Buttered Apples

This makes a fairly light ending to any big meal such as Christmas lunch or dinner. Serve the apples on slices of buttered toast, rounds of pastry or a bought pastry base. The dish should go into the oven just before you sit down to eat your starter.

Preparation time: 10 minutes
Cooking time: 45 – 60 minutes

8 dessert apples, halved and cored
60 ml (4 tablespoons) softened unsalted butter
30 – 45 ml (2 – 3 tablespoons) caster sugar
Cream or crème fraîche to serve, optional
Nuts of your choice, optional

Pre-heat the oven to 200°C/400°F/Gas 6. Place the apples on a non-stick baking sheet (or lightly buttered ordinary sheet) with the flat sides down. Spread the butter all over and sprinkle the sugar over in an even layer. Bake in the centre of the oven until the apples are lightly browned (around 45 – 60 minutes).

The apples can be eaten hot, warm or at room temperature; I like them best when they're just a bit warm to the touch. Serve with cream or crème fraîche and some chopped nuts, if you wish.

Peaches and Blueberries in Moscato Syrup

Another summer berry could be used instead of blueberries if you prefer. The peaches must be good and ripe.

Preparation time: 15 – 20 minutes

225 ml (8 fl oz) Moscato d'Asti wine
15 – 30 ml (1 – 2 tablespoons) caster sugar
A large pinch of ground cinnamon
Juice of ½ large lemon
10 – 12 ripe peaches, peeled if you wish, stones removed, chopped into 2.5 cm (1 in) chunks
1 kg (2 lb 2 oz) fresh blueberries, washed and dried
Basil leaves, to garnish, optional
Double cream or crème fraîche, to serve

Combine the wine with the sugar, cinnamon and lemon juice in a large mixing bowl and leave until the sugar is dissolved. Gently toss the fruit in this syrup and refrigerate until needed (no more than 3 hours).

When you're ready to eat, gently toss the fruit again and garnish with basil (if using). Serve with double cream or crème fraîche.

Grilled Peaches with Strawberry Jam

The best way to serve these is on a canapé or paste base, with a small jug of cream passed separately. Use a really good jam such as Bonne Maman, and try making it in summer with fresh peaches.

**Preparation time: 2 minutes
Cooking time: 5 minutes**

4 tinned peaches (8 halves), well drained
20 ml (4 teaspoons) caster sugar
30 ml (2 tablespoons) strawberry jam
8 canapés or pastry bases, optional
Double cream, to serve

Pre-heat the grill until it's blazing hot. Pat the cut surface of the peaches dry with a paper towel, then sprinkle with the sugar and place under the grill. Cook until the tops look 'toasted' and the sugar is bubbling merrily (around 5 minutes), then leave to cool for a few minutes. Spoon some jam into the hollow of each peach, place on the canapés or pastry bases (if using) and serve with cream.

Yoghurt-banana Brûlée

This recipe combines ideas from the Observer's *Nigel Slater and Shaun Hill, chef at the Merchants House, Ludlow, Shropshire. Bio yoghurt works better than Greek-style, and crème fraîche is better still.*

**Preparation time: 5 – 10 minutes
Cooking time: 2 – 3 minutes**

3 – 4 ripe bananas (depending on size)
60 ml (4 tablespoons) caster sugar
5 ml (1 teaspoon) ground cinnamon, optional
300 ml (10 fl oz) Bio yoghurt

Cut 2 bananas into slices around 2.5 mm (½ in) thick and use to line 4 ramekins, bottom and sides. If you want more banana and less yoghurt, use more slices to make a thicker layer on the bottom. Sprinkle with a fine dusting of sugar and cinnamon (if using). Now spoon on yoghurt to cover the banana completely, but keep it away from the rims of the ramekins. Refrigerate, uncovered, for 2 hours.

When you're ready to eat, pre-heat the grill until very hot. Slice the remaining banana very thinly (5 – 6 slices per ramekin). Arrange in overlapping layers on the tops of the ramekins and sprinkle on an even dusting of sugar around 2.5 mm (½ in) thick. Place under the grill and cook until the sugar is golden-brown. Remove immediately, and leave to cool for 5 – 10 minutes before eating.

Stir-fried Apples Flambé

This method works beautifully with pears, bananas and peaches and is particularly impressive when served on a large round or oval canapé – lightly buttered white toast. Flaming is optional but impressive. (NB: It's easier to clarify large amounts of butter than small, so you may want to make more and refrigerate the remainder.)

**Preparation time: 5 minutes
Cooking time: 5 – 8 minutes**

50 g (2 oz) butter
1 small orange
Juice of ½ lemon
450 g (1 lb) dessert apples ·
30 ml (2 tablespoons) sugar
60 ml (4 tablespoons) Calvados or Cognac
Single cream, to serve

Clarify the butter by placing it in a small saucepan and heating gently until completely melted. Turn off the heat and leave for 1 minute, then skim off the floating white scum. Carefully pour the clear butter into a clean vessel, leaving the white solids in the pan.

Cut the rind off the orange and squeeze out the juice. Put the orange and lemon juices in a large bowl. Cut the orange rind into very fine strips and set to one side. Peel, core and slice the apples, transferring them to the bowl with the juices, tossing well to prevent discolouration. When they're all peeled, heat the butter over a medium-high heat, add the apple slices and sugar then stir-fry until the apples are lightly coloured (3 – 5 minutes). They shouldn't get too deeply browned. The dessert can be prepared in advance up to this point.

To flame the apples, add the orange rind to the pan and re-heat if necessary. Warm the liqueur in a small pan and pour over the apples when they're really hot. If using a gas hob, turn the heat up high and tip the pan slightly until the flame ignites the liqueur. If your hob is electric, ignite the liqueur with a match. In either case, be careful. Carry the flaming pan to the table and, as soon as the flames have died down, serve with cream.

If you're not doing the pyrotechnics, use half the quantity of liqueur and cook down in the pan for 2 minutes or so.

Baked Pears with Chocolate

Orange Juice Whip

This can also be made with apple, pineapple or prune juice.

**Preparation time: 5 minutes
(plus freezing time)**

600 ml (1 pint) orange juice, preferably freshly squeezed
7.5 ml (1½ teaspoons) sugar
175 ml (6 fl oz) low-fat or Bio yoghurt
Curls of orange rind, to decorate, optional

Pour the orange juice into ice-cube trays and freeze completely. The cubes can be kept, in plastic bags, for up to 2 weeks.) When ready to eat, combine in the blender with the other ingredients. Blend until completely smooth, which may take some stirring and scraping with the blender off. Best if served immediately, but it can be frozen for a few hours. Decorate with curls of orange rind if you wish.

Frozen Fruit Fromage Frais

Use pears, apples or pineapple. The sugar can be increased if you wish.

**Preparation time: 10 minutes
Freezing time: 2 hours**

450 g (1 lb) fruit, peeled and cut into 2.5 cm (1 in) cubes
15 ml (1 tablespoon) lemon juice
15 ml (1 tablespoon) sugar
300 ml (10 fl oz) low-fat fromage frais or yoghurt

Toss the fruit with the lemon juice and sugar then place on 1 or 2 baking sheets. Freeze thoroughly (at least 2 hours). Blend the fruit in a food processor until smooth, then add the fromage frais or yoghurt and process just long enough to mix well. Serve immediately.

Baked Bananas in their Skins

There is no simpler pudding in the whole world, and few that are more delicious.

**Preparation time: 3 minutes
Cooking time: 25 – 35 minutes**

6 large, ripe bananas
100 ml (4 fl oz) single cream
5 ml (1 teaspoon) ground cinnamon
30 ml (2 tablespoons) sugar

Pre-heat the oven to 180°C/350°F/Gas 4. Put the bananas, unpeeled, in a large baking tray then cook in the centre of the oven for 25 – 35 minutes, until a knife pierces the fruit easily. Meanwhile, mix the cream, cinnamon and sugar, and leave for at least 10 minutes so the sugar has time to dissolve.

You can peel the bananas before serving, but in my experience your guests will enjoy doing the peeling themselves. Serve with the cinnamon cream.

You can also serve baked bananas with good vanilla ice cream, or with a Cointreau-flavoured whipped cream.

Baked Pears with Chocolate

Pears and chocolate make a classic combination. In this version, the pears are baked in their skins, peeled, and then draped with ribbons of melted chocolate just before serving.

**Preparation time: 5 minutes
Cooking time: 20 – 25 minutes**

4 good pears, not over-ripe
125 g (4 oz) best-quality cooking chocolate
100 ml (4 fl oz) single cream
Leaves, to garnish, optional

Pre-heat the oven to 200°C/400°F/Gas 6. Place the pears in a non-stick baking tin and bake until the fruit is just soft when pierced with a small, sharp knife (around 20 – 25 minutes).

Remove from the oven and leave to cool.

When you are getting ready to serve, break the chocolate into pieces and melt in a double boiler or – carefully – in a small, heavy pan. Do not let it burn.

Divide the cream between 4 serving plates, tilting them so the cream forms an even coating. Cut a flat section off the base of each pear, so it stands up on its own, then peel carefully using your fingers and a small, sharp knife. The skin should come away quite easily. Put each pear on a plate. When the chocolate is melted, use a spoon to dribble it over the pears in thin ribbons. Garnish with leaves dipped in chocolate if you wish. Serve immediately.

Cider-poached Pears

Cider-poached Pears

Use either sweet cider or dry cider according to your own preference.

Preparation time: 10 minutes
Cooking time: 20 – 25 minutes

600 ml (1 pint) cider
5 cm (2 in) piece cinnamon stick
15 – 30 ml (1 – 2 tablespoons) sugar, optional
4 juniper berries
1 piece star anise
2 cloves
2 medium-ripe pears, Williams or Comice
Cream, crème fraîche or Bio yoghurt, to serve

Put all the ingredients, except the pears, in a large pan and bring to the boil. Turn down the heat and simmer for 10 minutes. Meanwhile, peel the pears, halve lengthwise, and remove the cores. Using a very sharp, thin-bladed knife, make cuts at 5 mm (¼ in) intervals down the length of each half. The cuts should go all the way through but stop short of the tips, producing a fanned effect with the pears held together at the tip end.

Slip the pears gently into the poaching liquid and simmer, partly covered, until the fruit is soft but not mushy (around 10 – 15 minutes). Carefully remove with a slotted spoon and put in serving bowls. Turn up the heat under the liquid and boil down to around 100 ml (4 fl oz). Spoon some liquid onto each pear and leave to cool. Serve with cream, crème fraîche, or Bio yoghurt.

Pear and Citrus Granita

Granita, similar to sorbet, is one of the easiest of all desserts to make. This one has a very pure and rich flavour of the main ingredient and can be served either on its own or with Almond Biscuits (see page 183). You can use less sugar if you wish.

Preparation time: 5 minutes
Freezing time: 3 – 4 hours

4 large, ripe pears, around 1 kg (2 lb 2 oz) in weight
Juice of 2 large oranges
Juice of 1 lemon
120 ml (8 tablespoons) caster sugar
10 ml (2 teaspoons) pear liqueur or sweet white wine, optional

Peel and core the pears then cut into chunks. Put all the ingredients in your food processor and process to a very fine sludge. Pour into a large, flat dish and place in the freezer.

Check the granita after 2 hours and whisk thoroughly if ice crystals begin to form. Repeat every hour or so, bearing in mind that the sugar will prevent rock-solid freezing. Just before serving, give the mixture a final whisk and serve in ice-cold bowls or glasses .

Bread and Butter Pudding

There are a dozen ways of making this old favourite. My version isn't as rich as some, but it has the considerable virtue of being relatively light – which means you can eat more of it without hating yourself the next day.

Preparation time: 10 minutes
Cooking time: 1 ½ hours

2 eggs, size 1
700 ml (1¼ pints) milk, semi-skimmed if you prefer
50 g (2 oz) soft brown sugar, plus a little extra for sprinkling
50 g (2 oz) softened butter (2 good knobs)
6 – 8 thin slices white bread
85 g (3 oz) raisins, plus a little extra for sprinkling
5 ml (1 teaspoon) ground cinnamon

Use some of the butter to grease a baking dish about 15 x 25 cm (6 x 10 in) and the rest of it to butter the bread on 1 side only. Put half the slices in the baking dish, buttered side up and scatter on the raisins in an even layer. Top with the cinnamon, then the remaining slices of bread.

Beat the eggs with the milk and sugar until the sugar is completely dissolved. Pour into the baking dish, using more milk if the bread isn't completely covered, and leave for 1 hour. Sprinkle on extra sugar and raisins if you wish.

Pre-heat the oven to 150°C/300°F/Gas 2 and boil a kettle of water. Put the baking dish in a larger roasting tin and fill with water to the level of the custard in the dish. Bake in the upper third of the oven until the custard is set and a knife inserted at the centre comes out dry and very hot (around 1½ hours). Leave to rest for at least 20 minutes before serving.

Almond Biscuits, Fruit with Berry Sauce (page 167)

Almond Biscuits

These rich little numbers can be made without nuts, or with macadamias, peanuts or pine nuts instead of almonds.

**Preparation time:
20 – 30 minutes
Cooking time:
6 – 8 minutes**

125 g (4 oz) unsalted butter,
  softened, plus extra for greasing if
  necessary
6 fl oz sugar
2.5 ml (½ teaspoon) vanilla essence
1 egg, size 1
10 fl oz plain flour
2.5 ml (½ teaspoon) salt
2.5 ml (½ teaspoon) baking powder
Slivered almonds

Pre-heat the oven to 200°C/400°F/ Gas 6. Mash the butter in a mixing bowl with a wooden spoon until it is soft and pliable. Add the sugar in stages, blending thoroughly, then add the vanilla and egg. Keep mixing until you have a thick, wet sludge.

Put the flour, salt and baking powder in a sieve and tap onto the sludge in stages, blending well at each stage. When all the flour has been added, mix and stir for a good 3 – 4 minutes to make a completely homogeneous paste.

Butter a baking sheet, if you're not using a non-stick one. Scoop out around 5 ml (1 teaspoon) of dough and, using 2 teaspoons, form it into a neat oval. (Don't worry if there are rough bits around the edge: they'll disappear in baking.) Put the oval on the baking sheet and repeat the process, placing the ovals a good 2.5 cm (1 in) apart. When the sheet is full, press 1 or 2 almond slivers into each oval. Bake just above the centre of the oven until the biscuits are deeply browned around the edges and a somewhat lighter brown in the centre. Remove to a wire rack to cool and proceed with the rest of the biscuits. You should end up with around 40 in all.

Cream Cheese Tart with a Prune Compôte

This delicious two-part dessert is loosely based on a recipe in Julia Child's Mastering the Art of French Cooking. *It takes a bit of time, but not all that much – and the result is truly sensational.*

**Preparation time: 30 minutes
Cooking time: around 45 minutes**

250 g (9 oz) prunes
75 ml (5 tablespoons) sugar
50 ml (2 fl oz) ruby port
15 ml (1 tablespoon) Cognac
½ vanilla pod, split
225 g (8 oz) cream cheese
125 g (4 oz) unsalted butter, softened

125 g (4 oz) sugar
2 eggs
A large pinch of cinnamon
A large pinch of nutmeg
A large pinch of ground cloves, optional
275 g (10 oz) shortcrust pastry
Grated chocolate, to serve, optional

Soak the prunes in freshly boiled water for 20 minutes, then stone them if necessary. Put them in a pan with the 75 ml (5 tablespoons) sugar, port, Cognac, vanilla pod and 300 ml (10 fl oz) water and bring to the boil. Cook at a fast simmer until the water has reduced to a thick syrup (around 15 – 20 minutes). If the prunes are well softened before the liquid is thick enough, remove them and boil down the liquid separately. Leave to cool.

Meanwhile, mix the cream cheese, butter and sugar and then beat in the eggs and spices. Use the pastry to line a 23 cm (9 in) pie tin and refrigerate for 30 minutes. Prick the bottom all over with a fork, line with aluminium foil and weight down with dried beans. Bake blind on the middle shelf for 10 minutes, then remove the foil and bake again until the pastry is lightly coloured (around 10 minutes more). Remove the foil and leave to cool. The dish can be prepared in advance up to this point.

Pre-heat the oven to 200°C/400°F/Gas 6 and fill the pastry case with the cheese mixture. Bake just above the centre of the oven until a knife inserted in the cheese layer comes out clean and hot (around 25 minutes). This can be eaten straight from the oven, but I think it's best after around 30 minutes – still warm, but not scorching hot. Serve with the prunes on the side and with good cooking chocolate grated on top, if you wish.

Fruit Salad with Cassis

This is incredibly easy to make, if a bit fiddly. The oranges can be prepared 1 hour ahead.

**Preparation time: 15 – 20 minutes
Cooking time: 5 minutes**

175 ml (6 fl oz) water
100 ml (4 fl oz) sugar
30 ml (2 tablespoons) Crème de Cassis

4 large navel oranges
4 large, ripe peaches (preferably white)

Combine the water, sugar and Crème de Cassis in a small pan and bring to the boil, stirring occasionally until the sugar has dissolved. Boil down to reduce by around half, then turn off the heat and leave to cool.

Cut off the tops and bottoms of the oranges then peel with a sharp knife, taking away every bit of pith. Using a small, sharp knife held over the serving bowl, cut and pull the flesh from the segment skins. Remove any pips as you go along, and discard the navels. Prepare the peaches by skinning, halving and stoning them and cutting them into wedges around the same size as the orange segments. Toss gently with the oranges and, if not using immediately, cover the bowl tightly and refrigerate until needed.

To serve, toss the fruit with the sugar syrup. This can be served with sweet biscuits and cream, but it's perfectly good on its own.

Fruit Salad with Cassis (page 183)

Chocolate 'Custard'

This isn't a custard at all but a quick, light alternative made with milk and gelatine. The custard collapses somewhat when unmoulded, but still looks and tastes good.

Preparation time: 2 minutes
Cooking time: 5 minutes plus 3 – 4 hours setting time

450 ml (1 pint) milk
45 ml (3 tablespoons) soft brown sugar
20 g (scant 1 oz) best cooking chocolate, plus extra for grating
1¼ ml (¼ teaspoon) ground cinnamon
1 sachet gelatine
Grated chocolate, to decorate
Double cream, to serve

Put the milk in a saucepan with the sugar, chocolate and cinnamon. Heat gently, whisking constantly, until the chocolate has melted and the sugar is completely dissolved (around 4 minutes). Add the gelatine and whisk until dissolved (another minute or so), then pour into 4 small bowls and refrigerate until set (around 3 hours).

To serve, you can leave the custards in the bowls with chocolate grated on top and double cream passed separately. But they look much nicer if they are unmoulded onto small plates: run a thin-bladed knife round the edge of each bowl, put a plate over the top, and invert quickly. Grate some chocolate on top and serve immediately with the cream.

Apple Tortilla

This is something between a French dessert omelette and a Spanish tortilla – but should not be mistaken for either dish .

Preparation time: 5 minutes
Cooking time: 40 minutes

2 good dessert apples, cored, trimmed and cut into 5 mm (¼ in) slices
50 g (2 oz) unsalted butter (2 good knobs)
15 ml (1 tablespoon) self-raising flour
15 ml (1 tablespoon) soft brown sugar, plus extra for dusting
4 eggs
300 ml (10 fl oz) semi-skimmed milk

Pre-heat a heavy non-stick frying pan, about 25 cm (10 in) in diameter, over a medium heat. Put a generous layer of the dusting sugar on a large plate and press the apples into it. Working as quickly as possible, place them in the pan in a single layer. Cook until they're lightly browned (around 4 – 5 minutes), then turn and brown on the second side. They are done when the bubbles produced seem dry and sugary, rather than watery. Turn the heat off and leave to cool in the pan.

Meanwhile, melt the butter in a small pan and cook the flour gently until it loses its 'raw' smell (around 2 – 3 minutes). Add the 15 ml (1 tablespoon) of sugar and cook until it dissolves, then pour in the milk and cook, whisking constantly, until it's thick enough to coat the back of a spoon (around 10 minutes). Leave to cool for 15 minutes or so. The dessert can be prepared in advance up to this point.

Around half an hour before you want to eat, re-heat the apples and beat the eggs into the milk. Pour into the pan with the apples and cook at a low heat until the rim is set and bubbling, and the middle slightly liquid (around 25 minutes). Sprinkle with extra sugar (if you wish), and flash the tortilla under a medium-hot grill to brown the top and complete the cooking. Leave for a few minutes, then cut wedges straight from the pan to serve.

Steamed Lemon Pudding with Apricot Sauce

Steamed puddings are wonderfully simple and can be varied almost endlessly as to flavourings and sauces. They can also be baked or microwaved. Use the best apricot jam you can find for the sauce.

**Preparation time: 15 – 20 minutes
Cooking time: about 5 minutes in the microwave,
1 – 1 ½ hours in the oven or steamer**

175 g (6 oz) self-raising flour
85 g (3 oz) unsalted butter, cut into pieces, plus extra for greasing
45 ml (2 tablespoons) sugar
Salt
1 egg, size 1
100 ml (4 fl oz) milk
Rind of 1 lemon, finely chopped
75 ml (5 tablespoons) apricot jam
2.5 ml (½ teaspoon) vanilla essence

Mash the flour, butter and sugar with a pinch of salt until they're thoroughly blended. Beat in the egg, then gradually add the milk.

This can be done very quickly in a food processor, but you must take care not to over-beat the butter. Stir in the lemon rind last of all.

Generously butter a pudding basin and pour in the mixture, then cook as follows.

Steaming: Cover the dish with aluminium foil or greaseproof paper and tie with string. Place on a steaming rack over boiling water and cook for around 1½ hours.

Baking: Pre-heat the oven to 180°C/350°F/Gas 4 and put the basin in a pan of hot water. Bake, uncovered, for around 1 hour.

Microwaving: Cover the dish with greaseproof paper and tie with string. Cook at full power until well risen (around 5 minutes).

To make the sauce, put the jam and vanilla essence in a small pan with 75 ml (5 tablespoons) water. Bring to a boil, simmer for a few minutes and snip any large chunks of fruit with a pair of scissors. Re-heat gently before pouring over the pudding.

Teurgoule

Teurgoule is the rice pudding of Normandy, where the Confrèrie de la Teurgoule awards an annual prize for the best recipe. This one is adapted from Jane Sigal's Normandy Gastronomique, *and is made with a lower quantity of sugar than specified in the original. You can increase the sugar content if you wish.*

**Preparation time: 10 minutes
Cooking time: 8 hours**

125 g (4 oz) sugar
175 g (6 oz) pudding rice
A pinch of salt
15 ml (1 tablespoon) ground cinnamon
2 litres (3½ pints) milk
30 ml (2 tablespoons) double cream,
    optional

Pre-heat the oven to 140°C/275°F/Gas 1. Mix the sugar, rice, salt and cinnamon in a large, heavy casserole and gradually stir in the milk and the cream (if using). Place in the oven and cook, uncovered, overnight or for at least 8 hours. By that time the milk should have reduced by around 75 per cent. If it's still too runny, cook for another 1 – 2 hours with the heat turned up a little bit.

Steamed Lemon Pudding with Apricot Sauce

Index

almond biscuits 183
apple
  brown betty 171
  buttered 176
  chestnut stuffing 63
  stir-fried flambé 177
  tortilla 185
apricot
  browned banana with 173
  sauce 186
asparagus
  roasted 145
  salad 121
  spaghetti with prawns 128
aubergine
  grilled in pitta bread 149
  olive tart 98
  roulade of peppers 107
  stuffed peppers 72
  tomato layers 110
avocado
  ceviche 31
  dressing 161
  salsa 163

bacon
  barbecued brochettes 36
  penne with peppers 127
  potatoes and cheese 106
  sautéed chicken 51
  verdure affogate 109
  wild duck with shallots 60
baked bananas in their skins 179
baked basmati rice 134
baked chick peas with salsa 143
baked chicken and fennel 59
baked chicken with fresh herbs 54
baked pears with chocolate 179
baked root vegetables with ginger and
  red chilli 115
baked Spanish omelette 98
baked vegetables with herbs 105

banana
  baked 179
  browned with apricots 173
  yoghurt-banana brulée 177
barbecued chicken croquettes 53
barbecued ciabatta 154
barbecued prawn and bacon
  brochettes 36
barbecues 28, 69
basmati rice with whole spices 134
beans 11, 126 – 45
  baked chick peas 143
  basic beans 137
  black bean salsa 162
  borlotti bean salad 137
  frijoles refritos 136
  lamb and haricot beans 80
  leek and cannellini bean soup 24
  mung beans with spinach 141
  ribollita 25
  rice 136
  salad of baked tuna 29
  spicy black kidney beans 138
  warm bean salad 122
beef
  boeuf à la mode 72
  bulgogi-style 71
  fajitas 69
  Italianate burgers 72
  pasta sauce 130
  roast 72, 74
  salad 72
  sefrina 75
beetroot soup, spicy 21
berry sauce 167
black bean salsa 162
boeuf à la mode 72
borlotti bean salad 137
braised beef with rice and gremolata 71
braised chicory 113
braised pork with peppers and spices 85
brandade 41
bread and butter pudding 170, 181
browned bananas with apricots 173
bruschetta toppings 152
bulgogi-style sliced beef 71
burghal salad with peppers and herbs 120
buttered apples 176

cabbage and potato soup 24
cannellini gratin 138
carrot soup 21
Castilian steaks 74
celery salad with red pepper dressing 122
ceviche with avocado 31
charred soup 22
cheese 12, 148, 170
  biscuits 148, 157
  tomato pizza 91
chestnut
  apple stuffing 63
  stuffing 63
chicken
  baked 54, 59
  barbecued 53
  brochettes with watercress salad 57
  cucumbers with spicy peanut sauce 47
  flash-roasted 48
  forty cloves of garlic 56
  fragrant rice with 59
  'kung pao' thighs 47
  lemon 59
  pilaff with vegetables 51
  polenta and bagna cauda 54
  pollo con adobo 48
  roast 53
  sautéed with bacon and courgettes 51
  soup, Indonesian-style 22
  tajine with dried fruit 57
  Thai flavours 56
chilindrón 81
chocolate 170, 179
  brownie cake 173
  custard 185
  pots 173, 174
cholent 76
cider-poached pears 181
cinnamon fried rice with summer
  vegetables 133
Claridge's turkey 63
courgette
  spring onion sandwich 151
  tart with pesto 98
couscous 145

cream cheese tart with prune compôte 170, 183
Crème Caroline 17
crostini toppings 152
croûtons, parmesan 18
cucumber
  herb yoghurt 120
  salad with feta 120
curry
  quick 81
  Thai-style fish 33

desserts 170
dough 90, 91
dressings 35, 102, 119, 122, 161
duck
  bacon and shallots 60
  breasts 'au poivre' 51
  legs with prunes 61
duxelles 148, 151

egg parcels 157

feathered game 46 – 65
fennel
  baked chicken 59
  baked tuna salad 29
  cream sauce 130
  pan-fried mullet 41
  rigatoni with broccoli 133
  salad with gorgonzola 122
feta biscuits 152
figs with prosciutto and sour cream 157
fish 11, 28 – 43
  cutlets 38
  flash-roasted 33
  'paste' 149
  spread 41
  tartare with tomatoes 32
flash-roasted lamb fillet 78

flash-roasted Moroccan chicken 48
frijoles refritos 136
frozen fruit fromage frais 179
fruit 11, 170
  chicken tajine with dried fruit 57
  frozen fruit fromage frais 179
  miniature tarts 174
  salad with Cassis 183
fusilli
  fennel sauce 130
  tomato cream 132

game, feathered 46 – 65
gammon, perfect glazed 86
garlic
  ginger and spring onion salsa 162
  saffron soup 21
glazed gammon 86
goose, roasted 64
grains 126 – 45
gratins 102, 110, 113, 138
green olive paste 152
gremolata 71
griddled vegetables with goat's cheese 104
grilled aubergine in pitta 149
grilled leeks with goat's cheese 105
grilled peaches with jam 177
grilled sardines 41
grilled summer vegetables 103

hake in salsa verde 37
hasselback potatoes 107
herbs 10, 12, 120, 160
  soup 18
Hill, Shaun 63
Hom, Ken 65

Indonesian-style chicken soup 22
instant pea soup 21
instant spinach soup 18

instant yoghurt sauce 164
Italianate burgers 72

'kung pao' chicken thighs 47

lamb
  chilindrón 81
  flash-roasted fillet 78
  haricot beans 80
  noisettes with olives 76
  pot-roasted 78
  quick curry 81
  rack 76
  shanks with garlic 76
leek
  cannellini bean soup 24
  grilled with cheese 105
  mustard vinaigrette 113
  potato gratin 113
lemon chicken 59
lentilles de puy 141
lentils with smoked haddock 141
linguine with vegetables 128
low-fat fried fish 31
low-fat puréed vegetable soup 22

mango salsa 164
marinades 68, 78, 154
mashed potatoes and celeriac 114
meat 11, 68 – 86
melted vegetable sauce 167
merende 148
mérou à la Tahitienne 31
miniature fruit tarts 174
Moroccan-style sprouts 107
mullet (see red mullet)
mung beans with spinach 141
mushrooms 118, 148
mussels with shallot vinegar 39
my mother's chuck steak 69

new potatoes and mangetouts with
   creamy wild mushroom sauce 116
no-cook citrus cheesecake 171

oil 12, 160
olives 148
onion tart 96
orange juice whip 179

pan-fried mullet with fennel 41
pan-fried salmon with ginger 35
pan-roasted quail with grapes 60
parcel-roasted pheasant 60
parmesan croûtons 18
parsley 160
   butter sauce 161
   pesto 141
pasta 12, 126 – 45
   beef sauce 130
   onion salad 131
   salad 127, 131
   triple tomato sauce 128
pastry 90 – 8
pea soup, instant 21
peach in Moscato syrup 176
pear
   baked with chocolate 179
   cider-poached 181
   citrus granita 181
penne
   alla Romagna 130
   pepper and bacon 127
pepper
   aubergine-stuffed 72
   braised pork with spices 85
   burghal salad with herbs 120
   celery salad with dressing 122
   chilindrón 81
   penne with bacon 127

polenta with onion 145
   roasted 109
   roulade of aubergine 107
   sauce 167
   shredded with onion 103
   Spanish stuffed 85
   tart 97
pescado en escabeche 32
pesto 98, 141
pheasant, parcel-roasted 60
piadine 151
pickled walnut salsa 163
pico de gallo 163
pissaladière 94
pitta bread
   aubergine 149
   Italianate filling 157
pizzas 90 – 8
polenta 126, 143
   chicken with 54
   fingers 145
   peppers and onions 145
pollo con adobo 48
pork
   braised with peppers 85
   drunken 82
   fragrant kebabs 82
   kebabs 82
   pot-roasted 82
   quick curry 81
   Spanish stuffed peppers 85
   spiced with chutney 85
   sweet and spicy spare ribs 80
port wine jelly 152
pot-roasted leg of lamb 78
pot-roasted pork with chilli sauce 82
potato
   gratin 110
   salad 123
poultry 46 – 65
prawn
   barbecued 36
   spaghetti with 128
   tomato sauce and spices 43
prune compôte 183
puddings 170 – 86
pulses 11, 126 – 45
pumpkin 109

quail, pan-roasted 60

rack of lamb with mustard 76
raw fish salad 31
red, green and spicy salsa 162
red mullet
   pan-fried with fennel 41
   salad 29
   sherry vinegar 37
red pepper tart 97
red and purple pizza 92
refried beans 136
relishes 51, 160
remojón 39
ribollita 25
rice 12, 126
   baked basmati with saffron 134
   basmati with spices 134
   beans with 136
   braised beef with 71
   chicken 59
   cinnamon fried with vegetables 133
   fragrant with chicken 59
   Ken Hom's herb stuffing 65
   mould with herbs 133
   Spanish 136
   teurgoule 186
   wild salad 134
rigatoni with broccoli, fennel
   and lemon 133
roast beef 74
roast beef salad 72
roast chicken 53
roast goose 64
roasted red peppers 109
rosemary and garlic pizza 92
roulade of peppers and aubergines 107
Roux, Michel 65

salads 102, 170
baked tuna, red mullet, fennel
and beans 29
baussenque 119
borlotti bean 137
burghal with peppers and herbs 120
celery with red pepper dressing 122
chicken brochettes with watercress 57
chunky pasta 131
cucumber with feta cheese 120
fennel with gorgonzola 122
mixed asparagus 121
pasta with creamed onion 131
pasta with prosciutto 127
potato with sesame vinaigrette 123
raw fish 31
remojón 39
rich tomato 118
roast beef 72
seafood with red-oil dressing 35
warm bean 122
wild rice 134
salmon
en croûte 36
gravadlax with potatoes 43
pan-fried 35
salsas 37, 103, 143, 160 – 4
sardines, grilled 41
sauces 12, 13, 126, 160 – 7
bagna cauda 54
bulgogi-style sliced beef 71
creamy chilli 82
creamy wild mushroom 116
fennel cream 130
left-over beef 130
parsley butter 33
prawns with tomato 43
salsa verde 37
spicy peanut 47
spicy tomato 38
triple tomato 128
**sautéed chicken with bacon
and courgettes** 51
sautéed wild mushrooms 115
savoury tarts 90 – 8

scarpaccia viareggina 94, 148
seafood salad with red-oil dressing 35
sefrina 75
shellfish 28 – 43
shortcrust pastry 90, 94
shredded peppers with double onions 103
smoked fish 'paste' 149
snacks 148 – 57
sole, vegetable-topped 29
soups 16 – 25
spaghetti with prawns and asparagus 128
Spanish rice 136
Spanish stuffed peppers 85
spiced pork with chutney 85
spices 10, 11, 12, 13, 126
spicy beetroot soup 21
spicy black kidney beans 138
spicy vegetable stew 116
spinach
feta tart 97
lemon soup 18
mung beans with 141
soup with croûtons 18
spreads 41, 149, 152
sprouts, Moroccan-style 107
squid with chillies 43
steak
Castilian 74
cholent 76
my mother's chuck 69
steam-fried courgettes with tomatoes 104
steamed lemon pudding 186
stew, spicy vegetable 116
stir-fried apple flambé 177
stock 13, 16
store cupboard 10 – 13
stuffing 63, 65, 160
sweet potatoes with ginger 115
sweet and spicy spare ribs 80

tarts, savoury 90 – 8
teurgoule 186
Thai-style fish curry 33
tomato
salad 118

sauce 161
tarragon salsa 162
tonnato 149
toppings 152
tuna
herbs and olives 152
salad 29
turkey, Claridge's 63

vegetable soup, low-fat puréed 22
vegetable-topped lemon sole 29
vegetables 11, 12, 102 – 23
verdure affogate 109

warm bean salad 122
wild duck with bacon and shallots 60
wild rice salad 134

yellow pepper sauce 167
yoghurt 13, 120
banana brulée 177
instant sauce 164

Acknowledgements

To the memory of John Dally, Conal Walsh, and Kenny Everett

My relationship with SHE has changed since I wrote this book, as I left the magazine in the summer of 1995. What has not changed is my admiration and respect for Linda Kelsey, the editor of SHE. Linda loves food and has strong views on it. She guided my work on the magazine with unfailing wisdom, and it was a pleasure to work with her.

Nadia Marks and Yvonne Shaw-Binns, Associate Editor and Art Editor respectively, oversaw the task of making photographs to bring my recipes to life. Their talents – and those of photographers and stylists too numerous to name – are evident on every page of this book. Jan Boxshall, Managing Editor until February 1995, kept me on schedule and provided consistently helpful advice. And her successor Liz Gregory, a friend from way back, has taken on those chores with equal skill. Rachel Shattock, another old friend, has served as Deputy Editor since January 1995 and supplied invaluable guidance. The Sub-Editors at SHE handled my copy with care, in addition to carrying out their other tasks. Special thanks to Sheena Miller, Janice Battle, Sarah Clarke and Elaine Griffiths.

This book was done on a tight schedule which would not have been possible without the efforts of everyone at Pavilion. Many thanks to John Midgley, Rachel King, Fiona Brownlee, and copy editor Deborah Taylor. Thanks also to Anne Melbourne of the Enterprise Division, National Magazine Company, who made the contractual side of things simple and painless.

It's part of my work to keep up with developments at the major supermarkets, and their press officers make it easy to do that. I am deeply grateful to the following: at Marks and Spencer, Nick Herbert, Vivienne Jawett, and Melodie Schuster; at Safeway, Anne Bailey and Alison Hull; at Tesco, Kelly Murphy and Jan Noble; at Sainsbury, Diane Lamb, Andrea Mountford, and Louise Platt; at Waitrose, Wendy Harries-Jones.

Finally, people with no connection to the magazine. Matthew Fort, Food and Drink Editor of the *Guardian,* is a never-failing source of culinary and gastronomic wisdom. Anne Curtis, Victoria Whitcomb and Gail Simmonds have helped in ways they know all about. Numerous friends and relations have eaten the food and commented honestly. Rebecca, Alice and Ruth Ehrlich, my daughters, tolerate my hours in the kitchen and at the word processor.

My gratitude to Emma Dally, Deputy Editor of SHE from 1990 – 94, and my wife since 1980, is immeasurable and indescribable.